TRADING WEEKLY OPTIONS

Founded in 1807, John Wiley & Sons is the oldest independent publishing company in the United States. With offices in North America, Europe, Australia and Asia, Wiley is globally committed to developing and marketing print and electronic products and services for our customers' professional and personal knowledge and understanding.

The Wiley Trading series features books by traders who have survived the market's ever changing temperament and have prospered—some by reinventing systems, others by getting back to basics. Whether a novice trader, professional, or somewhere in-between, these books will provide the advice and strategies needed to prosper today and well into the future.

For more on this series, visit our website at www.WileyTrading.com.

TRADING WEEKLY OPTIONS

Pricing Characteristics and
Short-Term Trading Strategies

Russell Rhoads, CFA

WILEY

ISBN 9781118616123 (Hardcover)
ISBN 9781118727171 (ePDF)
ISBN 9781118727386 (ePub)

Printed in the United States of America.
10 9 8 7 6 5 4 3 2 1

To Maggie—
You always inspire me to do better than
anyone would have ever expected.

CONTENTS

Short-dated options have taken off in popularity since being introduced on stocks and exchange-traded funds in the summer of 2010. By some accounts, up to 20 percent of daily trading volume may be attributed to these options. Short-term stock traders who shied away from options have come to embrace the shorter-dated contracts. Also, historically, there have been certain trading strategies that would only be implemented the week of expiration. Now every week is expiration week for options on almost 200 markets!

The first half of this book introduces or reviews option-pricing factors and characteristics of option trading when contacts have just a few days remaining until expiration. Time decay and time value are very different near expiration than when options have weeks or months remaining until expiration.

The second half of this book discusses strategies and how they may be implemented using options with just a few days remaining until expiration. Also discussed are strategies that combine longer-dated options with contracts that have a few days remaining until expiration. Short-term stocks and option traders should be trying to take advantage of the time-decay characteristics of short-dated options and this book highlights methods to do so.

Finally, visiting the website that accompanies this book is strongly encouraged. The website highlights some advanced strategies that combine contracts on unique exchange trade funds along with a consistent update on short-term events, such as earnings announcements, that may offer short-term, catalyst-trading opportunities. See the About the Website section for more information about the website.

ACKNOWLEDGMENTS

The opportunity to write this book would not have come to me without a tremendous amount of help from Kevin Commins. I will be forever indebted to him for giving me the opportunity to work with Wiley. Meg Freeborn has been a patient guide for the third time and I appreciate her patience with this project.

I am very fortunate to work with a wonderful group of people at the Options Institute. In alphabetical order: Taja Beane, Jim Bittman, Laura Johnson, Barbara Kalicki, Michelle Kaufmann, Mary Kearney, Peter Lusk, Pam Quintero, and Deb Peters are a wonderful group to work with. Also the past two summers I have had wonderful interns. Both Sean Knudson and Allison Michel were helpful with this book. The combination of all these people has enabled me to set a longevity employment record at the CBOE.

Finally, at home I promise Merribeth, Maggie, and Emmy that this is the last summer with no vacation because I'm busy writing a book.

CHAPTER 1

Introducing Weekly Options

■ Evolution of Weekly Options

On Friday October 28, 2005, the Chicago Board Options Exchange (CBOE) launched the first weekly contract. Weekly contracts were first launched in 2005 on the S&P 500 (SPX) and S&P 100 (OEX) market indexes. The popular thinking, however, is that weekly, or short-dated, options have only been available since the summer of 2010 because many traders focus on equity options and only became aware of short-dated options when they became available on stocks. Weekly options on exchange traded funds followed shortly after short dated options on stocks the following month. When shorter dated options in equities and exchange-traded funds (ETFs) hit the markets in 2010, many more traders started to pay attention to these contracts and rapid growth in trading volume quickly followed.

Weeklys is a term that is specific to options trading at CBOE and is actually a service mark of CBOE. However it is a term that seems to have taken on general meaning for all short dated option contracts. Other option exchanges list short-dated options as well but they use different terminology. For instance, the NYSE ARCA Options exchange uses the term Short Term Options Series. Other than the name, contracts listed at this exchange or any other option exchange that start trading on Thursday and expire the following Friday have all the same characteristics as weeklys.

From 2005 until 2010 SPX and OEX Weeklys were the only weekly option contracts listed at CBOE or any other options exchange in the United

States. Toward the end of this five-year period that precedes the introduction of equity weeklys in 2010, the average daily volume of SPX Weeklys was around 16,000 contracts and the average daily volume of OEX Weeklys was just over 15,000 contracts. In late 2012 the average daily volume for SPX Weeklys had jumped to 100,000 contracts—some days with volume topping 200,000 contracts. Also, as a percentage of total SPX option trading, short dated SPX options had grown to over 20 percent of average daily volume as of late 2012.

After weekly options on equities were introduced, there was another change to the structure of the options that has probably aided in the success of these contracts. Originally these contracts would be issued on a Friday morning the week before they were set to expire. After about a month of weekly options on stocks being listed on a Friday morning and typically expiring the following Friday, the decision was made to list these contracts a day earlier on Thursdays. This final change resulted in what is commonly thought of as weekly options, weeklys, or short-dated options. There are some other small deviations on this that will be discussed in the next couple of chapters.

Barring a holiday, a weekly option series will begin trading on the market opening on a Thursday and cease trading the following Friday. The result is an option contract that has a life of seven trading days between listing and expiration. In addition to the seven trading day options that are listed for expiration on nonstandard expiration weeks there are also some series that are listed to assure there are five expiration weeks in a row. If a stock or market has options expiring in five consecutive weeks, it is commonly referred to as having serial options available for trading.

■ Popularity of Weekly Options

Many academic studies have been commissioned to determine what makes a successful listed derivative product. Needless to say, exchanges are very curious to know what the right formula is to bringing traders, investors, and liquidity providers together to trade a financial product. Although there is much time, thought, and effort that goes into a new exchange-listed product, the success or failure seems to have an aspect of luck as well. At first glance, the rapid acceptance of short-dated options on equities is a bit perplexing. Weeklys had been around for years on SPX and OEX and without attracting the dramatic volume that equity options did. However, considering what strategies are most popular with equity options relative to strategies with options on indexes, there is an understanding how the emergence of short-term options on stocks fueled the eventual growth for both short-dated equity and index option contracts.

Figure 1.1 compares the daily SPX Put–Call Ratio trading to equity-option trading at CBOE for the first six months in 2012. A put–call ratio is calculated by dividing the volume of put options traded by the number of call options traded in a particular period. The higher line on this chart represents a ratio of SPX puts to SPX calls traded each day. The lower line on this chart represents a ratio of equity put option volume divided by equity call option volume each day.

Note the higher line representing the SPX Put–Call Ratio; it is consistently above 1.00 and often above 2.00. The SPX Put–Call Ratio over 1.00 is interpreted as more SPX put options trade in a day than SPX call options. If total SPX option volume is 600,000 contracts in a single day and the SPX Put–Call Ratio equals 2.00 that would mean twice as many SPX put options than call contracts traded in a single day. For a day with the total volume at 600,000 this would mean 400,000 puts and 200,000 calls traded on the day.

Now consider the solid line that represents equity put volume divided by equity call volume. The light gray line is under 1.00 on a pretty consistent basis. This means that more equity call options trade than equity put options on a daily basis. If 3,000,000 equity options trade in a single day at the CBOE and the Equity Put–call ratio equals 0.50, then half as many equity put options as the number of call options traded on the day. For a day

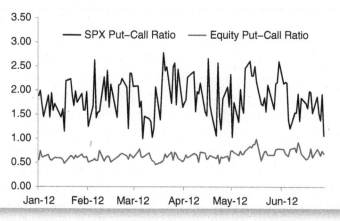

FIGURE 1.1   **SPX and Equity Put–Call Ratios, January 2012 to June 2012**
Source: www.CBOE.com.

with 3,000,000 contracts changing hands this would mean put volume was 1,000,000 and call volume 2,000,000. So how does this relate to the success of short-dated options since 2010?

Before joining the Options Institute at the CBOE, my career spanned a wide variety of trading and institutional investment firms. The majority of the firms I worked for would use equity and index options in completely different ways. If a portfolio manager gave the trading desk a ticket to trade index options, this trade was going to be a trade using SPX put options. With very few exceptions the trade would involve using put options to hedge a portfolio. The hedge would often be a very straightforward opening purchase of out-of-the-money SPX put options. In the case that the order was to buy index options, it would be a purchase of SPX puts to close out a long position.

If an order ticket was given to the desk to trade equity options it would be to trade a call option. This order would typically be an opening transaction that involved selling calls versus shares that were currently owned. This is a very common strategy known as a covered call. Portfolio managers often work with target prices to exit stocks or possibly lower their exposure to the stock. A method of exiting the stock is to sell a call option and take on the obligation to sell shares. If the covered call is held until expiration, it would either be assigned with shares being called away or expire with no value and a profit to the portfolio. If a buy order came in for an equity call option, it would be to close out the trade. Closing out the covered call would involve a purchase of call options to close out the obligation to sell the underlying shares that goes along with that trade.

When selling a call option against shares of stock that is owned, one secondary motivation will be to benefit from the time decay of the option contract. In certain circumstances it makes sense to focus on the nearest expiring option contract when considering a covered call. Sometimes this would result in a trade not being executed. The next expiration date may be too far out on the calendar or the premium received would not make sense to have an obligation to sell shares for the time until expiration. Now for over 200 equity securities there are always options that will be expiring in a very short period of time which gives more flexibility to considering a covered call. These shorter dated call options are ideal for taking advantage of time decay. This short-dated time decay is the basis of several other strategies covered in this book.

Equity call options are often used for covered calls while the most common use of index options is to hedge portfolios. The daily volume for SPX put contracts is consistently higher than the volume of SPX calls because hedging is a primary motivator to trade index options. Also, since the majority of index option trading is on the put side and, for hedging purposes, the attractiveness of index options that have only a few days until expiration may not have been apparent before the introduction of short-dated equity options.

Generally a portfolio manager would want to hedge a portfolio for more than just a few days. Because of the longer time frame relative to expiration a portfolio manager would not see the value in buying short-dated puts to gain portfolio protection. However, under several scenarios SPX Weeklys make sense for hedging purposes. Index options will be fully introduced in Chapter 3. Chapter 24 will discuss how SPX Weeklys actually make sense and are being used for hedging purposes. The recognition of the use of shorter dated SPX options for hedging purposes has resulted in steady volume growth for SPX Weeklys. Figure 1.2 is a chart depicting the average daily volume for SPX Weeklys from January 2010 to November 2012.

A slight drop in SPX Weeklys volume may be seen between May 2010 and June 2010. This may be attributed to weeklys being offered for the first time on broad-based exchange-traded funds. On June 4, 2010, CBOE began trading weekly options on four exchange-traded funds—Standard and Poor's Depositary Receipts (SPY), DIAMONDS Trust Series 1 (DIA), NASDAQ-100 Index Tracking Stock (QQQ), and iShares Russell 2000

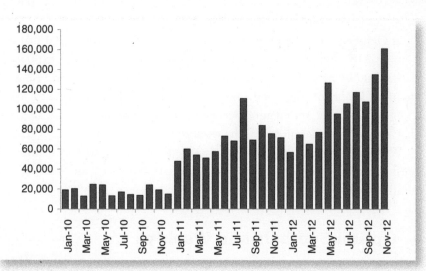

FIGURE 1.2 Average Daily Volume for SPX Weeklys, January 2010 to November 2012

Source: www.CBOE.com.

Index Fund (IWM). It is very possible that these new weekly options that give traders similar exposure to the overall market as SPX option contracts initially took some volume from SPX Weeklys. However, as overall acceptance of weekly options emerged in early 2011, volume in SPX Weeklys began to increase at a rapid pace.

■ Option Expiration Dates Explained

Officially, standard option contracts expire on the third Saturday following the third Friday of the month. This date was selected as there is always a third Friday and it is least likely to be a market holiday week. When weekly options were introduced the expiration date was actually designated to be on Friday. This is a subtle difference between standard option contracts since the markets are not open on Saturdays. Basically this does not have much of an impact for most traders because Friday would typically be the last day to trade either standard or short-dated option contracts.

Saturday expiration is becoming a bit antiquated as it was implemented back when the recordkeeping process was very labor intensive. With the emergence of technology, standard options not officially expiring until 11:59 A.M. the Saturday following the third Friday of the month has become an outdated process. For individuals, the difference between non-third-Friday options and standard option contracts is not too much when it comes to expiration, but for firms this is something that has to be tracked.

In October 2012 the Options Clearing Corporation announced that beginning with options expiring after February 2015 the official expiration date would be moved from the third Saturday following the third Friday to the third Friday of the month. In October 2012 there were January 2015 Long-term Equity AnticiPation Securities (LEAPS) options already in place that had Saturday designated as the expiration date.

With those contracts in place it made sense to keep Saturday expiration until after those contacts expire. When those contracts expire Saturday expiration will be history.

■ Option Symbols and Weeklys

When I am out speaking on behalf of CBOE or the Options Industry Council, I will expound on the benefits of weekly options and also mention they have only been around for equities for only a couple of years. A common question I will get is what took so long for exchanges to list weekly options on equities. The answer is rooted in option symbols.

Until 2010 specific option contracts consisted of symbols that had five letters. This effort was known as the Options Symbology Initiative and was enacted and coordinated by the Options Clearing Corporation. The reason behind this change was simple. We had run out of symbols. Also, symbols for option contracts had no logic. The Option Symbology Initiative also added some logic to the appearance of option symbols.

Prior to 2010 an option contract would consist of five letters. The first three letters would represent the underlying stock or index. Having three letters represent a stock had issues, as there are many four-letter stock tickers. Also, many of those four-letter stocks are the most actively traded options series around. The fourth letter would represent both the expiration date and whether the option was a call or a put. Finally the fifth letter would represent the strike price. This worked well with a limited number of expirations, strike prices, and stocks that had active option markets. However, as time went by some stocks would need multiple root symbols due to a LEAPS trade or due to a massive number of strike prices. With only 26 letters in the alphabet tickers could run out quickly on stocks like AAPL, AMZN, or GOOG. The system had run its course and was overdue to be updated. After much effort and cooperation the method of creating options symbols changed.

The new symbology method for options that was rolled out in 2010 resulted in tickers that have over 20 characters. The number of characters would depend on the underlying stock symbol. As an example, the ticker symbol for a YHOO October 15 call that expires on the standard (third Saturday following the third Friday) expiration date in October follows, with the components broken out.

YHOO121020C00015000
YHOO: Stock-ticker symbol
12: Expiration year (2012)
10: Expiration month (October = 10)
20: Expiration day (the twentieth of October)
C: Call option (P for put option)
00015000: Strike price of 15

These different components of an option symbol are pretty straightforward with the exception of the strike price. The strike price section has several zeros before and after the actual strike price of 15. These zeros before

15 can accommodate higher strike prices using the spaces to the left of the 15 on the strike price. Also the last three spaces that are occupied by zeros on this example allow strike prices that go out three decimal places. Upon first thought, having so many places for the strike price may not appear logical, but consider a split that adjusts the strike price. Going out three decimal places allows for a bit more accuracy in the case of an unusual stock split such as a 3 for 1 split.

Before the new symbology convention in 2010 the expiration date was signified by a single letter. Now the expiration date is indicated by six spaces that replicate and appear in a fairly normal date format. Suddenly the ability to customize options contracts existed as the ability to create a symbol for any expiration date existed.

The Options Symbology Initiative was phased in over a few months in the first half of 2010. The final phase was completed on May 14, 2010, and at this point all option symbols had been changed over to the new much longer and comprehensive format. It is no coincidence that weeklys on equities debuted at the end of May. This was conveniently just a couple of weeks after the change in the format of tickers for option contracts was completed.

Now that short-dated options are available traders have a wide variety of strategies they can implement based on a variety of market and individual stock outlooks. With options consistently trading that have very little time left to expiration, short-term strategies with a bullish, bearish, or neutral outlook can be implemented with a different focus than in the past when only standard option contracts were available for trading.

CHAPTER 2

Short-Term Index Options

Short-dated options, under the name weeklys, were first launched on indexes in 2005. In 2010, weeklys were introduced on stocks and then exchange-traded funds. Once short-dated options were offered on equity products, the popularity of weeklys began to take off. The two original weeklys options were listed on the S&P 500 (SPX) and S&P 100 (OEX) indexes. Both continue to be listed, with SPX and OEX options having been expanded to include several consecutive weeks of short-dated option series. In addition to SPX and OEX, S&P 100 European Style (XEO) short-dated options are available for trading, along with short-dated options on the Nasdaq-100 (NDX), Russell 2000 (RUT), and Dow Jones Industrial Average (DJX). Each of these has their own unique features so they will be briefly covered individually.

■ Dow Jones Industrial Average (DJX)

The typical symbol associated with the Dow Jones Industrial Average is DJIA. However, options on this index are signified using the ticker DJX. DJX is the symbol used for index options that are based on the DJIA. In addition to having a different ticker, the level of DJX is 1/100th that of the commonly quoted DJIA. For example if the DJIA closes at 13,500, DJX will be quoted at 135.00. This adjustment is made because the trading value of an option on an index quoted at 135.00 would be more reasonable than an option quoted on an index trading at 13,500. Therefore DJX is a modified version of the DJIA, but tracks the performance of the larger index. Weekly options on the DJX begin trading on a Thursday morning and are European style, A.M.-settled contracts. They typically cease trading on a Thursday afternoon and are cash settled based on the opening prices of the stocks in the index the following morning.

■ Russell 2000 (RUT)

The Russell 2000 is generally considered a benchmark for mid- and small-cap or domestic stocks in the United States. The RUT is a subset of the Russell 3000 index, which is an index comprised of the 3,000 largest public companies in the United States. The 2,000 smallest of these 3,000 stocks are what make up the RUT. As the 1,000 largest publicly traded companies are excluded from this index the RUT has gained the notoriety as a small-cap index. Also, because smaller public companies are the components of the Russell 2000 it is also considered an indication of domestic business conditions, in contrast to indexes like the Dow Jones Industrial Average or S&P 500. RUT options are issued on a rolling basis so there will always be five consecutive weeks in the future that have options expiring. Options on RUT begin trading on a Thursday morning and are European style, A.M.-settled contracts. They typically cease trading on a Thursday afternoon and are cash settled based on the opening prices of the stocks in the index the following morning. RUT options are also listed so they will always be expiring over the next five consecutive weeks. This serial expiration follows the method of listing options introduced by CBOE on SPX and OEX.

■ NASDAQ-100 (NDX)

The NDX is comprised of the 100 largest nonfinancial companies listed on the NASDAQ market. This index is more of a proxy of the performance of technology companies, as many of the largest members of this index are well-known technology companies. Because of the large concentration of technology companies, the NDX tends to be a bit more volatile than the S&P 500, which offers different trading opportunities than SPX options. Weekly options on the NDX begin trading on a Thursday morning and are European style, A.M.-settled contracts. On a nonholiday trading week, NDX options will cease trading on a Thursday afternoon and are cash settled based on the opening prices of the stocks in the index the following morning.

■ S&P 100 Weeklys (OEX and XEO)

The S&P 100 Index was originally a proprietary index of CBOE before being brought into the Standard & Poor's group of indexes. As a CBOE index it was created to represent the performance of the 100 largest publicly traded stocks that have listed options. The result is an index that basically represents the performance of the largest stocks in the S&P 500 index. Depending on market conditions, the S&P 100 index will represent over 50 percent of the performance of the S&P 500 Index. That is, the market capitalization of the stocks in the S&P 100 covers over half the market capitalization of the 500 stocks in the S&P 500. The result is a pretty close correlation between the performance of the S&P 100 and S&P 500 indexes.

There are two different types of S&P 100 index options listed. OEX options are American style while XEO options are European style. Weeklys on OEX and XEO are both P.M.-settled contracts that trade through expiration, which is based on the closing index level, typically on a Friday. Both OEX and XEO options are listed so that there will always be options expiring the following next five weeks.

The European- versus American-style options do actually make a difference when trading OEX or XEO Weeklys. The risk in early exercise can result in subtle pricing differences between the two.

The quotes in Table 2.1 are the midpoint of the bid–ask spread on OEX and XEO options near the close on October 11, 2012. The S&P 100 was at 658.28 and the options have six trading days left to expiration.

Note the XEO options consistently have a lower premium than the OEX contracts. This is due to the difference between the exercise styles of the two types of options. OEX options may be exercised any day up until expiration while XEO options cannot. The cutoff time to exercise OEX options is 3:20 central time—20 minutes after the equity market closes and the closing value for the S&P 100 has been determined. The risk of being assigned a

TABLE 2.1	OEX and XEO Option Premium Comparisons			
OEX Call	XEO Call	Strike	XEO Put	OEX Put
10.95	10.60	650	2.05	2.15
7.00	6.80	655	3.25	3.35
4.10	3.85	660	5.45	5.65
2.15	1.85	665	8.45	8.90
0.95	0.75	670	12.40	12.95

short-option position is always present. With equity options the potential goes up with dividend payments and this can be anticipated. However, with respect to OEX options, the possibility of early assignment is not necessarily something that can be weighed in advance.

For example, Exxon Mobile (XOM) is one of the largest components of the S&P 100 index, accounting for about 5 percent of the market capitalization of the index. If at 3:00 OEX closes at 605.00 and just after the close XOM releases negative news that will result in a much lower price the next day it may make sense for a holder of a 600 strike call that has just a few days until expiration to exercise that call. If it appears the bad news in XOM is going to knock the stock down 20 percent that could take 1 percent out of the S&P 100, which would result in the S&P 100 opening under 600 the following day, but also result in the 600 strike call going from in the money by 5 points to having no intrinsic value. Noting this distinct possibility it may make sense to exercise the 600 strike call and receive 5 points ($500) for an option that is likely to lose value the following day. Many other factors can play into this, but this is a simple scenario that illustrates why there is early-exercise risk for OEX options. This could also work in the opposite directly with bullish news on a big S&P 100 component stock and the holder of an OEX put option.

■ S&P 500 (SPX, SPXPM, SPXW)

SPX Option contracts are consistently the most actively traded index option contracts in the United States with average daily volume around 700,000 contracts in 2012. Even more impressive, this comes close to $100 billion in notional value changing hands in the S&P 500 index option markets on a daily basis. For a little more context, the average daily volume for SPY comes to about $20 billion or one-fifth that of SPX option trading.

In October 2011, CBOE introduced P.M.-settled electronically traded SPX options using the ticker SPXPM. These options were offered as an electronically traded P.M.- settled alternative to standard SPX options. Beginning in the first quarter of 2013 SPX Weeklys began listing under the ticker SPXPM. This was a logical step made by CBOE as SPX Weeklys and SPXPM options both shared P.M. settlement as the characteristic that differentiates those options from SPX standard A.M.-settled contracts.

There is a noticeable difference between standard SPX options that expire on the third Friday and SPXPM options. Both are European-style options. Standard SPX options are A.M.-settled and cease trading on a Thursday afternoon while SPX Weeklys are P.M.-settled and trade through the close on expiration Friday. This means on the third Friday each month there will be SPX options settled based on the market opening prices and SPXPM options that settle on the close of the market.

SPXPM options were the first index (or equity) option series to be offered that would have five consecutive expiration dates in a row. This was offered in May 2012 and since that time this sort of listing of option contracts has been expanded to other indexes (OEX, XEO, RUT) as well as many equity related products.

There are also SPXPM contracts that are listed to expire at the end of each quarter. This means there are actually index options that expire on the market close at the end of a quarter, which is convenient for money managers who are judged from quarter to quarter. If the quarter ends on a Friday then that day the weekly SPXPM options will not be listed for that date. There are a lot of moving parts here so an example is probably in order. If it is December 31, 2012, then the following expirations are trading through the end of the first quarter in 2013:

January 4, 2013—Weekly SPX
January 11, 2013—Weekly SPX
January 18, 2013—SPXPM and Standard SPX
January 25, 2013—Weekly SPX
February 1, 2013—Weekly SPX
February 16, 2013—SPXPM and Standard SPX
March 16, 2013—SPXPM and Standard SPX
March 28, 2013—Quarterly SPX

In addition to the expirations listed above there were several more SPX and SPX-related series expiring for years beyond March 28, 2013.

■ Index Option Comparisons

For all the small differences that have been pointed out regarding the different broad based indexes, the day-to-day performance of these indexes is highly correlated. So if the expectation is that each index will perform in the same manner as the other indexes, how do we go about choosing the right index option to trade? Table 2.2 may help clear things up a little.

TABLE 2.2 Short-Dated Index Option Comparison

Index Series	A.M./P.M. Settlement	Multiple Weeks	American/European
DJX	A.M.	No	European
OEX	P.M.	Yes	American
XEO	P.M.	Yes	European
RUT	A.M.	Yes	European
SPXPM	P.M.	Yes	European
NDX	A.M.	No	European

In addition to the parameters of the specific contract, another thing to consider, if choosing an index option series to trade, is the level of the index. Many traders begin trading options through equity options and an experienced equity-option trader can tell you that there is a difference between trading options on a stock trading at 700.00 versus trading options on a stock with a market price of 30.00. These five indexes actually are quoted at a variety of prices that provide some alternatives based on a trader's comfort level.

The following quotes represent the closing index levels range for September 28, 2012.

DJX—134.37
OEX/XEO—663.80
RUT—837.45
SPX—1,440.67
NDX—2,799.19

As a reminder, DJX is 1/100th the level of the Dow Jones Industrial Average. It is also the lowest underlying value of the five indexes that have weekly options available. If you are interested in index options, DJX options may be a good starting alternative. The low index quote results in low option premiums as well. This would be similar to trading options on any number of stocks that have a price around 134. In addition, due to the close pricing, DJX options offer an easy alternative to SPY option contracts for those considering making a change from ETF options to index-option trading. Finally, there are dollar strikes for DJX options so many alternatives are available.

Moving up the price ladder, the S&P 100 and RUT option series have underlying markets in the upper hundreds. These premiums will be lower than SPX or NDX options and may also offer a trader getting acquainted with index options a good place to start. OEX options have been around for some time and still have a good crowd trading them at CBOE. Another difference between OEX/XEO options and RUT is the volatility of the two indexes. Although correlated, the Russell 2000 tends to have higher volatility than the large-cap-dominated S&P 100 index. The result of this is lower option premiums for OEX and XEO options based on the lower implied volatility levels.

As an academic exercise the respective volatility indexes for these five indexes were used to determine the cost of a 30-day at-the-money call. The results are:

DJX 30-day 134.37 call = 2.25
XEO 30-day 663.80 call = 11.33
OEX 30-day 663.80 call = 11.44
RUT 30-day 837.45 call = 19.12
SPX 30-day 1,440.67 call = 26.50
NDX 30-day 2,799.19 call = 55.58

With these six choices the premium for a 30-day at-the-money call option ranges from 2.25 for DJX to 55.58 for NDX; in dollar-per-contract range that comes to $225 versus $5,558. This is an incredibly wide range of premiums for at the money option contracts that result in exposure to the U.S. equity market.

SPX options are the most liquid index option market of the five indexes discussed in this chapter. They also have many more expiration dates available, which allows for even more flexibility compared to the other four indexes. However, there is a large notional value (over 1,400 at the time of writing this book). Another benefit of SPX relative to the other indexes is the availability of more expiration dates. This just adds some flexibility based on the timing outlook behind any sort of SPX trade.

The five indexes all offer broad based exposure to U.S. stock markets and are highly correlated, but not 100 percent. Table 2.3 is a matrix showing the correlation of these indexes from January 2000 through December 2012.

TABLE 2.3 Daily Index Correlations January 1, 2000 to December 31, 2012

	OEX	DJX	RUT	NDX
SPX	0.9930	0.9691	0.8977	0.8333
OEX		0.9702	0.8687	0.8353
DJX			0.8382	0.7503
RUT				0.7954

Not surprisingly, the two indexes that are most correlated are the S&P 100 and S&P 500. The correlation between the two is 0.9930—almost perfectly correlated. This strong relationship should be expected as all 100 stocks from the S&P 100 are included in the S&P 500 and these 100 stocks represent well over half the market capitalization of the S&P 500.

Day-to-day performance of the Dow Jones Industrial Average closely matches both the S&P 100 and S&P 500. Large-cap stocks dominate these three indexes so the correlation would be expected. The performance correlation begins to disconnect a bit with the other two indexes. The Russell 2000 matches up with the first three indexes, but not to the same high degree. RUT is diversified and covers all industries like the larger cap dominated indexes. Finally, the NASDAQ-100 is still well correlated, but is the least correlated of the five indexes. Recall there are no financial stocks in the NDX and the index only includes stocks that are primarily listed on the NASDAQ stock market.

■ Comparing Index and Exchange-Traded Fund Options

For every index option series discussed in this chapter there is an equivalent exchange-traded fund with performance based on a similar market. The most actively traded of this group of exchange-traded funds is the SPDR S&P 500 ETF Trust (SPY). There is a common misperception in the market place that SPX Index options and options on SPY are the same thing. Both have performance based on the S&P 500 Index, but beyond that there are several differences. Notional contract size, exercise style, the underlying delivery method, and potential tax treatment for profits are all significant differences between broad-based indexes and options on comparable exchange-traded funds.

SPY is quoted at a price very close to one-tenth the value of the S&P 500 while the level of SPX is the value of the S&P 500. Due to this a comparable option on SPY will have a dollar cost that is close to one-tenth the value of an SPX option that would be traded with a similar outlook. As a basic example consider if the S&P 500 is at 1,500 combined with the pricing of the following two options:

SPY Jun 150 call @ 3.00
SPX Jun 1,500 call @ 30.00

The dollar cost of the SPY Jun 150 call would be $300 while the dollar cost of the SPX Jun 1,500 call would be $3,000. However, the SPY option represents \$15,000 of market value while the SPX option represents \$150,000 of market value. Also, the premium for both options is equal to 2 percent of the notional value. Therefore, for both options to break even the market needs to be 2 percent higher than the strike price. In order to have the same exposure of a single SPX option, 10 comparable SPY options would need to be traded.

Stock and exchange-traded fund options traded in the United States are known as American-style options. An American-style option can be exercised by a holder on any business day prior to expiration. All the broad-based index options discussed in this chapter, with the exception of OEX options, are European-style option contracts. European-style options may not be exercised until expiration. Since European-style contracts may not be exercised until expiration this means that a holder of a short position in a European-style contract will have the risk of being assigned on their short-option position. This is a distinct advantage when initiating a spread trade with index options versus ETF options.

When exercised or assigned the holder of a position in options on exchange-traded funds will purchase or sell shares of the underlying. This is known as physical delivery where the actual shares are delivered. The exercise process for index options results in a cash transfer. There is no share transfer to deal with just a dollar profit and loss. Considering many short-term option positions, especially spread trades, may need to be held through expiration for a full profit to be realized, this is a distinct advantage for index options over exchange-traded fund options.

The topic of taxes on profits is something that is worth mentioning before closing this chapter on index options. Trading profits on options on broad-based indexes receive a special type of tax treatment relative to other types of option contracts. The difference exists when comparing index options to options on exchange-traded funds and equities.

According to *Taxes and Investing*, which is published by the Options Industry Council, options on broad-based indexes are classified as 1256 contracts and receive different tax treatment than options on exchange-traded funds or stocks. This is commonly referred to as 60/40 tax treatment, which means that 60 percent of any gain is treated as a long-term profit with the remaining 40 percent treated as a short-term profit. This is true for a trade that lasts just a few minutes or a trade that goes on for several years. The potential tax benefit comes from short-term trades. Since the short-dated options are only listed for a few days or at the most weeks traded for seven days the benefit is always in place for trades using weeklys.

A copy of *Taxes and Investing* may be downloaded from www.cboe.com /LearnCenter/pdf/TaxesandInvesting.pdf. Of course tax laws may have changed since the writing of this book and a tax professional should always be consulted on topics such as this.

Short-dated index options give traders an opportunity to trade short-term market opinions. The six contracts available for trading have a variety of notional values and volatility histories, so there should be an index option series that meets the needs of all levels of option traders. Finally, note the significant differences between broad-based index options and comparable exchange-traded fund options. If a trader has been trading options on ETFs, they are doing themselves a disservice by not at least exploring comparable index options.

CHAPTER 3

Weekly Options on Equities and Exchange-Traded Products

Once short-dated options were introduced on stocks—exchange-traded funds (ETFs) and exchange-traded notes (ETNs)—their popularity and volume growth came very quickly. Initially only a handful of equity products had short-dated options available, but this list has quickly expanded to include over 200 equities with short-dated options available. In addition to options that typically are listed on a Thursday to expire the following Friday, there are a number of stocks and exchange-traded funds that have options expiring several weeks in a row, much like the format used for index options.

■ Stocks

Among the early stocks that had weekly options listed were high-volume traders such as Apple (AAPL), Google (GOOG), and Amazon (AMZN). The list would often change from week to week based on which stocks may be in the news or have an earnings announcement scheduled for the following week. The various options exchanges would list short-dated options based on their belief of which stocks would generate interest in trading options with just a few days to expiration. A good example of this, and an interesting stock that would continuously show up on the list of stocks with weekly options, was on BP p.l.c. (BP), previously known as British Petroleum.

Typically, BP would not have been a very volatile stock that would have garnered attention of option traders. It certainly would not have been the sort of stock that short-term traders would be interested in. However, this was the summer of 2010 and BP was in the news. It was the summer of the Gulf Oil spill and BP stock was trading based on the most recent news surrounding that event. This actually illustrates one of the reasons for the popularity of stock options with only a few days left to expiration. These options are a great vehicle for traders to attempt to take advantage of quick moves in the underlying stock. Being aware of stocks in the news, exchanges wisely choose stocks that are moving on new information to be among those with weekly options available. Although there are now well over 200 stocks with short-dated options available, from time to time new names will have short-dated options available based on market conditions.

■ Exchange-Traded Products

Governments will often establish frameworks of rules and then challenge companies to report information, which governments deem the general public has a right to know, but for which they are reluctant to set up full-scale codes and regulations. In these cases, the framework provides a detailed structure within which companies can report environmental performance.

The term exchange-traded product (ETPs) is used as an encompassing term to cover both exchange-traded funds and exchange-traded notes. There are some unique features of ETFs and ETNs that differentiate the two, but the similarity is what is important in this book. What they have in common is they both trade like a stock and both have listed options markets. The main difference is in the structure and when considering trading an ETP for the first time a trader should always perform a little due diligence on the product.

The first ETF, introduced in 1993, was the SPDR S&P 500 ETF Trust (SPY), which is commonly referred to as the Spyder due to its ticker symbol SPY.

This was the first of hundreds of successful exchange-traded funds introduced to the marketplace. As of early 2012 the total value under ETF management was over $1 trillion.

Exchange-traded notes were introduced in 2006 and have become popular trading and investing vehicles. Although they trade like equities, ETNs are actually structured as fixed income obligations with the payout of that obligation based on the performance of a strategy. Typically the strategy will have some sort of index that the ETN is charged with matching.

■ Leveraged Exchange-Traded Products

Leveraged exchange-traded funds are specifically created in order to have a daily performance that is possibly two or three times the underlying market. What can and does occur with the leveraged products is a disconnection in performance versus the underlying index as time passes. The issue here is the daily performance part. To illustrate this consider a leveraged ETF that will give an investor double the daily return of the XYZ Index. To clearly illustrate the difference between expectations in performance consider if XYZ Index is at 100.00 and the leveraged XYZ ETF that returns two times the XYZ index daily return is also at 100.00.

If XYZ Index drops 10 percent in a day the index would move down from 100.00 to 90.00. The leveraged XYZ ETF would lose 20 percent on the day as the performance is twice that of the underlying index. Therefore the leveraged XYZ ETF price has trade down from 100.00 to 80.00. If the following day the XYZ Index rebounds by 5 percent this would result in the XYZ Index moving up from 90.00 to 94.50. The leveraged ETF should return two times the index performance on this day and trade up 10 percent. Therefore the leverage ETF would increase by 10 percent or 8.00 points and the closing price would move up to 88.00 from 80.00.

Now compare the net price change for the XYZ Index and leveraged XYZ ETF over this two-day period. The XYZ Index has dropped from 100.00 to 94.50—a loss of 5.50. A loss of 5.50 on an index that started at 100.00 results in a loss of 5.50 percent. The leveraged XYZ ETF has moved down from 100.00 to 88.00 for a drop of 12.00. A 12.00 drop on an ETF that was initially trading at 100.00 would represent a loss of 12 percent. So the ETF that was matching two times the daily performance of XYZ Index is down more than twice as much as the leveraged ETF. If the ETF were to perfectly match the index performance over this time period it would have lost 11 percent, not 12 percent. For short-dated option positions this may not be as much of a factor as for a long-term position. However, this understanding is important if you plan on trading either a leveraged ETF or the options on one of these ETFs.

Inverse Exchange-Traded Products

When an investor purchases an inverse exchange-traded fund or note they gain exposure that is opposite to the performance of the underlying index. An inverse ETP is a fairly straightforward method of gaining exposure to performance that would be the inverse of a long position in the underlying index. Tracking errors for these funds exist, but are minimal compared to the goal of the fund. However, the majority (if not all, depending on the current list of equities with short-dated options) of inverse ETPs are leveraged as well. Be aware the leveraged performance issues that were discussed in the previous section may exist for inverse-leveraged ETPs as well.

Volatility-Related Exchange-Traded Products

Volatility being treated as an asset class is an emerging area for the financial markets. One method of taking a volatility-related position is through trading one of the exchange-traded products that is based on a volatility strategy index. There are several available, but one regularly shows up on the list of stocks with short-dated options available. That one is the iPath S&P 500 VIX Short-Term Futures Exchange Traded Note which is commonly known by the ticker VXX.

The VXX ETN has been available since early 2009 and is structured to match the performance of an index, not VIX. The performance of VXX is based on holding a portfolio of futures contracts on the CBOE Volatility Index. Due to the nature of VIX futures pricing, VXX suffers from performance issues relative to the performance of VIX or even VIX futures. Some days VXX will lose value in a low volatility environment, even if VIX or the VIX futures rise on the day. Investors come away a bit confused about the intent of VXX on days where VIX rises and VXX drops. Figure 3.1 is a diagram that shows the typical curve that is associated with VIX futures relative to VIX.

The strategy VXX follows involves weighting a position in the front two-month VIX futures contracts to match a 30-day outlook. On the chart above this are the January and February futures contracts. VIX futures are listed to expire every month. Therefore the front month future will often have less than 30 days to expiration while the second month future will have more than 30 days. The managers of VXX will rebalance the portfolio to match a 30-day average weighting of VIX in the portfolio. This rebalancing will happen on a daily basis.

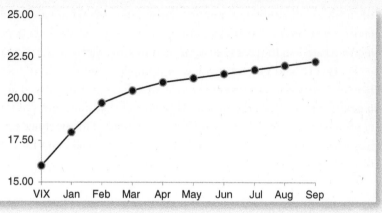

FIGURE 3.1   VIX Futures Pricing Curve

The curve in Figure 3.1 is typical of the pricing of VIX futures. There are times the shape of this curve changes, but when VIX is low, or there is a neutral to bullish stock market, the VIX curve will take on this shape, which is referred to as *contango* by traders. When in contango the price of the future being sold is going to be lower than the future being purchased each day. Eventually the second month will become the front month and those futures will be sold. This constant rebalancing when VIX futures are in contango is a persistent problem for VXX.

However, when VIX futures rise quickly, often VXX does too. It is a good method of obtaining long exposure to VIX if you expect a quick move to the upside that is followed to the upside by the futures contacts. When this happens the curve looks like Figure 3.2. Note in this depiction of VIX futures that prices

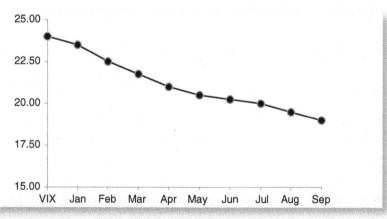

FIGURE 3.2   VIX Futures Pricing Curve in Backwardation

the front month are at a premium relative to the second month. In addition to benefitting from increased VIX futures prices, VXX will also experience a price increase based on the premium of the first month relative to the second month.

When VIX and VIX futures increase in price and the curve inverts VXX benefits greatly and is a good investment vehicle to trade if you anticipate a quick move in VIX to the upside. However, if that move does not happen, a continued price grind lower in VXX will persist. Finally, short-term short-biased trades on VXX have proven fruitful after a spike in VIX and VIX futures has resulted in a subsequent rally in VXX.

■ Summary

The number of available stocks and exchange-traded products with short-dated options continues to expand. Option strategies based on stocks or vanilla exchange-traded funds are fairly straightforward. However, many unique exchange-traded products have short-dated option contracts available. A trader should be sure to have a full understanding of the underlying market you are trading before putting money to work in short dated option contracts.

CHAPTER 4

Option-Pricing Factors and Short-Dated Option Contracts

The market value of an option is ultimately decided by the marketplace. If an option or any other financial asset is perceived as undervalued it will attract buyers which should push the price higher. Conversely, if a financial asset is overpriced it may induce selling. The point is that market forces ultimately determine the value of an option contract. However, there are pricing factors that traders take into account when determining whether they believe an option's price is too high or too low relative to their expectations. These factors can be entered into an option-pricing calculator with the output being the trader's theoretical value of an option. If this theoretical value is different than market prices a trade may result.

Option pricing factors we'll discuss include the following:

Underlying Market Price
Option Strike Price
Days to Expiration
Implied Volatility
Interest Rates
Dividends

Some of these factors change over the life of an option. The market price of the underlying stock or market will be expected to change. As time passes, days to expiration will also change, but at a known rate. The implied volatility, which is determined by the price of an option, will also change over time.

Other pricing factors will be unchanged or will stay in a fairly narrow range. This is especially true of short-dated options. The strike price is set in stone and will not change. The interest rate input is based on the risk-free interest rate, which does change periodically, but often these changes are well known in advance. A change in interest rates is often properly anticipated by the market and option prices may already be pricing in the change to a certain extent. Also, dividends tend to be known in advance, but at times there are some surprise dividend payments or changes in dividends that occur.

■ Underlying Market Price

Any option trade begins with a price forecast for the underlying market. After determining a price outlook, a trader should proceed to consider different option strategies. A market or individual stock may move higher, lower, or not at all. In all three cases there are option trades available to take advantage of the forecast. With respect to short-dated options this price forecast will need to play out over a very short period of time. The bonus is for short term price projections, an option with less time to expiration often gives better results for a quick trade.

If XYZ is trading at 35.00 a 35 strike call option with four trading days left to expiration may be trading for 0.50. All else being the same, a 35 strike call option with 19 trading days until expiration may be trading for 1.10. Now if the forecast was for XYZ to rise by 2.00 points over the next two days the expectation would be that the 4-day call would be at 2.00 while the 19-day call would be trading for 2.35. Table 4.1 summarizes these price moves.

TABLE 4.1 Four- and 19-Day Call Option Price Change Comparison		
	XYZ @ 35.00	XYZ @ 37.00
XYZ 4-Day 35 Call	0.50	2.00
XYZ 19-Day 35 Call	1.10	2.35

Based on an outlook that a stock is going to rise 2.00 the call with very little time to expiration would cost 0.50. If XYZ rises two points in two days the XYZ 4-day 35 call would have a premium of 2.00. There is basically no time value remaining as the contract is in-the-money with only two days until expiration. The result would be a profit of 1.50 based on a cost of 0.50.

The 19-day call with more time to expiration would have a higher premium costing 1.10. This contract would have some time value left and be trading at 2.35 based on the two-point stock price rise in two days. Considering these two options as a use of capital, the XYZ 4-day call returns 300 percent of the 0.50 premium paid, while the XYZ 19-Day call returns 114 percent of the 1.10 premium that would be paid for this contract. Of course there is less time to be correct on the price forecast for XYZ with the 4-day option versus the 19-day call.

■ Days to Expiration

It goes without saying that a difference between longer- and shorter-dated options has to do with the days left to expiration. Another big difference can be the behavior of the time value of these option contracts. Time decay (or lack of time decay) is often a major consideration when taking an option position. Now that shorter-dated option contracts are consistently available on a wide variety of equities and indexes there are more opportunities to take advantage of time decay. Table 4.2 uses the same option contracts in the earlier pricing example with the 35 strike call options representing at the money calls.

The difference in this example is that the price comparisons between the options are based on the stock price not changing, just a change in the number of days to expiration. With the passage of two days and no change in the stock price or any other option pricing factors, the XYZ 4-day 35 call loses 0.15 with the price dropping from 0.50 to 0.35. The longer-dated XYZ 19-day 35 call price moves from 1.10 to 1.05, for a drop of only 0.05. This sort of time decay behavior is typical of at-the-money option contracts

TABLE 4.2   4- and 19-Day Call Option Time Decay Comparison

	Current Price	Two Days Later
XYZ 4-Day 35 Call	0.50	0.35
XYZ 19-Day 35 Call	1.10	1.05

and is a key component to the popularity of shorter-dated option contracts. Chapter 5 will offer a more comprehensive analysis of how time to expiration and time decay are unique for options with just a few days until expiration.

■ Implied Volatility

The most difficult concept for option traders at all levels is implied volatility. When, all else being the same in the market place, an option price increases this increase is attributed to an increase in implied volatility. The actual option price increase will be based on market participants increasing their demand for the options. When there are more buyers than sellers for any financial asset the price will rise. For options this increased demand will be stated as an increase in the implied volatility of the option. This works as well if options are considered overpriced. More sellers will enter the market and push the price down. The lower option premium will also be attributed to a change in implied volatility.

This section will touch on implied volatility a bit and then Chapter 6 will dive into how implied volatility behaves specifically with options that have just a few days left to expiration.

Table 4.3 is a comparison of similar option contracts with either 7 or 22 trading days remaining until expiration.

This table shows different option premiums for comparable call and put options that have either 7 or 22 days left to expiration. For each 5 percent increase in implied volatility the premium for the seven-day options increase by 0.10. Notice this holds true for both put and call options, higher implied volatility has the same directional impaction on the price of both types of options. The impact on the contracts that have 22 days left to expiration is a bit more significant. In fact, it is two times the impact that implied volatility changes have on the seven-day contract. For each 5 percent increase in implied volatility, each of these options increases in value by 0.20.

TABLE 4.3 Different Implied Volatilities and Option Pricing			
XYZ @ 35.00	25%	30%	35%
XYZ 7-Day 35 Call	0.60	0.70	0.80
XYZ 7-Day 35 Put	0.59	0.69	0.79
XYZ 22-Day 35 Call	1.05	1.25	1.45
XYZ 22-Day 35 Put	1.02	1.22	1.42

The longer the time to expiration the more impact a change in implied volatility has on the price of an option contract. This is a direct function of changes in implied volatility, only impacting the time value component of an option contract.

■ Interest Rates

Interest rates and the time value of money will have an impact on the value of an option contract. Higher interest rates result in higher call premiums and lower put premiums. A call option is the right to own a stock at a certain price in the future. Interest rates have an impact on the future expected price of a stock as there is a tradeoff between earning a risk free rate of interest or taking on risk and being rewarded with a return above the risk-free rate. Therefore the future expected value of a stock would be higher if the risk free rate is higher and this expected value would be lower if the risk-free rate is lower. This is one method of explaining why call premiums will be higher relative to put premiums in the case of higher interest rates. Also, the farther out the expiration date, the more an impact in interest rates will have on the price of an option.

Due to the short time to expiration for weeklys a change in interest rates will not have much of an impact on the premium of a short-dated option. Table 4.4 is an example of the difference between two similar call and put options with the risk-free interest rate at 1 percent and 2 percent.

Table 4.4 compares the price differences for two at-the-money options with seven trading days left to expiration. With the risk-free rate at 1.00 percent a 7-day 35 call would be worth 0.70. If the interest rate moves from 1.00 percent to 2.00 percent then, all else being the same, the option premium would increase by 0.01. The 7-day 35 put would be trading at 0.69 with the risk-free interest rate at 1.00 percent; it would be 0.01 lower if the risk-free rate were at 2.00 percent. The major point here is that interest rate changes do influence option premiums, but will not have much of an impact on shorter dated options.

TABLE 4.4	Option Premiums at a Risk-Free Rate of 1 Percent and 2 Percent	
Stock @ 35.00	1.00%	2.00%
7-Day 35 Call	0.70	0.71
7-Day 35 Put	0.69	0.68

■ Dividends

When a company pays a dividend the stock price adjusts the following day. The day the price of a stock adjusts for a dividend is called the ex-dividend date. There are some exceptions to this, but in regular stock trading an investor needs to purchase shares of a stock before the ex-dividend date. The ex-dividend date is the first date that a new purchaser of shares will not be entitled to a dividend, even though the dividend is going to be paid at a later date. This is why the stock price adjusts downward by the amount of a dividend on the ex-dividend date.

Option holders do not participate in dividends. If an owner of a call option wants to receive a dividend they may exercise their call before the ex-dividend date. This means they would purchase shares and no longer hold the call option. They would now be a shareholder. Because stock prices adjust downward on the ex-dividend date this has an impact on call and put prices. Dividends push put prices higher and call prices lower as put option prices benefit from lower stock prices and call option premiums come under pressure when a stock price moves down.

Option premiums typically anticipate the payment of a dividend through a discounted call premium and higher put price. However, if an option contract is set to expire before a dividend is paid then dividends have no impact on an option's price. Short-dated options will often have no dividend payment incorporated into the life of the option.

The theoretical value of a short-dated option contract is determined using the same inputs that may be used to determine the value of a long-dated option contract. However, the factors that would be expected to change have a different sort of impact on these short-dated options. Price changes in the underlying market may have more of an impact on option prices, time decay behaves differently, and a trader may be less concerned about changes in implied volatility when trading an option with very little time left to expiration.

CHAPTER 5

Time Decay and Short-Dated Options

Time value and time decay are two of the biggest differences between option contracts that have just a few trading days left until expiration and options that expire several weeks or even months in the future. For most short-dated options, time to expiration is never longer than seven full trading days while a standard option contact may have up to nine months remaining until expiration. When LEAPS are thrown into the discussion the time to expiration may be measured in years.

The time left until expiration will often have a direct impact on the value of an option contract, depending on the strike price of the option relative to where the underlying security is trading. Typically when there is more time left until expiration, there is more value for an option contract. However, the time to expiration also influences how the time value of an option changes as the contract approaches expiration. This is known as time decay.

Many option strategies are implemented to take advantage of time decay. The rapid acceptance and volume growth of short-dated options with only a few days left until expiration may be attributed to strategies that take advantage of or are able to avoid the influence of time decay. The majority of trades that include weekly options involve strategies that are based on either taking advantage of time decay or avoiding the impact of time decay on a position.

■ Behavior of Time Decay

The rate of time decay is not uniform for all option contracts. There are some pricing factors that have more influence on time decay. The most straightforward of those factors is the price of the underlying stock or index relative to the strike price of the option contract. There are specific terms used to describe the strike price of an option relative to the underlying market. An option may be referred to as either being in-the-money (ITM), out-of-the-money (OTM), or at-the-money (ATM). An option contract would be considered in-the-money if it would make economic sense to exercise the option at expiration. The right to buy stock XYZ at 40 would be represented by a XYZ 40 call. If XYZ were trading at 50.00 at expiration then the XYZ 40 call would be in-the-money and exercised.

Out-of-the-money is the opposite of in-the-money. An out-of-the-money option would not be exercised at expiration as there would be no economic value in exercising an OTM contract. For example, with XYZ trading at 50.00 an XYZ 60 call represents the right to buy XYZ at 60.00. This would not be exercised at expiration as it does not make sense to pay 60.00 for a stock that is trading in the open market at 50.00. This XYZ 60 call has no value if exercised so it would be considered an out-of-the-money option.

Finally, an at-the-money option is defined as an option contract that has a strike price that is equal to the market price of the underlying stock. For example if XYZ is trading at 50.00 the XYZ 50 call would be considered at-the-money. Since stocks do not always (in fact rarely) trade at round numbers like 50.00, traders will often refer to the option contract that has the nearest strike price to the underlying market as being the at-the-money option. For instance, if XYZ were trading at 50.13 the XYZ 50 call would still be considered an at-the-money option by many traders.

Time decay occurs differently for at-the-money options relative to in-the-money or out-of-the-money option contracts. Table 5.1 compares time decay over a variety of periods for ITM, ATM, and OTM option contracts over 22 trading days. The time period of 22 trading days is chosen as that is approximately the number of trading days in a month. Also, for the figures in the table there is an assumption that no other pricing factors change over the 22-day period. The goal is to isolate the behavior of time value over this time period.

TABLE 5.1	Time Decay for ITM/ATM/OTM Calls					
Stock @ 45.00	22 Days	17 Days	12 Days	7 Days	2 Days	Expiration
ITM—44 Call	2.15	1.96	1.74	1.48	1.14	1.00
ATM—45 Call	1.61	1.41	1.19	0.90	0.48	0.00
OTM—46 Call	1.17	0.98	0.76	0.50	0.14	0.00

Note that the 44 call is 1.00 in-the-money at the beginning and end of the time period covered on this table. Over the full 22-day period the ITM 44 call premium goes from 2.15 to 1.00—a loss of 1.15, all of which would be attributed to time decay. The price of the OTM 46 call starts out at 1.17 and ends up at 0.00 at expiration. This is a loss of 1.17 and close to the time value loss that occurs over this 22-day period for the in-the-money 44 call. This sort of time decay behavior is typical of in-the-money and out-of-the-money option contracts that are equally in and out of the money.

The loss of time value (and the option premium) for at-the-money option contracts is unique relative to in-the-money and out-of-the-money contracts. For ITM and OTM options the premium drops at a fairly linear rate. Time decay is different for ATM option contracts. ATM options experience time decay in a less linear fashion and the loss of value actually accelerates as expiration approaches. This can be seen on the table as between 22 and 17 days to expiration the ATM 45 call loses 0.20 of value. Over the last two days until expiration the same contract drops by 0.48. Figure 5.1 shows a graphical comparison of the loss in value for an out-of-the-money contract and at-the-money option.

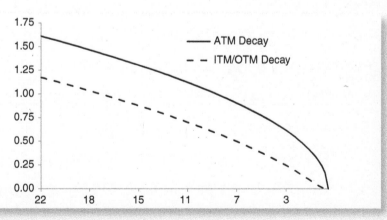

FIGURE 5.1   Twenty-Two-Day Time Decay Comparison

The chart is a graphical representation of the data used in Table 5.1. The dashed line on this figure represents OTM time decay, but could just as easily show the loss of time value for ITM as both lose value at a very similar rate. Note the solid line that shows how the value of an ITM contract drops. As expiration approaches the loss of premium begins to accelerate. This book primarily focuses on options that only have seven days of trading life and various strategies that are short term in nature. Table 5.2 compares the time decay for these same three option contracts over seven days leading up to expiration.

As in the 22-trading-day example, time decay is linear and similar for the ITM and OTM call options. The ATM contract is where the time decay really has some interesting behavior. With seven days until expiration, the premium for the ATM 45 call would be 0.90. All else being the same, the premium drops by 0.06 over the course of a day. That is, if the stock price does not change, only the passage of a single day occurs, the option price will be 0.84 the following day, when there are six days remaining to expiration. Note the decay over the final two days into expiration. With two days to go, the option is priced at 0.48 and 0.34 of value comes out of the contract over the final day of trading. This loss of 0.34 of the final day is a dramatic drop when compared to the 0.06 price change from day 7 to day 6.

Figure 5.1 takes the ATM and OTM data from Table 5.2 for a graphical time decay comparison. Much like the chart showing 22-day time decay the linear versus nonlinear behavior of OTM versus ATM time decay is apparent. Also, like that previous example, ATM time decay accelerates as expiration approaches.

TABLE 5.2	ITM/ATM/OTM 7-Day Time Decay		
Days to Expiration	ITM—44 Call	ATM—45 Call	OTM—46 Call
7	1.48	0.90	0.50
6	1.42	0.84	0.44
5	1.36	0.76	0.37
4	1.29	0.68	0.30
3	1.22	0.59	0.22
2	1.14	0.48	0.14
1	1.05	0.34	0.05
0	1.00	0.00	0.00

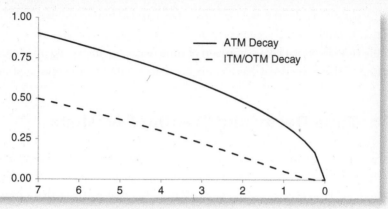

FIGURE 5.2 Seven-Day Time Decay Comparison

■ Weekends and Time Decay

In this book I avoid the issue of weekends by only focusing on trading days for time value examples. However, many pricing models include weekends in the total number of days until expiration. A question that often arises is how do professional traders, especially market makers, account for time decay? The answer is not fully quantifiable but more of a subtle tweaking of pricing models as weekends approach.

Through discussions with market makers and other professional option traders I have found many traders begin to account for weekend time decay on Friday. Typically they will begin to alter their models based on how volatile the underlying market is and rely on experience to begin to take weekend time decay into account. As Friday afternoon progresses the time value of an option contract approaches the number of days remaining to expiration from Monday morning, excluding Saturday and Sunday from consideration.

This is actually an important factor for individual option traders as well. Throughout this book there will be trading examples that are motivated by taking advantage of time decay in one form or another. Something to keep in mind when considering a short position in a short-dated option contract is whether to trade before or after the weekend. If a trader is considering a short position in an option, initiating a trader late on a Friday may not be an ideal time for option selling. There is always market or specific stock event risk that exists for any position and there is a little potential market or stock-event risk that may be attributed to a weekend. Because of this, it may make sense to wait until Monday morning to initiate a short-term trade once the weekend has passed. Again, this is more of a subjective judgment call, but if the motivation behind a trade is to benefit from time decay, late Friday afternoon is not the time to try to take advantage of time decay for the weekend. A good portion of that time decay has already been discounted by the option premium.

■ Time Decay and Trading Decisions

So far this chapter has focused mainly on how the time value of an option deteriorates based on where the strike price is relative to the underlying market. However, the time to expiration is a major factor that can have implications on taking advantage of time decay as well. There was a glimpse of this in the previous section, but the following example highlights how time to expiration impacts time decay.

Consider if XYZ is trading at 45.00 and a trader is long 100 shares of XYZ. They have a neutral outlook for the stock price over the next 22 trading days. With this the trader decides to sell a call option against their holding in XYZ to bring in some income. Using the pricing from the previous examples in this chapter the resulting covered call positions is:

Long 100 XYZ @ 45.00
Short 1 XYZ 22-day call @ 1.61

Before weekly options this may have been the best and only choice based on the trader's outlook. However, there is a potentially better alternative using short-dated options. It turns out in this example that XYZ also has short-dated options available and the XYZ 7-day call is trading at 0.90. An alternative to selling the 22-day call to create a covered call scenario may be:

Long 100 XYZ @ 45.00
Short 1 XYZ 7-day call @ 0.90

Instead of taking in 1.61, only 0.90 of income could be garnered from selling a call option. However, the 7-day call is going to expire and there will be still be 15 trading days left for the trader's outlook of a neutral stock price. At that point, with a correct neutral outlook on XYZ, another short-dated option contract with five days left to expiration might be sold. The premium in this case would be 0.76. With 15 days left for the neutral XYZ, outlook the new position is:

Long 100 XYZ @ 45.00
Short 1 XYZ 5-day call @ 0.76

Selling a 5-day call could be repeated again two more times over this 22-day period. Backing up to the beginning of this 22-day forecast there are two decisions to compare. One would be selling the 22-day call with the other decision being a systematic selling of shorter dated XYZ calls. The two decisions are illustrated here:

22 Days—Sell 1 XYZ 22-day call @ 1.61
Net Income = 1.61

or

22 Days—Sell 1 XYZ 7-day call @ 0.90
15 Days—Sell 1 XYZ 5-day call @ 0.76
10 Days—Sell 1 XYZ 5-day call @ 0.76
5 Days—Sell 1 XYZ 5-day call @ 0.76
Net Income = 3.18

Admittedly, this is an academic example where the price of the underlying is steady. Also, under real market conditions the other pricing factors that influence the price of XYZ options would change. The stock price would not consistently be at 45.00 and the implied volatility of XYZ options would move around. The goal here is to focus on how to make time decay work for a trader. For at-the-money option contracts time decay works for a trader very effectively as the contract approaches expiration. Short-dated options, by their nature, are always very close to expiration.

■ Avoiding Time Decay

In addition to using short-dated options to take advantage of time decay, it is also possible to take long positions in these contracts and avoid having time work against a position. Typically in-the-money option contracts that have little time left to expiration will have very little time value. Table 5.3 uses an option-pricing calculator to determine premiums for options that have seven trading days remaining to expiration with a stock trading at 20.00 and implied volatility of 25.00 percent.

Based on the factors used to generate these option prices the 19 call has only 0.05 of time value and the 18 call only 0.01. In reality the market would probably have an offer side that had 0.05 to 0.10 of time value built in. However if a trader is bullish on XYZ over the next few days he could take a long position in either of those call options and not have too much time decay working against him. The put premiums have very little time

TABLE 5.3	Theoretical Option Premiums
Contract	Premium
17 call	3.00
18 call	2.01
19 call	1.05
20 call	0.34
20 put	0.33
21 put	1.05
22 put	2.01
23 put	3.00

value as well and would offer a very inexpensive method of taking a short term bearish position on XYZ.

The behavior of time decay varies depending on the time to expiration along with where the underlying market is trading relative to an option's strike price. For at-the-money options there is an opportunity to take advantage of the rapid time-decay characteristics that are common for the last few days of life for an option. In-the-money options may have little time value due to the lack of time left to expiration and these contracts may be a good method of taking a bearish or bullish position through purchasing a put or call option.

CHAPTER 6

Implied Volatility and Weekly Options

Implied volatility is often described as a risk factor that is associated with the market price of an option. However, it is not exactly a measure of risk in the sense that most traders think of risk. When traders or investors think of risk they generally are contemplating the potential for loss in an investment. As a measure of risk implied volatility can be used to estimate how much downside price action the option market is pricing in for a certain stock or market. However, implied volatility may also be used to determine how much of a potential price rise is being priced in by the option market as well. Implied volatility is an indication of what sort of price movement—higher or lower—is being anticipated out of the underlying market over the life of an option contract. Higher implied volatility is an indication that there is more price action in both directions expected out of the underlying market.

■ Time to Expiration and Implied Volatility

There is a direct relationship between option premiums and implied volatility. When implied volatility moves up the result is higher option premiums and when there is lower implied volatility priced into an option contract option premiums are lower. An option price change that is attributed to changes in implied volatility will only have an impact on the time value of an option contract. Since volatility-based price changes only impact the time-value component of an option contract, when an option has less time left to expiration a price change based on a change in implied volatility would be less than a price change that would occur in an option that has more time to expiration.

Take for example the two option contracts below. These two calls are at-the-money options on the same underlying. The prices of these two call options are based on XYZ trading at 50.00 and the implied volatility of the options at 20 percent. One has four trading days to expiration and the other has 24 trading days until expiration. Other than that all pricing factors are the same for both options.

XYZ 4-day 50 call @ 0.50
XYZ 24-day 50 call @ 1.25

Keeping all factors in place, what if a large buyer of these two XYZ call options comes into the market and buys these calls? They will continue buying these calls until the implied volatility reaches 25 percent. This buying would have a different dollar impact on the option premiums. The 4-day call would increase in value by 0.10 and then the implied volatility of this call would be 25 percent. The 24-day call would gain 0.30 until the implied volatility is 25 percent.

XYZ 4-day 50 call @ 0.60 +0.10
XYZ 24-day 50 call @ 1.55 +0.30

The first example shows the impact of a change in implied volatility for at-the-money option contracts. The more an option strike price differs from the underlying market, the lower the time value of that option. This actually works in both directions, higher and lower, starting with a situation where the call strikes are higher than the underlying market. If XYZ were trading at 48.00 instead of 50.00 the two 50 strike call options with implied volatility at 20 percent would have the following premiums:

XYZ 4-day 50 call @ 0.05
XYZ 24-day 50 call @ 0.50

As with the at-the-money contracts, the premiums for these calls are all time value, but there is less time value than there was for the at-the-money options. If the same trading situation occurred where a buyer came in and purchased both calls until implied volatility moved up to 25 percent then the options would have the following price changes:

XYZ 4-day 50 call @ 0.10 +0.05
XYZ 24-day 50 call @ 0.75 +0.25

The 4-day call gains 0.05 and the 24-day call gains 0.25 to reach an implied volatility of 25 percent. Both premium gains are a little less than the price change for the at-the-money options that resulted in implied volatility at 25 percent.

An in-the-money option also has less time value than an at-the-money contract. The in-the-money options will be priced higher, but this is a function of the option being in-the-money. If the underlying stock is at a premium to the strike price of a call option there will be a combination of intrinsic and time value to the option contact. Continuing with expirations four and 24 days in the future the contract prices below are based on XYZ trading at 52.00.

XYZ 4-day 50 call @ 2.05
XYZ 24-day 50 call @ 2.55

With XYZ trading at 52.00 both calls have 2.00 of intrinsic value. The XYZ 4-day 50 call is quoted at 2.05 and only 0.05 of this 2.05 may be attributed to time value. The XYZ 24-day 50 call has 2.00 of intrinsic value and 0.55 of time value. A 5 percent jump in implied volatility has the following impact on the two option premiums:

XYZ 4-day 50 call @ 2.10 +0.05
XYZ 24-day 50 call @ 2.80 +0.25

Like the out-of-the-money contract, the price changes for both options are a little less than the price change for the at-the-money contract. Since the 4-day option only has 0.10 of time value it will have a smaller expansion of time value based on the 5 percent increase in implied volatility. The 24-day option increases more in value due to there being more time left to expiration.

■ Interpreting Implied Volatility

Implied volatility is an annualized figure that takes the market price of an option contract and projects the expected price range for the underlying market over the life of the option contract. This projection is one standard deviation so statistically this projection should be accurate 68.2 percent of the time. For example, consider stock XYZ trading at 40.00 and the implied volatility of an option contract that expires a year from today is 30 percent. To determine standard deviation in terms of points all we need to do is multiply the implied volatility times the price level of the stock. In this case it would be .30 × 40.00 with a result being 12.00 points. Therefore, statistically the market is pricing in with 68.2 percent certainty that XYZ will close between up 12.00 points and down 12.00 points a year from today. Another way to interpret this is that XYZ should be between 28.00 and 52.00 with 68.2 percent certainty a year from today. The math behind this is pretty easy:

Expected Upside Range   = Stock Price + (Stock Price × Implied Volatility)

Expected Downside Range = Stock Price − (Stock Price × Implied Volatility)

Applying the formula to the examples laid out in the text gives:

$52.00 = 40.00 + (40.00 \times .30)$
$28.00 = 40.00 − (40.00 \times .30)$

The implied volatility on our stock tells us that with 68.2 percent certainty XYZ should close in a range between up or down 12.00 points a year from today. Statistics would describe this range as being up or down one standard deviation a year from now. Again, in this case one standard deviation is equal to 12.00 points.

Statistics also tells us that with 95.4 percent certainty an outcome will land between up and down two standard deviations and with 99.7 percent certainty an outcome should be between up and down three standard deviations. Converting a projected one standard deviation price range to two and three standard deviations involves basic multiplication. Using our example where one standard deviation is equal to 12.00 points, we can determine a two standard deviation price move as 24.00 points (2 × 12.00), and a three standard deviation move as 36.00 (3 × 12.00) points. For the 40.00 stock this means that with 95.4 percent confidence the stock should be between 16.00 and 64.00 a year from today. For example:

$16.00 = 40.00 − (2 \times 12.00)$
$64.00 = 40.00 + (2 \times 12.00)$

Finally, the market is pricing in with 99.7 percent certainty that the 40.00 stock should close between 4.00 and 76.00. This is determined through the following equations:

$4.00 = 40.00 − (3 \times 12.00)$
$76.00 = 40.00 + (3 \times 12.00)$

The previous example involved taking the implied volatility of a one-year option and showing what it tells us regarding the expected price movement of the underlying security for a year. We rarely have an option contract that expires a year to the date from this very moment. Also, it is probably rare that we are trading with a forecast that involves targeting a price in exactly a year. Since implied volatility is an annualized number, we need a method of converting that number to match up to different time periods. This method involves a little more math than just dividing the annualized implied volatility by the number of days in a year, but do not be too alarmed—the formula is not nearly as overwhelming as one may think.

At a very basic level implied volatility is an annualized number that can be easily converted to any time period, even a single day. The common formula used to convert implied volatility projections to just a few days appears below.

Stock Price × Implied Volatility × (Square Root (Days to Expiration) / Square Root (Days in Year))

A common question is whether to use calendar days or trading days for this formula. Typically longer-dated options will use calendar days and short-term options are better suited using trading days. Because this book focuses mainly on short-term option trades, the number of trading days is used consistently.

■ Behavior of Implied Volatility

The CBOE Volatility Index, commonly known as VIX, is an index created by CBOE that calculates a standard 30-day implied volatility as indicated by S&P 500 Index (SPX) option prices. VIX has been termed the *fear index* by the popular press due to the inverse relationship between price changes in the S&P 500 and VIX. It is called the fear index because during approximately 80 percent of trading days the S&P 500 and VIX move in opposite directions. Due to this highly publicized inverse relationship the assumption exists that all stocks have this sort of inverse relationship between the price performance of all trading instruments and the implied volatility of option prices. This assumption is not accurate, at least not in the case of equity options.

In addition to VIX, CBOE publishes several volatility related indexes and has five volatility indexes that are based on the implied volatility of option prices on individual stocks. Those stocks are Amazon (AMZN), Apple (AAPL), Google (GOOG), Goldman Sachs (GS), and IBM (IBM). Table 6.1

TABLE 6.1 Comparison of Equity Volatility Indexes and Underlying Markets—September 30, 2011 to September 28, 2012

Underlying Market	Days Higher	Volatility Index Lower	% Opposite	Days Lower	Volatility Index Higher	% Opposite	% Total Opposite
S&P 500	134	106	79.10	117	91	77.78	78.49
AAPL	135	93	68.89	116	67	57.76	63.75
AMZN	124	80	64.52	125	77	61.60	63.05
GOOG	138	89	64.49	113	79	69.91	66.93
GS	126	93	73.81	125	79	63.20	68.53
IBM	128	94	73.44	123	88	71.54	72.51

is a basic comparison of the daily price performance of the S&P 500 to VIX along with the daily performance of these five stocks compared to their respective volatility indexes.

Again, the common belief is that option prices react in a way that implied volatility rises when the underlying market moves lower. This is not necessarily true across the board. For IBM and the S&P 500 implied volatility moves opposite to the price reaction of the underlying for over 70 percent of trading days. For AAPL and AMZN this relationship is closer to 60 percent of trading days. Traders who focus on a small number of stocks will get a feel for how those stocks trade; option traders will get a feel for how the options change based on changes in implied volatility. In both cases the nature of price and implied volatility changes is unique to the individual market or stock.

CBOE also calculates and quotes volatility indexes on various exchange-traded funds. (See Table 6.2.) The CBOE Crude Oil ETF Volatility Index (OVX) measure market expectation of the volatility of oil prices based on options that trade on the United States Oil Fund (USO). The CBOE Gold ETF Volatility Index (GVZ) measures market expectations of the volatility for the price of gold by applying VIX methodology to options on SPDR Gold Shares (GLD) exchange-traded fund. Finally, the CBOE EuroCurrency ETF Volatility Index (EVZ) is a volatility measure of the $US/Euro currency exchange rate based on option trading on the CurrencyShares Euro Trust (FXE) exchange-traded fund. There are several more volatility indexes based on exchange-traded funds that may be found at www.cboe.com/volatility.

The nature of implied volatility varies based on the underlying market. A blanket statement stating that a trader should expect an increase in implied volatility when there is a price drop in the underlying market is misleading. For options on broad-based indexes or exchange-traded

TABLE 6.2		Comparison of ETF Volatility Indexes and Underlying Markets—November 30, 2011 to September 28, 2012						
Underlying	Higher	Volatility Index Lower	% Opposite	Lower	Volatility Index Higher	% Opposite	% Total Opposite
S&P 500	134	106	79.10	117	91	77.78	78.49
FXE	119	84	70.59	131	80	61.07	65.60
GVZ	135	84	62.22	116	64	55.17	58.96
USO	129	95	73.64	120	75	62.50	68.27

funds there is an inverse and mostly reactionary relationship between underlying price action and implied volatility. When considering the relationship between stocks and implied volatility, option-implied volatility is more anticipatory since it is based on an expected price move in the underlying stock.

The best example of implied volatility of stock options being anticipatory is option price activity around a corporate earnings report. Stock price changes (higher or lower) are often headline-grabbing events around earnings reports. If a stock typically trades in a 1 percent range on an average trading day, option prices will reflect this sort of price action when there is not an event on the horizon. If the same stock moves an average of 10 percent in reaction to the company's earnings report option prices will reflect this sort of anticipated trading activity as an earnings announcement date becomes imminent. Option premiums will be at higher than normal levels based on the pending news announcement and increase in implied volatility. This concept will be expanded on in Chapter 18 which focuses on using short-dated options to trade events such as earnings announcements.

■ Implied Volatility across Expiration Dates and Strike Prices

Different options on the same underlying market almost always have different implied volatilities. This statement is true for contracts that have different strike prices as well as for options with different expiration dates. This difference in levels of implied volatility is commonly referred to as the volatility skew. Since options may have different strike prices and different expirations, there are two different types of skew based on these two parameters.

Vertical Skew

Vertical skew refers to different levels of implied volatility as indicated by prices of options contracts that have the same expiration date but different strike prices. The difference between the implied volatility of options with different strike prices comes down to the demand for those contracts. When options are in higher demand the prices move up and the result is higher implied volatility. This holds true for options on different underlying markets as well as for option contracts on the same market versus other individual option contracts.

The figures in Table 6.3 are the respective implied volatility levels for December SPX options approximately a month before expiration. Also at this time, the S&P 500 was close to 1,390.

These are not the only SPX options that were listed for standard December expiration in 2012, but they are a good sample to show the different implied volatilities that are indicated by the market prices of each option. The first strike price on this table is the 1,335 call and put contracts. The implied volatility of these two options is 16.36 percent and 16.33 percent. Up at the 1,455 strike price the implied volatility for the call is 11.25 percent and the put options is 11.59 percent, an average of about 5 percentage points lower than the 1,335 strike contracts. As the strike prices increase the implied

TABLE 6.3	December SPX Implied Volatility Levels				
1,335 C	16.36%	1,375 C	14.15%	1,415 C	12.34%
1,335 P	16.33%	1,375 P	14.20%	1,415 P	12.30%
1,340 C	16.14%	1,380 C	13.90%	1,420 C	12.15%
1,340 P	16.12%	1,380 P	14.04%	1,420 P	12.10%
1,345 C	15.89%	1,385 C	13.67%	1,425 C	12.00%
1,345 P	15.83%	1,385 P	13.78%	1,425 P	11.91%
1,350 C	15.60%	**1,390 C**	**13.43%**	1,430 C	11.79%
1,350 P	15.51%	**1,390 P**	**13.57%**	1,430 P	11.86%
1,355 C	15.32%	1,395 C	13.22%	1,435 C	11.69%
1,355 P	15.26%	1,395 P	13.39%	1,435 P	11.67%
1,360 C	14.89%	1,400 C	12.96%	1,440 C	11.53%
1,360 P	15.04%	1,400 P	13.14%	1,440 P	11.57%
1,365 C	14.69%	1,405 C	12.80%	1,450 C	11.33%
1,365 P	14.77%	1,405 P	12.85%	1,450 P	11.17%
1,370 C	14.47%	1,410 C	12.57%	1,455 C	11.25%
1,370 P	14.55%	1,410 P	12.69%	1,455 P	11.59%

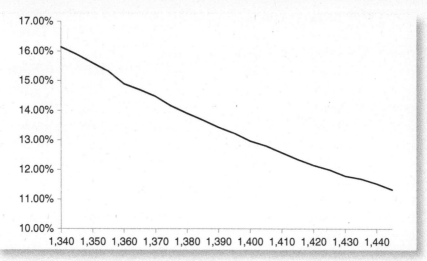

FIGURE 6.1 SPX December 2012 SKEW

volatility indicated by these option contracts drops. This change in the implied volatility is referred to as the skew for December SPX Option contacts. Figure 6.1 charts the skew of the December 2012 SPX option contracts.

The shape of the curve in this figure is fairly common when comparing the implied volatility of equity index options for out of the money puts and calls. This is due to the nature of trading in index option contracts where more puts than calls are traded, and the put trading is usually a result of portfolio managers turning to SPX options for portfolio protection. The most common methods of using options to protect a portfolio involve purchasing put options and the result is more demand for out-of-the money SPX put options than demand for out-of-the-money SPX call options. The shape of this curve is a graphical display of the trading activity in SPX option contracts.

Vertical skew is a little different with respect to other markets. With individual stocks the skew may be a little less dramatic than for options on indexes.

AAPL was trading close to 560 when Table 6.4 was created and there was about a month until December expiration. The 560 put and call are highlighted to signify they are the at-the-money option contracts. The implied volatility on the low end of the strike prices represented is 33.91 percent for the 510 call and 32.77 percent for the 510 Put. Note at different strike prices there will be higher implied volatility for the call or put depending on market factors, but they are always very close to each other due to arbitrage that exists when put and call prices get out of line with each other. A chart of AAPL skew for December expiration appears in Figure 6.2.

TABLE 6.4   December AAPL Implied Volatility Levels

510 C	33.91%	545 C	30.63%	580 C	29.62%
510 P	32.77%	545 P	30.46%	580 P	29.02%
515 C	31.98%	550 C	30.72%	585 C	29.46%
515 P	32.34%	550 P	30.24%	585 P	28.97%
520 C	32.46%	555 C	30.54%	590 C	29.43%
520 P	32.00%	555 P	30.03%	590 P	28.92%
525 C	31.26%	560 C	30.40%	595 C	29.38%
525 P	31.61%	560 P	29.78%	595 P	28.69%
530 C	31.84%	565 C	30.10%	600 C	29.31%
530 P	31.26%	565 P	29.68%	600 P	29.22%
535 C	31.46%	570 C	29.88%	605 C	29.41%
535 P	31.00%	570 P	29.43%	605 P	29.43%
540 C	31.10%	575 C	29.75%	610 C	29.35%
540 P	30.62%	575 P	29.20%	610 P	28.48%

The shape of AAPL's skew chart is similar to that of the overall equity market. The interesting thing is the reason behind this shape for equities. While the major use of index options involves purchasing out-of-the-money put options, the most common use of equity options involves selling call options to create a covered call. Therefore, buying pressure on puts impacts the shape of a chart of skew for market indexes, while selling pressure on call options has a big influence on the skew for individual stock option series.

A market behaves differently with respect to the behavior of implied volatility is gold. The SPDR Gold Shares (GLD) is an excellent way for individuals to have exposure to the price of gold in their personal portfolio.

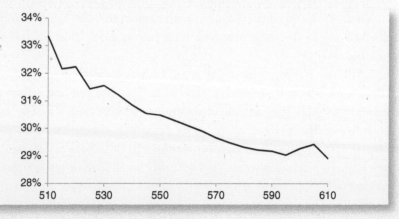

FIGURE 6.2   AAPL December 2012 SKEW

TABLE 6.5 December GLD Implied Volatility Levels

165 C	12.77%	**170 C**	**12.18%**
165 P	12.43%	**170 P**	**12.02%**
166 C	12.43%	171 C	12.24%
166 P	12.23%	171 P	12.04%
167 C	12.27%	172 C	12.35%
167 P	12.11%	172 P	12.14%
168 C	12.19%	173 C	12.49%
168 P	12.02%	173 P	12.18%
169 C	**12.20%**	174 C	12.70%
169 P	**11.98%**	174 P	12.53%

GLD tracks the spot price of gold and is backed by physical gold held in a secure and secret location. Gold is a unique asset relative to other investable markets and the option price behavior and the subsequent impact on implied volatility is unusual as well. Note Table 6.5, which shows the implied volatility GLD options a month before expiration with GLD trading at 169.61. Based on GLD being between 169.00 and 170.00 both strikes are highlighted and considered at-the-money.

Note the implied volatility skew does not have much shape at all. The 165 strike options have very similar implied-volatility levels as the 174 put and call. As the strike prices approach the underlying price, the implied volatility levels actually drop. In fact, as seen in Figure 6.3, the volatility chart looks more like a smile than being skewed in a certain direction.

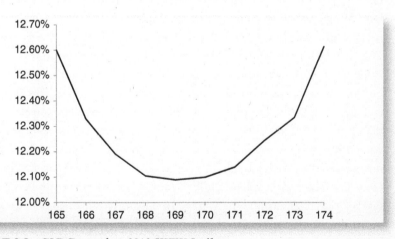

FIGURE 6.3   GLD December 2012 SKEW Smile

This is not a typical shape that is created when charting a skew chart for stocks or market indexes. However, for markets where different participants need to hedge in different ways, skew will often look more like a smile. Consider the price of gold. Some market participants will want to hedge against a drop in gold prices, such as mining companies. On the other side, consumers of gold such as jewelry producers may want to hedge against higher gold prices. Hedging against a drop in the price of gold would result in purchasing put options. Hedging against a rise would involve buying call options. Therefore in the case of an asset like gold, demand for options is the same based on higher or lower prices and the result is a shape that appears like a smile when charting the implied volatility of options.

Horizontal Skew

Vertical skew is important when considering different options that share an underlying and expiration, but what will be more relevant throughout this book is horizontal skew. Horizontal skew refers to different levels of implied volatility based on the expiration date of option contracts. This type of implied volatility difference is significant with respect to trading of short-dated options versus long-dated options. The focus of this book is on short-dated option contracts. Many of the strategies presented in later chapters relate to spread trades that involve one expiration series versus another expiration series. An understanding of horizontal skew is vital to trading those types of spreads.

SPX option contracts have a typical pattern with respect to horizontal skew. Near-dated options usually have a lower implied volatility level than farther-dated options. (See Table 6.6.) This is typical, but not an absolute rule. When volatility runs up quickly based on a market event, it usually reverts back to a lower level. This reversion may show up in near-dated options having higher implied volatility than longer-dated options.

Figure 6.4 shows the horizontal skew for SPX options expiration going out just over two years from when the data was recorded. This illustration is not to time scale, but does depict how implied volatility is usually higher than farther out and lower for near-dated contracts. An exception to this is when the market experiences near-term spikes in volatility. In those periods nearer-dated volatility tends to rise relative to volatility on farther-dated contracts. The reason behind this behavior is that over time implied volatility tends to oscillate around an average or mean. This average level may vary over time, but the reversion shows up in farther-dated volatility not running up in cases of spikes in near dated volatility.

Expiration	1,375 Call	1,375 Put	1,400 Call	1,400 Put	1,425 Call	1,425 Put
11/30/2012	15.01%	15.09%	13.44%	13.39%	12.53%	12.31%
12/7/2012	14.83%	15.00%	13.44%	13.52%	12.38%	12.77%
12/14/2012	14.78%	14.83%	13.47%	13.56%	12.47%	12.59%
12/21/2012	14.15%	14.20%	12.96%	13.14%	12.00%	11.91%
12/31/2012	14.31%	14.24%	13.15%	13.05%	12.05%	12.07%
1/19/2013	14.81%	14.70%	13.77%	13.60%	12.79%	12.55%
2/16/2013	15.48%	15.61%	14.55%	14.73%	13.73%	13.87%
3/16/2013	15.96%	16.37%	15.19%	15.58%	14.41%	14.83%
3/28/2013	16.37%	16.66%	15.61%	15.90%	14.83%	15.16%
6/22/2013	16.93%	17.77%	16.32%	17.19%	15.72%	16.61%
6/28/2013	17.07%	17.94%	16.47%	17.32%	15.85%	16.71%
9/21/2013	17.32%	18.69%	16.82%	18.21%	16.31%	17.73%
9/30/2013	17.40%	18.81%	16.87%	18.27%	16.42%	17.75%
12/21/2013	17.52%	19.39%	17.08%	18.99%	16.64%	18.60%
1/18/2014	17.52%	19.39%	17.07%	19.01%	16.68%	18.63%
6/21/2014	17.92%	20.29%	17.59%	19.97%	17.21%	19.67%
12/20/2014	18.17%	21.00%	17.87%	20.69%	17.59%	20.43%

TABLE 6.6 SPX Implied Volatilities across Different Expirations

For individual equity options volatility also normally rises when expiration is farther out. Table 6.7 shows the implied volatility for various option contracts trading on AAPL when the stock was close to 560.00.

Near-dated options have lower implied volatility and when the implied volatility increases up to a point that coincides with the first series available that expires after AAPL would report earnings. (See Figure 6.5.) Options that have an

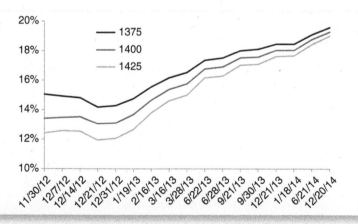

FIGURE 6.4 SPX Horizontal Skew

TABLE 6.7   Horizontal Skew for AAPL

Expiration	530 Put	530 Call	560 Put	560 Call	590 Put	590 Call
11/30/2012	29.87%	28.91%	28.43%	27.65%	28.36%	29.75%
12/7/2012	31.40%	30.66%	29.85%	29.54%	29.10%	28.24%
12/14/2012	31.62%	30.96%	30.13%	29.66%	29.27%	28.58%
12/21/2012	31.84%	31.26%	30.40%	29.78%	29.43%	28.92%
12/28/2012	31.42%	32.13%	30.58%	30.83%	29.63%	29.56%
1/18/2013	33.24%	32.64%	32.07%	31.47%	31.25%	30.66%
2/15/2013	36.99%	35.27%	35.86%	34.36%	35.23%	33.83%
3/15/2013	35.48%	34.35%	34.45%	33.79%	33.64%	32.87%
4/19/2013	34.65%	34.04%	33.82%	33.22%	33.25%	32.67%
6/21/2013	34.22%	33.43%	33.53%	32.85%	32.65%	32.36%
7/19/2013	33.99%	33.36%	33.10%	33.09%	32.57%	32.44%
12/20/2013	34.27%	34.18%	33.70%	33.77%	33.04%	33.14%
1/17/2014	35.02%	34.98%	34.35%	34.62%	33.86%	34.25%
1/16/2015	36.26%	36.70%	35.87%	36.56%	35.32%	36.14%

expiration date closest to, but following an earnings announcement have higher implied volatilities as traders focus on those contracts to trade the earnings event. Then the implied volatility indicated by AAPL option premiums trends down a little and picks up again as expiration dates are farther out in the future.

Finally, Table 6.8 shows the implied volatility for a wide variety of options on GLD. The skew behaves differently for GLD across time like it does across strike prices.

Note the chart depicting GLD option prices across expirations (Figure 6.6). The implied volatility of near-dated options is high and then drops a bit.

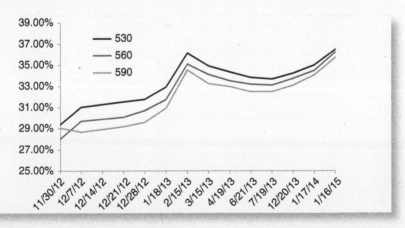

FIGURE 6.5   AAPL Horizontal Skew

TABLE 6.8 Horizontal Skew for GLD

Expiration	166 Call	166 Put	170 Call	170 Put	174 Call	174 Put
11/30/2012	14.30%	13.53%	12.49%	12.19%	14.21%	11.64%
12/7/2012	13.59%	12.88%	12.52%	12.25%	13.25%	12.82%
12/14/2012	12.72%	12.52%	12.37%	12.06%	12.77%	12.61%
12/21/2012	12.43%	12.23%	12.18%	12.02%	12.70%	12.53%
12/31/2012	12.06%	11.94%	11.88%	11.74%	12.24%	11.99%
1/19/2013	12.55%	12.45%	12.55%	12.47%	12.86%	12.71%
2/16/2013	13.26%	13.17%	13.26%	13.20%	13.52%	13.45%
3/16/2013	13.99%	13.91%	14.07%	13.94%	14.28%	14.23%
3/28/2013	14.18%	14.20%	14.28%	14.25%	14.45%	14.51%
6/22/2013	15.42%	15.74%	15.52%	15.86%	15.69%	16.10%
6/28/2013	15.53%	15.94%	15.62%	16.05%	15.83%	16.24%
9/21/2013	16.37%	17.12%	16.51%	17.29%	16.66%	17.43%
9/30/2013	16.49%	17.29%	16.55%	17.41%	16.73%	17.59%
12/21/2013	17.45%	18.60%	17.60%	18.73%	17.74%	18.92%
1/18/2014	17.77%	19.04%	17.93%	19.16%	18.10%	19.33%
1/17/2015	21.94%	20.31%	20.23%	22.30%	20.49%	22.46%

As time to expiration expands the implied volatility of GLD options continues to trend higher.

Implied volatility is an important part of option trading and it can have an impact on whether a trade turns out to be profitable or a loss. Just as different markets trade differently, the implied volatility indicated by option pricing may differ across asset classes. Taking things a little further, implied volatility behaves differently for different individual stocks as well.

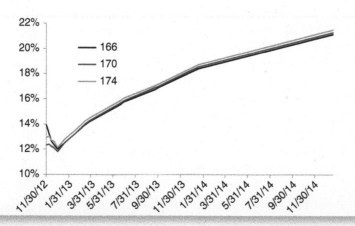

FIGURE 6.6   GLD Horizontal Skew

CHAPTER 7

Developing Your Trading Plan

Every option trade begins with an outlook for the underlying stock. This is the first thing I try to emphasize with any trader embarking on trading options. It may appear I am repeating myself on this subject and that is because I am. I think it is also a good reminder for all levels of option trader. This outlook will have a timing component along with a price outlook for the underlying market. There also may be a forecast for implied volatility when there is a short-term trade that is expected to exit before expiration. However, even before a trade is established there should be some sort of overall trading plan.

The plan should help dictate from a high level what trades will be initiated. The components that will be dictated include what underlying markets will be traded, what strategies will be used, and how trading decisions will be made. The maximum amount of capital attributed to each trade would be known from the trading plan. Trading should be enjoyable to you, but the main reason you probably decided to focus on the markets or even buy this book is because you want to make money trading options. Any endeavor that is entered into to make a profit should be approached as a business. For a trader the trading plan is like their business plan.

This chapter will focus on developing a high-level trading plan that will be focused on trading short-dated options. The first decision to make will be what markets to trade. The next will be what types of option strategies will be implemented based on different outlooks. Finally, some general thoughts behind developing trading ideas will be demonstrated.

■ Markets to Trade

A trap that many individual traders fall into is trying to trade too many markets. With well over 3,000 underlying securities and markets that have option trading this is an easy trap to fall into. For instance, someone on a business network makes a very bullish or bearish recommendation on a certain stock. Many traders, who may have never even traded or possibly even heard of this stock, may take this recommendation to heart as the expert on TV must know what they are talking about. This trader may actually consider some sort of bullish or bearish strategy based on the expert's comments. This is not how to go about approaching trading as a business and definitely is not a path to financial success through trading the financial markets.

My belief is that if individual traders are to succeed in the markets they should approach the markets with a focus. This focus starts with what markets will analyze, monitor, and, when appropriate, trade. One way an individual can compete with professional trading firms is by focusing on a very small number of stocks. Keep in mind that most professional traders try to profit by trading as many markets as they feel they can handle. Also, as a professional they have more of an incentive to consider more opportunities to trade than an individual. An individual trading as a part-time endeavor does not have to fully rely on trading profits to survive. If an individual has a very narrow focus, even just four or five underlying instruments, I think it helps a trader maintain an advantage on the competition.

When someone is asked to name a successful investor or trader the name Warren Buffett will inevitably come into the conversation. According to SEC filings, Warren Buffett's firm, Berkshire Hathaway, held about $90 billion in publicly traded stocks. His portfolio has about 40 stocks, but just over two-thirds of Berkshire Hathaway's portfolio consists of four stocks. Wells Fargo (WFC—20.7%), The Coca-Cola Company (KO—18.9%), International Business Machines (IBM—15.7%), and American Express (AXP—12.8%).

Admittedly, Warren Buffett approaches the markets differently than traders looking to trade short-dated options. However, this focus on a very limited number of companies gives him an edge on the markets. That is not the only edge Buffett operates with, but being focused does work in his favor. A short-term option trader can take this lesson and apply it to their trading plan as well. Buffett believes his focus on a few companies helps him manage risk, focusing on just a few stocks or markets to trade should work the same for an individual trader.

I typically suggest a trader begin trading new strategies by focusing
more than five individual stocks, ETFs, or index markets. A starting
would be the list of stocks with available weekly options. Both the C...cago
Board Options Exchange (CBOE) and Options Clearing Corporation
(OCC) provide lists of securities that have short-dated options available for
trading. For this exercise the OCC's list is a good one to work from, as their
list includes the date that weekly options first became available on a stock or
ETF. Nothing would be more frustrating than getting up to speed on trading short-dated options on a stock and then suddenly having weekly options
not offered anymore. The OCC's list can be found at www.theocc.com
/webapps/weekly-options. The CBOE's list has its own merits as it shows
which markets have more than one short dated expiration series available.
Also, the CBOE list is easily exported to excel. Their list can be found at
www.cboe.com/weeklys.

The mixture of underlying markets should offer different types of
opportunities. The stocks that are chosen to be part of your trading universe
should come from a variety of industries. Short-term stock price changes
tend to be influenced by the overall market and their particular market sector more than the fundamentals that drive the company. If you choose to
focus on five restaurant companies the number of trading opportunities may
be limited. If a news item moves one of these stocks, it will probably have a
similar impact on the stock of their competitors. Focusing on one industry
will not result in much diversification of trading opportunities.

Also, you should try to choose stocks that have a variety of earnings
reporting dates. A good portion of S&P 500 stocks report their earnings
two to three weeks after the end of the calendar quarter. Many retailers
close their quarterly books at the end of January, April, July, and October.
A couple of good resources to explore when a company typically reports
earnings are www.reuters.com/finance/markets/earnings and www
.whispernumber.com

Also, in addition to earnings reports, many retailers report their sales on
a monthly basis. Announcements like earnings and sales are always good for
extra volatility and trading opportunities. The retailer that I always like to
focus on is Wal-Mart (WMT).

Another factor that may come into play would be some sort of familiar-
ity with the company or the products the company produces. I grew up
in Memphis, Tennessee, and have always been very familiar with FedEx
Corporation (FDX). It's the largest employer in my hometown, and everyone has a relative or acquaintance that works for FedEx.

I have already mentioned two companies that make my personal list. In addition to FDX and WMT I also will put Chevron Corporation (CVX) on my list. Any energy stock would be sufficient to add to the mix, but the price level of CVX actually made it my choice. I personally like to focus on trading options on stocks with a quoted price that is high relative to the average stock. When I went through this exercise WMT was close to 75.00, FDX near 95.00, and CVX was trading around 125.00. Finally, my group of stocks covers some diverse industries; also, their earnings announcements are spread out so I can focus on trading earnings individually around each stock.

I wanted to have some sort of commodity exposure and probably the most liquid exchange-traded fund that is based on a commodity is the SPDR Gold Shares ETF (GLD). Finally, my index option series is the S&P 500 Index (SPX). The S&P 500 is a professional benchmark that I have watched my whole career. Also, SPX options are often 90 percent of the daily index option-trading volume (excluding VIX), so this is by far the most liquid of the index markets.

This exercise where I selected a group of underlying markets to focus on is unique to my background and market interest. Everyone's universe of stocks, ETFs, and indexes will be different; I am just showing the process one would go through in order to select their own trading universe.

Also, there will consistently be the temptation to add stocks or markets that are in the news. Until feeling completely comfortable with your small universe it would be best to avoid giving into that temptation.

■ Trading Strategies

The outlook for an underlying market will dictate the strategies utilized. Theoretically there are an unlimited number of strategies that may be implemented using option contracts. However, it is best to have a handful of strategies that will be used based on an outlook. This could be considered the tools you are going to use to trade based on your market outlook.

The choice of what strategy to use should go beyond buying a call when bullish or buying a put when bearish on a market. Remember when buying an option you are often paying up for time value and exposing yourself to time decay. I am not saying all a trader should do is sell options, but I do believe traders should utilize—at minimum—spread strategies that involve short-option positions as part of the strategies they choose to implement.

Trading Decisions

The reasons for implementing a trade vary from trader to trader. Some have fundamental outlooks on companies believing that business trends will cause the stock price to rise or drop. It has been shown that stock prices do correlate with the fundamentals of a company over the long term. However, good portions of stock price changes over the short term have little to do with the long-term fundamentals of a company. A good option market related method of benefitting from a long-term outlook for a stock is either taking a position in the stock or taking a position in the longer dated options known as LEAPS. These types of long-term positions will be discussed somewhat later in this book, but in conjunction with taking positions in short-dated options.

The bulk of this book is about short-term trading and for short-term trading technical analysis is a better method than fundamental analysis for trade selection. Every technician has their own favorite indicators or methods and you should develop your own methods as well. Throughout the rest of this book I will introduce some methods that will help traders decide on the near-term price movements of an underlying market. What is covered is only scratching the surface of what methods are available to you.

Capital and Risk Management

Short-term trading should comprise a portion of your total net investment capital, but definitely not all of your capital. Each person has their own risk tolerance levels and investment goals. Within this context there should be a certain amount of capital allocated to your short-term option-trading program.

Also, there should be a decision made regarding how much capital will be risked on each trade. Many option trades will result in a 100 percent loss. Keep this in mind when determining how much capital will be risked on each trade. I have seen traders use anywhere between 2 and 10 percent as the capital allocated to each trade.

Keeping a Trading Record

Several proprietary firms I have worked with strongly encourage traders to keep a journal or other type of record of their trading. This would involve writing down the reason for particular trades along with the outcome. Part of the outcome would be just how well the trader followed their initial entry plan. If journaling sounds a bit too much like keeping a diary or is something that you know from experience you will have a difficult time maintaining you might consider a spreadsheet. The method of record keeping not nearly as important as just making sure you have a method to keep up with your trading results.

Whatever the approach, the trading record could contain all the columns with important information related to each trade. Information related to entering a trade would include the reason for the trade, entry price on the option, the price of the underlying market, current overall stock market conditions, and the reason for the trade. Also, upon entering a trade there should be an exit plan in place. The exit plan should have scenarios where the trade works and is not working. A target price based on the option position or the underlying market can be the positive outcome. A stop loss based on time, underlying price, or option pricing can represent the negative outcome that would prompt exiting the trade. When exiting the trade the price of the underlying, the exit price on the option contract, and underlying market conditions, should all be recorded. Finally, notes should be made about how well the original plan was followed and how the plan was followed. Trading on your own means you do not have anyone to answer to except yourself. Keeping some sort of record of your trading will help you be accountable.

This exercise should be simple enough that it is not a burdensome task each time a new trade is entered. At the same time your trading record should be comprehensive enough that when reviewing your trading history you are able to understand what is working and not working and how disciplined you have been following your original trading plans.

■ Tying It All Together

The pieces should all fall together in a way that your trading activity is treated in a businesslike manner. If you have this structure in place, it should make the trading part a bit easier and more organized. Once the organization is in place you should decide how much time you plan on contributing to your short-term option trading. Setting aside a scheduled time each week to work on your trading program will also help you maintain a consistency that is needed to implement a successful trading program. Finally, if you have all the pieces in place all you really will need to do is focus on the universe of markets you are trading and plan and execute trades based on market conditions.

CHAPTER 8

Long Option Trades

L ong option strategies are usually the first trades introduced to those new to option trading. Buying both a call option with a bullish outlook and buying a put option where there is a bearish outlook will be introduced in this chapter. Although there are better first, live-option trades, such as a covered call, buying a call or put is a good introduction to how the option markets work. These long trades are a good first step when discussing the mechanics of option trading. With the introduction of short-dated options a long option trade may actually make sense as a first live trade. One of the reasons short-dated options have taken off in popularity is because traders may come very close to a long or short position on a stock when trading an option that has very little time left to expiration. By their very nature, weekly options always have very little time left to expiration.

If a trader has a long or short opinion on a stock or market one of the most basic methods of trading that outlook is the purchase of a call or put option. When purchasing an option there is often a time value component that needs to be overcome in order for the trade to become profitable. This can be true for trades that are only anticipated to last a day or two, but the amount of time value that an option has in the premium may be at a level where, when combined with the price outlook for the underlying market, it makes doing a trade prohibitive. Time decay is always a concern and potential obstacle when taking a long option position.

Many traders who are new to the option market will buy a call or put based on a bullish or bearish outlook. They may get the direction of the underlying market or stock correct. However, the outcome of the trade may result in a loss due to the selection of an option that has too much time value. When long an option contract, whether it is a put or a call, the trader is subject to time decay to the potential detriment of a trade. There are two methods of limiting exposure to time decay. The more complex is an option-spread trade that will be discussed in later chapters. The simpler method involves trading an in-the-money, short-dated option. That is the focus of this chapter.

■ Long Call

The most basic option trade is purchasing a call. When there is a bullish outlook for a stock the first trade considered for all levels of option trader may be purchasing a call. If the pricing factors, specifically time value, does not result in a long-call position being cost prohibitive then this may be the best trading alternative. After an outlook for a stock has been determined, at least two alternative option trades should be considered. This example, using shares of Boeing (BA), focuses on a short-term outlook and options that have five trading days until expiration.

On Friday five days before the following weekly options expire BA stock closed at 70.05. If a trader has a view that shares of BA are going to trade higher the following week they may consider buying call options. Since BA has weekly options expiring the following Friday then these options match up perfectly to an outlook of BA over 71.50 over the next five trading days. The available call options with five trading days to expiration are shown in Table 8.1.

The 5-day BA 65.00 call is offered at a price where the there is only 0.10 of time value. If bullish on BA over the following week then 0.10 of time value would need to be overcome in order to make a profit off this trade. The meaning of overcoming this is that the stock would need to trade at least 0.10 higher. In this case the breakeven level for this trade would be

TABLE 8.1 Boeing 5-Day Option Quotes

Option	Bid	Ask	Time Value
BA 65.00 Call	4.95	5.15	0.10
BA 67.50 Call	2.55	2.70	0.15
BA 70.00 Call	0.65	0.70	0.65
BA 72.50 Call	0.09	0.11	0.11

70.15. Also, at the price target of 71.50 the BA 65.00 call would be trading at 6.50. The result would be a profit of 1.35 on a cost of 5.15. This profit turns out to be a return of 26 percent.

The BA 67.50 call is offered at 2.70 that translated this call option into having 0.15 of time value. This option is not as deep in-the-money as the 65.00 call which results in 0.05 more in time value. Considering the low time values, both of these call options are inexpensive ways to benefit from a move to the upside in BA over the following week. However, the benefit of the BA 67.50 call becomes more obvious when the price target of 71.50 is considered. With the stock at 71.50 near expiration the BA 67.50 call would be trading at 4.00 at expiration. This would be a gain of 1.30 on a cost of 2.70 for a return of 48 percent. The percentage return is definitely superior to the 65.00 call. Also, remember when an option is purchased, the maximum potential loss is equal to the premium paid for the contract. Therefore the dollar risk of the BA 65.00 call (5.15) is much higher than the dollar risk of the BA 67.50 call (2.70).

Since BA is trading at 70.05 the BA 70.00 call is the closest strike to the underlying and would be considered by traders to be the at-the-money contract. Remember that at-the-money option contracts will have more time value than the out-of-the-money and in-the-money option contacts. This option is trading at 0.70 so there is 0.05 of intrinsic value. The result for a long trade in this option would be 0.65 of time premium to overcome for a long position to be a profit. The stock would need to climb to 70.70 for the trade to break even, a much higher level than the first two contracts considered. However, there is a leverage benefit to this contact. If correct and BA trades to 71.50, the BA 70.00 call would be trading for 1.50. Paying 0.70 for an option expected to be trading at 1.50 results in a profit of 0.80. As this is a profit of over 100 percent, the option is more attractive on a leverage basis. This looks very tempting, but leverage works both ways, as the stock has to move higher by 0.65 just to break even on the trade. Whether this is the option to buy based on the price target of 71.50 depends on a trader's conviction about their bullish outlook.

The BA 72.50 call is offered at 0.11 with 100 percent of this premium being attributed to time value, but notice that this option is out-of-the-money by 2.45. In other words on a position held until expiration, a profit on this trade would only be realized if BA moves up by more than 2.56. This is outside the price target expected from BA so the 72.50 call is definitely counted out. A full comparison of these four option choices appears in Table 8.2.

TABLE 8.2	Break Even and Option Profit Comparisons				
Option	Premium	Time Value	Breakeven	Profit @ 71.50	% Profit @ 71.50
BA 65.00 Call	5.15	0.10	70.10	1.35	26
BA 67.50 Call	2.70	0.15	70.20	1.30	48
BA 70.00 Call	0.70	0.65	70.70	0.80	114
BA 72.50 Call	0.11	0.11	72.61	0.00	0

The ultimate decision comes down to buying the BA 67.50 call or BA 70.00 call. Each has benefits and drawbacks. The BA 67.50 call would break even if the stock trades only 0.15 higher and would only lose 0.15 if the stock does not move at all over the following week. It is always prudent to consider the outcome if the stock does not behave as planned. The BA 70.00 call has a lower premium and better return if the trade works out. However, the stock has to trade up by 0.65 for this trade to break even and if the stock is only 0.05 lower at expiration the whole premium would be lost. Figure 8.1 shows payoff diagram comparisons for buying both the BA 67.50 call and BA 70.00 call.

Payoff diagrams like this one are always great methods to compare two different strategies based on the same outlook. This chart illustrates the difference between buying a BA 67.50 call and BA 70.00 for a short-term trade. The stock is trading very close to the breakeven level on the 67.50 call while there is a little more price performance that must be overcome to break even for a trade that buys the 70.00 call. Also note the different downside results that show up on the left side of the diagram. One nonquantitative factor that will figure into the final trading decision relates to the confidence a trader has in the price forecast for the underlying stock.

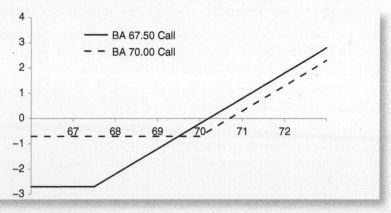

FIGURE 8.1   BA 67.50 Call and BA 70.00 Call Payoff Diagram Comparison

	Option/	Time		Profit	% Profit
Option/Stock	Stock Cost	Value	Breakeven	@ 71.50	@ 71.50
BA Stock	70.05	0.00	70.05	1.45	2
BA 67.50 Call	2.70	0.15	70.20	1.30	48
BA 70.00 Call	0.70	0.65	70.70	0.80	114

TABLE 8.3 Breakeven and Profit Comparisons between Options and Stock

There is one alternative that has not been mentioned yet. Why not just buy the stock? There is no time value in share ownership and the profit or loss at expiration is easy to determine. However, there are a couple of aspects to share ownership that can make buying a call option more attractive. Table 8.3 compares purchasing shares to the two long call option alternatives.

One advantage of buying a call based on the five-day outlook can be seen in the final column. Buying shares of BA would cost 70.05 with a profit of 1.45. This dollar profit is higher than the dollar profit for the two option alternatives, but as a use of capital it falls short. A perfect result would only be a 2% return on the capital implemented. Also, theoretically the potential loss on shares of BA could be 70.05. Admittedly if BA shares lose all value in a five-day period there is probably more to worry about in the world than trading, but a dramatic drop in shares could result in a loss greater than the premiums for the two option contracts. Whenever an option is purchased the most that may be lost is the premium paid for that option.

■ Long Put

A consideration in the option markets when a trader has a bearish outlook on a stock would be to purchase a put. This, like the long call, is the most basic of methods to trade a bearish opinion on the direction of a stock. As with any option trade, an outlook for the underlying stock or market along with the timing of that outlook would come into consideration when buying a put.

Consider Yahoo! (YHOO) trading at 17.19 on a Friday afternoon. A trader has a bearish outlook for the following week on shares of YHOO. Specifically the trader expects YHOO shares to trade down to 16.50 the following week. With this outlook a trader checks out quotes on YHOO weekly options that expire the following Friday. These option quotes along with the time value of each contract appear in Table 8.4.

TABLE 8.4 — Yahoo 5-Day Option Quotes

Option	Bid	Ask	Time Value
YHOO 17 Put	0.13	0.15	0.15
YHOO 18 Put	0.87	0.92	0.11
YHOO 19 Put	1.86	1.90	0.09
YHOO 20 Put	2.85	2.92	0.11

As with the first long call example there is very little time value in many of these short-dated option choices. If the focus is on paying up as little as possible for time value then the YHOO 19 put is the superior choice by two cents. The YHOO 19 put is offered at 1.90 that results in time value of just 0.09. However, offered at 0.92 the YHOO 18 put costs less than half the 19 strike put and only has 0.02 more of time premium. Another consideration is that the YHOO 18 put also gives a trader more leverage if the target price of 16.50 is reached. The YHOO 18 put would be worth 1.50 if the stock trades down to 16.50 for a profit of 0.58 on a cost of 0.92 or about 63 percent. Also, the higher strike options have comparable time value but also have a higher dollar premium which actually adds more risk to the trade if YHOO stock moves up dramatically and a lower percent return on the option cost if the stock hits the target price of 16.50.

Finally, there is the out-of-the-money YHOO 17 put that is trading at 0.15 (Table 8.5). This option has the closest strike price to where the stock is trading, but is still 0.19 out of the money. All 0.15 of the premium is time value and the stock actually must trade down to 16.85 for the trade just to break even. There is more risk that this trade may not work out, but on the flip side if the stock does trade down to 16.50 the result is a profit of 0.35 on a cost of 0.15 or a return of over 200 percent.

The decision in this case would come down to the amount of conviction a trader had regarding their outlook. The more conviction a trader has in

TABLE 8.5 — Breakeven and Option Profit Comparisons

Option	Premium	Time Value	Breakeven	Profit @ 16.50	% Profit @ 16.50
YHOO 17.00 Put	0.15	0.15	16.85	0.35	233
YHOO 18.00 Put	0.92	0.11	17.08	0.58	63
YHOO 19.00 Put	1.90	0.09	17.10	0.60	31
YHOO 20.00 Put	2.92	0.11	17.08	0.38	13

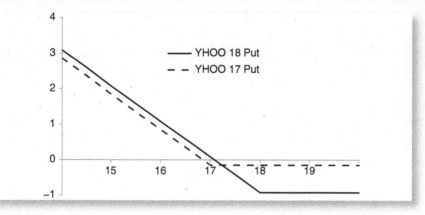

FIGURE 8.2 YHOO 17.00 Put and YHOO 18.00 Put Payoff Comparison

the 16.50 target price the more likely they may be to buy the YHOO 17 put instead of the YHOO 18 put. Figure 8.2 shows the payout for these two alternatives.

On the payoff diagram the profit and loss difference is pretty narrow on the left side. The left side is the section where YHOO share prices are dropping and both trades work well. The risk is displayed fairly well as a higher stock price has a bigger impact on the 18 put than on the 17 put.

Finally, an alternative to purchasing a put would be shorting shares of YHOO at 17.19. Selling short is not for the faint of heart, as the losses that may be incurred through a short position are theoretically unlimited. Purchasing a put option would result in dollar risk equal to the premium paid for the option. Also, often there would be more capital tied up in a short sale than in a situation where a short sale is implemented. If a put option may be purchased with very little time value in the contract and a time frame that matches up to a trader's outlook it is probably a better alternative than selling shares short.

The majority of long option trades are subjected to some sort of time decay. Short-dated in-the-money options and out-of-the-money options are alternatives that allow a trader the ability to trade a short-term outlook and have little exposure to time decay. With the introduction of weekly options many short-term traders have started to take advantage of using options in place of long or short stock positions.

CHAPTER 9

Short Option Trades

When an option contract is sold, the seller takes on an obligation. The seller receives a premium or payment in exchange for taking on the obligation. If a call option is sold then an obligation is taken on. In the case of selling an equity call option the result is an obligation to sell a stock at a certain price any time up to expiration of that option contract. Conversely when a put option is sold the result is the obligation to purchase a stock at a certain price anytime up to the expiration date. The buyer of the option contract obtains a right. When a holder of an option decides to exercise their right a holder of a short position in that option has to make good on that right. This is referred to as *being assigned*.

Being assigned on a short option position may not necessarily be a negative outcome for a trade. Whether this is considered a negative relates to the motivation behind selling the option. When a put option is sold the seller takes on the obligation to buy a stock at a certain price. If the seller of that put would like to own the shares over the long term, then being assigned would result in a long stock position. If the intent of the trade is to take a long position in a stock, then assignment would be considered a positive event.

Another motivation behind selling options may be to collect income. The end game here is for the option to expire with no value and a profit being made equal to the premium collected when the option is sold. If this is the reason the option was sold in the first place was for income and not to be assigned then this would not be a positive outcome for the option seller.

As a side note, there is a common misperception regarding how many options expire out-of-the-money. According to the Options Clearing Corporation (OCC) in 2012 only 7.2 percent of option positions that were opened were exercised. Many market observers assume this means that 92.8 percent of options expire. If this were true we could all retire early through selling options. However, after an option position is opened one of three things results when the option position is retired. First it may be exercised and we know that 7.2 percent of option positions that were opened in 2012 ended up being exercised. Second, the option may expire with no value. In 2012, 21.3 percent of option positions expired with no value. Third, it may actually be closed out through selling a long or buying back a short option position. In the case of 71.5 percent of option positions that were opened in 2012 the positions were exited through closing transactions. The closing transactions may have resulted in a profit or a loss, but definitely would not have resulted in a position expiring with no value. Finally, these statistics that are compiled by the OCC are fairly consistent over history.

Unfortunately, many option traders are not approved for a variety of option-selling strategies. Brokerage firms consider uncovered option positions to be too risky for individual traders. There is some validity to this argument. However, option-selling strategies have proven to be a source of profitability for option traders of all levels. If not pure short positions, at minimum, there should be spread trades that have a short option as one of the components of the trade.

■ Short Call

A seller of a call option takes on an obligation to sell a stock at a certain price over the life of an option contract. A short call position can be covered or uncovered. Referring to a short call being covered means that the shares that would be sold if assigned on the short call are owned. This strategy is commonly referred to as a *covered call* or a *buy-write* and is discussed extensively in the next chapter.

If a call option is sold and the stock is not currently owned this is known as a *naked short call position*. Theoretically this is a very risky trade as a stock price may rise to unlimited levels. This potential risk is a valid reason that many brokers do not allow individual traders the ability to take on short call positions. However, for a skilled and experienced trader a naked short call option position may be an appropriate strategy.

The only motivation behind selling an uncovered call position can be that the stock does not trade or settle above the option-strike price. For example, on a Friday morning shares of Baidu, Inc. (BIDU) were trading at 84.90. The 5-day 85 call that expires the following Friday could be sold for 1.30. If a trader believed that shares of BIDU were going to hit resistance at 85.00 and not trade above this price during the following week they may consider selling this call option. The motivation behind this trade is for the option to expire out-of-the-money and result in a profit that is equal to the premium received. In this case a correct outlook would result in a profit of 1.30. However there is risk involved in this trade that shows up in the potential payoffs at expiration in Table 9.1.

The hopeful outcome of this trade is for BIDU to remain under 85.00 and the call option to expire out-of-the-money. The trader's risk is that shares of BIDU trade much higher over the next few days closing above 85.00. At any price level over 85.00 the short call will be in-the-money. Since this is a short position the in-the-money amount works against the position holder. The breakeven level for this trade is 86.30 where the short 85 call would be 1.30 in-the-money. Over 86.30 this trade turns into a losing prospect. Figure 9.1 shows the payoff diagram with of this short-call position. The risk that is to the upside is prominently displayed here.

This payoff diagram shows the potential profit or loss of this short call trade. If BIDU settles the following Friday above 85.00 then short positions in the expiring 85 call will be assigned. As a short call position holder the trader will most likely end up selling BIDU at 85.00 if the call is in-the-money at expiration. The intent of this trade was to earn trading income, not a short position in BIDU. To avoid having a short position in BIDU stock, the trader needs to cover their short position if it appears the option is going to be in-the-money at expiration.

Selling a call option is truly a risky trade considering the potential downside if the stock rallies. However, it is an appropriate method of

TABLE 9.1	Short BIDU 85 Call Payoff at Expiration		
BIDU	Short 85 Call Value	Income	Profit/Loss
80.00	0.00	1.30	1.30
85.00	0.00	1.30	1.30
90.00	−5.00	1.30	−3.70
95.00	−10.00	1.30	−8.70
100.00	−15.00	1.30	−13.70

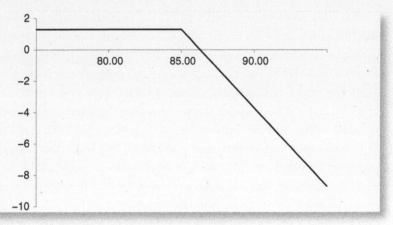

FIGURE 9.1 Short BIDU One-Week 85 Call Payoff

trading options for experienced traders that can control the risk associated with this sort of trade. Finally, because of the potential risk behind this trade, positions should be monitored closely and a strict stop-loss plan put in place.

■ Short Put

A naked short put position may also be viewed as a fairly risky trade. In an academic sense the risk is not as great as a naked short call position. A stock price may never go below zero so *substantial* is the term used for the risk associated with a short put. There may be two motivations for selling a put option short and both will be discussed in this chapter. First, just as with a short call option, a put option may be sold with the belief that the option will be out-of-the-money at expiration. Another way to state this is a short put position may be initiated based on an outlook that a stock is going to be above a certain price at expiration. The other motivation is to own a stock. This motivation will be addressed after covering selling a put for income.

The first example will address a situation where a trader believes a stock will be above a certain price level over the course of the following week. About midday on Friday, shares of Chipotle Mexican Grill (CMG) were trading at 366.75. If a trader had an outlook that CMG would stay over the 360.00 level for the next week he might consider selling a CMG 5-day 360 put. The CMG 5-day 360 put, could be sold for 2.25 in this instance. As long as CMG closes the following Friday over 360.00 and

TABLE 9.2	Short CMG 360 Put Payoff at Expiration		
CMG	Short 360 Put	Income	Profit/Loss
345.00	−15.00	2.25	−12.75
350.00	−10.00	2.25	−7.75
355.00	−5.00	2.25	−2.75
360.00	0.00	2.25	2.25
365.00	0.00	2.25	2.25

the short position has not been assigned, the profit will be equal to the premium received of 2.25. Table 9.2 shows the profit and loss for this trade at a variety of levels.

The risk for this trade is that CMG is below 360 at expiration. As there is a short position in the 360 put, lower price levels for CMG works against the short put option position holder. The theoretical very worst-case scenario is that CMG goes to 0.00, at which point the trade would be down 357.75. That is technically defined as a substantial loss. The payoff diagram for this CMG trade appears in Figure 9.2.

Any type of option, not just weekly options, can utilize the strategy being discussed here. However, there can be an advantage to selling weekly options. This CMG trade is a prime example. In addition to the weekly-option series there are also standard-option series that expire on CMG in two weeks and seven weeks. The pricing of those options appears in Table 9.3.

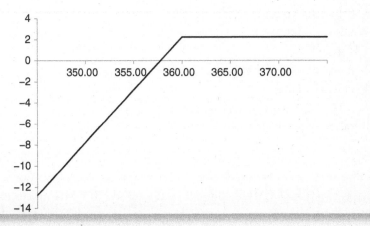

FIGURE 9.2 Short CMG 360 Put Payoff

TABLE 9.3	Three Different CMG 360 Put Option Quotes
	360 Put Bid
5-Day	2.25
10-Day	3.70
35-Day	9.50

When selling options the time decay of various potential contracts should be considered. The closer the strike price is to where the underlying stock is trading, the more a trader should focus on the impact of the passage of time on the option premium. As discussed in the chapter on time decay, a good portion of the benefit from time decay of at-the-money options comes over the last few days leading up to expiration. Of course weekly options consistently only have a few days left to expiration.

Consider the same outlook that was present for CMG in the previous example. However, change the time frame from 5 to 10 trading days. So the outlook for selling a CMG 360 put is based on the expectation of CMG trading over 360 for the next 10 days instead of just 5. The CMG 10-day 360 put could be sold for 3.70. However, another alternative exists, although this alternative is a little more dynamic. Instead of selling the CMG 10-day 360 put for 3.70 a trader could sell the 5-day 360 put for 2.25 and then plan on selling another option with similar time decay characteristics five trading days later. If CMG is at a similar price level an assumption may be made that another CMG 5-day 360 put could be sold for 2.25. The difference would be 0.80 more in income. In summary:

Choice 1
Sell 1 CMG 10-day 360 put @ 3.70
Total Income = 3.70
Choice 2
Sell 1 CMG 5-day 360 put @ 2.25
Five Days Later
Sell 1 CMG 5-day 360 put @ 2.25
Total Income = 4.50

Maybe 0.80 is not much to get excited about when there is going to be another trade that needs to be executed over the course of two weeks. Also, there is the risk of CMG taking off to the upside. If CMG moves dramatically higher in the first week, then the second put option that would need to be sold may not bring in much premium. On the flip side there is also the risk that CMG drops very quickly and the trader has only taken in 2.25 as opposed to 3.70. The result is that lower premium has been taken in to offset the losses incurred by the stock price drop. There are many variables that come into play here.

The bigger the time difference between expirations the more magnified the difference between time decay of the near-dated option and the farther-dated option. For instance, compare the CMG 5-day 360 put bid at 2.25 and the CMG 35-day 360 put bid at 9.50. If there is an outlook that CMG is going to stay over 360 for the next 35 days, a CMG 35-day 360 put could be sold for 9.50. However, the 5-day option could be sold seven consecutive times with the outcome being income of 15.75 (7 × 2.25). Instead of showing seven consecutive transactions this difference is highlighted in the payoff diagram in Figure 9.3.

The lower line represents selling a single CMG 35-day 360 put at 9.50 while the upper line represents hypothetically selling a CMG 5-day 360 put at 2.25 and having that opportunity for several consecutive weeks. This is admittedly a stretch as the price of CMG will move around and the odds are against being continuously being able to sell the 360 put for the same premium. This comparison is more to demonstrate the time decay difference between long-dated and short-dated options.

The CMG example is a speculative bullish trade based on CMG trading higher or at minimum being over a certain price at expiration. As with

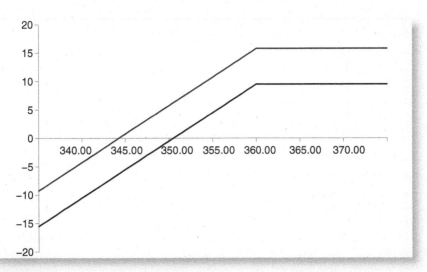

FIGURE 9.3 Short CMG 35-Day 360 Put versus Seven CMG 5-Day 360 Puts Payoff

shorting a call option based on a price outlook for the underlying market, this is a fairly risky trade and not appropriate for less sophisticated traders.

■ Selling a Put to Purchase Shares

The other motivation for selling a put is more appropriate for individual investors. This second motivation involves being a willing owner of the underlying stock at a certain price. This involves selling a put option with a strike price at a level where an investor would be happy to purchase the shares. If the stock price is under that strike price at expiration the result would be assignment at a price where the trader is willing to own shares. In this instance being assigned would actually be a positive outcome as the goal is to own the shares. The other potential outcome in this scenario is to not have to make good on the obligation to buy the stock that goes along with a short put position.

For example, shares of Facebook (FB) are trading at 28.30 on a Friday. A trader likes shares of FB for the long term, but thinks the stock may dip a little below 28.00 the following week. Based on this outlook they decide to take on the obligation to buy shares of FB the following Friday at 28.00. The trade involves selling a FB 5-day 28 put for 0.35. (See Table 9.4.)

Since the goal behind this trade involves obtaining a long position in FB at a lower price than the market, a column has been added to this payoff table. This column spells out what happens at expiration regarding the resulting position in the underlying stock. At any price above 28.00 at expiration this FB 5-day 28 put will expire with no value. The result will also be no position in FB stock. Below 28.00 the shares would be put to the trader, but at a price where the trader would be willing to take a long position in shares of FB. (See Figure 9.4.)

The risk for this trade is the same as selling a put as a bullish trade. A trader that has a bullish outlook on a stock and sells a put purely for income

TABLE 9.4	Short FB 28 Put Payoff at Expiration			
FB	Short 28 Put	Income	Profit/Loss	Stock Position
26.00	−2.00	0.35	−1.65	Long 100
27.00	−1.00	0.35	−0.65	Long 100
28.00	0.00	0.35	0.35	No Position
29.00	0.00	0.35	0.35	No Position
30.00	0.00	0.35	0.35	No Position

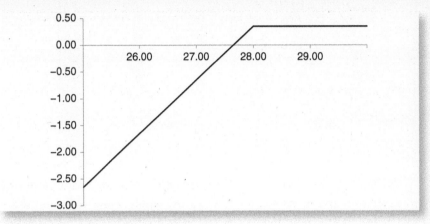

FIGURE 9.4 FB Weekly 28 Put Payoff

would do so with no intent of being assigned on the stock. Their only risk is price risk to the downside. For a trader that is selling a put with the hope of owning shares there is another risk. That would be the risk of not owning the shares even if the stock traded below 28.00 over the life of the option. Sticking with FB consider this scenario.

A trader sells the FB 5-day 28 put for 0.35 with the hope that the stock closes under 28.00 upon expiration the following Friday. The result would be purchasing shares with a net effective cost of 27.65. It is possible that FB shares could trade below 28.00 during the following week, but then finish the week above 28.00. In this case, if there is no early assignment on the short put, the put option would expire and shares would not be owned. There is still a profit of 0.35, but the end goal was to own shares under 28.00 if the opportunity presented itself.

Once an option position is opened up it may be closed out at any time up until expiration. If a trader aggressively wants to buy shares of FB they may always close out the short put and purchase shares. For example, if FB is trading at 27.90 the Thursday before expiration and a trader wants to make sure he does not miss the stock he may buy back the short position in the FB 5-day 28 put and then purchase shares of FB in the open market. This is always an alternative. In fact at that point it would be very possible that due to time decay the FB 28 put could be bought back for less than the 0.35 that was taken in when the put was sold. In this pricing example with two days remaining to expiration the FB 28 put may be repurchased for 0.30 or a small profit of 0.05.

TABLE 9.5	Five Consecutively Expiring FB 28 Put Option Quotes
	FB 28 Put Bid
5-Day	0.35
10-Day	0.48
15-Day	0.60
20-Day	0.70
25-Day	0.80

Of course a short put may be initiated with options that have more time to expiration and more income may be the result. However using short-dated options can result in more flexibility and more potential income than using long-dated options. Sticking with FB, there is also a contract that expires every Friday for five consecutive weeks, also known as serial options. The bid price for each of these options appears in Table 9.5.

Maybe our trader is not happy with 0.35 of income and is willing to sell the FB 10-day 28 put for 0.48. He is content to wait a couple of weeks for the outcome of this trade. There is a risk of FB trading below 28.00 and then above 28.00 over the next 10 days. This could result in the trader missing the stock when a chance to buy it below 28.00 existed. He can also always buy back the put option if he is afraid of missing the stock. Using the same example as buying back the FB 5-day put has an interesting result.

On the Thursday following the Friday where the FB 10-day put is sold for 0.48 FB has traded down to 27.90. In this case there are seven trading days remaining until the expiration of this short put. Due to the price drop in FB to 27.90 and the lack of time decay that this slightly longer dated put has experienced the short FB 28 put would actually be trading at 0.55. This is a premium higher than where the put option was sold. The result of covering this short put position would actually be a small loss.

Short-dated options offer pretty dramatic time decay features for at-the-money and near at-the-money contracts. Also, these contracts have more flexibility as far as exiting a short position with a profit. The popularity of weekly or short-dated options is a direct result of the combination of these two benefits.

All option trades should begin with a price and time outlook for the underlying market. An added dimension to this outlook might be the time decay benefit and added flexibility. Even if a trader has a two-month outlook for a stock, they may want to consider short-dated options to potentially increase their profitability through rapid time decay. In addition there is much more flexibility that goes along with an option position that has only a few days remaining until expiration.

■ CBOE PutWrite Index

The Chicago Board Options Exchange created an index to track the performance of a strategy that consistently sells S&P 500 Index (SPX) options versus a cash portfolio. The CBOE PutWrite Index (PUT) was created in 2007, but there is data on the index going back to June 1986. PUT simulates a portfolio that consistently holds Treasury bills in cash and on the third Friday of each month sells at-the-money SPX put options that expire on the third Friday of the following month. The specific put option that is sold in this process is the closest strike on the downside relative to where the S&P 500 is quoted.

When at-the-money options are sold the time decay of those options is expected to accelerate as the option's expiration date is approached. If the S&P 500 is relatively flat over the life of this option, the time-decay benefit of the short option position will be mostly realized in the last few days before expiration. With weekly options available it is possible to get more time decay benefit from index options above what the PUT index experiences.

Figure 9.5 shows the performance of PUT versus the total return of an investment in the S&P 500 from January 1, 2000, through December 31,

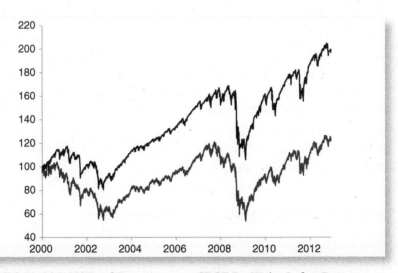

FIGURE 9.5   S&P 500 Total Return versus CBOE PutWrite Index Return

2012. An investment of $100 that results in the total return from the S&P 500 would result in a portfolio worth close to $124. Taking $100 an applying it to a portfolio that replicates the PUT index return would result in a portfolio worth just under $200 at the end of this comparison period.

Selling a put option often requires a fairly high level of approval from a brokerage firm as is it considered a high-risk strategy. This is unfortunate because a consistent strategy of selling put options on the S&P 500 has been shown to achieve returns that are superior to both buy-write strategies or buying and holding a market portfolio. It is also a good method of lowering the cost of entering a stock through selling a put and being assigned on the short position.

Option positions that determine the performance of the PUT index are rolled or initiated on the third Friday of each month. The put option pricing that is used to calculate the PUT index is based on a 30-minute, volume-weighted average price that is calculated between 10:30 A.M. and 11:00 A.M. on that third Friday. For comparison purposes I am using the closing price of the S&P 500 and relevant index options on that date.

On June 21, 2013, the S&P 500 closed at 1,592.43. The closest strike below the index option would be 1,590. Standard July expiration is on July 20 so replicating the PUT index strategy using closing prices would result in selling the SPX July 20 1,590 put for 30.80. If we chose to take an approach that involves selling weekly options in place of selling the next standard option expiration then a SPX June 28 1,590 put would be sold at 17.60.

There are 19 trading days between June 21 and July 19 and 5 trading days between June 21 and June 28. The 19-day put option would yield 30.80 in premium while the 5-day put would bring in 17.60. There are many ways to attempt to display the difference in time-decay benefit between selling the 1,590 put that expires on June 28 and the same put that expires on July 20. Probably the easiest is to isolate the time decay of both options between June 21 and June 28. The two option values in Table 9.6 use the admittedly unrealistic assumption that the S&P 500 is unchanged over the five trading days between June 21st and June 28th.

TABLE 9.6 SPX June 28 and July 19 1,590 Put Values

	June 21	June 28	Change
June 28 1,590 Put	17.60	0.00	−17.60
July 19 1,590 Put	30.80	26.30	−4.50

Over the following week that ends on June 28, the 5-day put option would lose all value and expire worthless. In the unrealistic world that the S&P 500 is unchanged over five days this option would lose almost four times as much value as the option expiring on July 19. The time decay benefit of using a short-dated option to replicate the PutWrite Index rather than the one-month contract is indisputable. Of course there are always instances where the market may be more volatile and other market factors would result in the longer dated option being a better choice, but for time decay benefits a 5-day near at-the-money option is going to be the preferred choice.

■ Tying Short-Dated Option Selling Together

For at-the-money and near at-the-money contracts using a short-dated option gives a trader extra time decay benefits that were not as consistently available before weekly options were introduced. Uncovered short-option strategies are not for inexperienced traders as they need to be constantly monitored. The risk of a large stock or market move combined with the leverage of option contracts means that option sellers should approach short option strategies with a risk management plan in place. They should also follow that plan when a trade goes against them.

In a case where an investor wants to purchase shares at a lower price, a cash-secured put is an excellent method to take in some income while taking on the obligation to purchase shares. There are some risks that the stock may be missed if the price dips below the strike price and then closes over the strike at expiration. Finally, as displayed by the PUT index, put-selling strategies on the market have been shown to outperform buy and hold strategies. Shortening the time frame related to the once a month systematic option selling that occurs with the PUT index results in more dramatic time decay benefits than selling long-dated options.

CHAPTER 10

Covered Calls and Buy-Writes

When weekly options first came out on stocks in mid-2010, my first impression was these short-dated contracts were going to be excellent candidates for actively selling call options against long stock positions. Time decay for at-the-money and close to at-the-money option contracts will accelerate as an option approaches the expiration date. With the introduction of short dated options there are always contracts available for trading that have just a few days remaining until expiration. In addition to the benefit of rapid time decay for short-dated options, the covered call is one of most common uses of options on individual stocks. Therefore it is pure logic that at-the-money weekly options make perfect sense for covered-call strategies.

83

■ Covered Call Basics

A covered call is a combination of two positions: long stock and short a call option against those shares. The term *covered* applies to the long-stock position covering the obligation that goes along with a short call. Another common term for this trade is a buy-write, which indicates the stock was purchased in conjunction with selling the call option. In either case a covered call or buy-write, the short-call option results in the obligation to sell shares at a certain price any time up to and including the expiration date. The seller of the call option receives a premium in exchange of taking on the obligation of selling the stock at a set price up to and including expiration.

As a basic example consider a trader owning 100 shares of XYZ trading at 44.50. A covered call would be created if a call option were sold against that long position. For illustration's sake, a trader decides to take on the obligation to sell their 100 shares at 45.00 any time up to and including August expiration by selling short 1 XYZ Aug 45 call for 2.00. The covered call position is:

Long 100 XYZ at 44.50
Short 1 XYZ Aug 45 call at 2.00

There are actually four potential outcomes for this covered call position:

1. First, the trader that has sold this call option may buy the call option back in the open market. Exiting the call at some point before expiration will result in the trader no longer having an obligation to sell shares. The profit or loss outcome would depend on the price where the trader covered their short call in conjunction with the price change of the underlying stock. If the stock has traded down or there has been enough time decay, the XYZ Aug 45 call might be trading at a price lower than where it was sold short and the trader will have a profit. If XYZ has traded up then the XYZ Aug 45 call may be trading at a much higher price and the short call would be covered at a loss, but the stock price appreciation may offset a portion of this loss.

2. The second potential outcome involves early assignment. If a holder of the XYZ Aug 45 call decides they would like to exercise their right to buy shares of XYZ at 45.00 before the expiration date they will inform their broker that they would like to exercise their option. The broker will inform the Options Clearing Corporation (OCC) of this early exercise. The OCC then randomly selects a brokerage firm that has an open short position in the XYZ Aug 45 call. The brokerage firm then selects one of their customers that have a short position in this contract. This holder of the short-call position will then be assigned on this obligation. They must sell or deliver 100 shares to the party that exercised the option. If the goal behind selling the call option was to sell shares this could be considered a positive outcome to the trade.

3. The third outcome is very similar to the second outcome. If XYZ is over 45.00 at August expiration then the OCC will automatically exercise all of the XYZ Aug 45 call options. This occurs unless a holder informs their broker not to exercise the contract. If a trader has a covered call and the stock price is higher than the strike price at expiration, they

should assume they would be exercised on this obligation although there is always the possibility that it may not happen. The holder of a call always has the right to say they do not want to exercise a call at expiration; they would do this if the stock price is very close to the strike price and the fees associated with exercising the call are greater than the in-the-money amount of the call. In the case of automatic exercise, shares will be called away and the holder will receive the strike price as the payment for those shares.

4. The final potential outcome occurs at expiration as well. If XYZ is trading under 45.00 at August expiration then the option contract will expire with no value. The 2.00 income taken in for selling the XYZ Aug 45 call is a profit and the trader is still long 100 shares of XYZ. The overall covered-call profit or loss depends on the price change that would have occurred in XYZ.

Table 10.1 shows the net profit or loss for this covered-call position at expiration of the XYZ Aug 45 call at a variety of prices. At any price below and including 45.00 the option will expire out-of-the-money. Above 45.00 there is intrinsic value at expiration and this value works against a short position in the option. Note that the profit from the long position in XYZ stock is offset by the short position in the XYZ Aug 45 call. Also, note that as the stock moves lower in price there is a net loss in the covered-call position. Figure 10.1 is a payoff diagram that shows the profit or loss for this covered call.

At any price from 45.00 and higher the maximum profit for this covered call trade is capped at 2.50. The trader received 2.00 and there was a 0.50 profit for the stock appreciation up to 45.00 a share. Also note on the left side of the diagram there is exposure to the downside if XYZ loses value. The breakeven on this trade is 42.50, based on the 2.00 premium that was received when the call option was sold.

TABLE 10.1	Long XYZ + Short XYZ Aug 45 Call Payoff			
XYZ	XYZ Profit/ Loss	XYZ 45 Call Value	Income	Covered Call Profit/Loss
40.00	−4.50	0.00	2.00	−2.50
42.50	−2.00	0.00	2.00	0.00
45.00	0.50	0.00	2.00	2.50
47.50	3.00	−2.50	2.00	2.50
50.00	5.50	−5.00	2.00	2.50

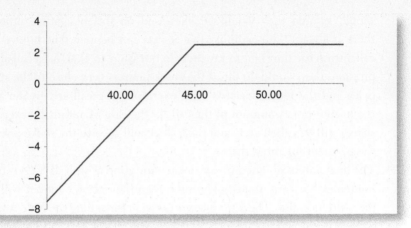

FIGURE 10.1 Long XYZ + Short XYZ Aug 45 Call Payoff

■ Covered Call Trading Examples

Again, a call option will be sold against a long position in a stock for one or two reasons. First, a trader has a price where they are a willing seller of their shares and would like to take in some income in return for taking on the obligation to sell their shares at that price. The other motivation would be that a trader believes their stock will not trade over a certain price in the near term and would like to generate portfolio income on their long position. In both cases short-dated options offer some advantages over options with more time to expiration when creating a covered call.

On a Friday shares of Freeport-McMoRan Copper & Gold (FCX) were trading at 31.70. A shareholder decides that they would be a willing seller of their shares of FCX at 32.00 over the next 10 days. This is a case where the motivation is to exit shares and the seller of a call option will be pleased if FCX is trading over 32.00 at expiration. In addition to the short-dated expiration that occurs in 5 trading days on the following Friday, there is a standard expiration date in 10 trading days. The bid prices for these two FCX 32 calls appear in Table 10.2.

TABLE 10.2	Next Two Expiration FCX 32 Call Bid Prices
Expiration	**32 Call Bid**
5-Day	0.50
10-Day	0.75

TABLE 10.3	Daily Premiums for FCX 32 Call		
Days	Premium	Days	Premium
10	0.75	5	0.50
9	0.70	4	0.43
8	0.65	3	0.35
7	0.60	2	0.26
6	0.55	1	0.16

The FCX 10-day 32 call matches up with the time frame of this trade, but the FCX 5-day 32 call has a couple of advantages. First, there is a time decay advantage. Remember having time decay work for a trader is a major motivating factor behind the short call option part of a covered call.

Both options are slightly out-of-the-money contracts so 100 percent of the premium is attributed to time value. Both options will expire with no value if the stock price does not move at all between now and expiration. The FCX 5-day 32 call has 0.50 of time value. The FCX 10-day 32 call has 0.75 of time value and twice as many trading days remaining to expiration. Table 10.3 demonstrates the daily time decay for the 5-day and 10-day options over the following five trading days.

Note in the table 0.05 of time decay comes out of the premium for the FCX 32 call for each day between 10 days remaining until expiration and 5 days remaining until expiration. After five days to expiration the time decay accelerates into expiration. A graph depicting 10 days of time decay is displayed in Figure 10.2.

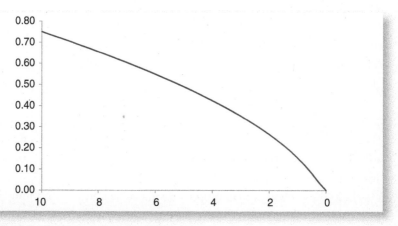

FIGURE 10.2 FCX 32 Call 10-Day Time Decay

Both the figure and table showing the time decay of the FCX 32 call rely on the stock not changing prices and not changing in implied volatility. Both of which are unrealistic assumptions, but the point is to isolate time decay and show how the last five days of time decay outpace the first five days of time decay.

Another advantage of the five-day contract over the 10-day option is the motivation behind this trade—exiting the stock. Shares will most likely be called away if the stock price is higher than the option strike price at expiration. The key point is if the stock price is at this level at expiration. It is very possible that FCX could trade over 32.00 while a short-call position is on, but close under 32.00 at expiration, would result in shares not being called away or sold. If the 10-day call is sold to create the covered call, shares need to be over 32.00 at expiration in 10 days to assure shares will be called away. If the plan is to sell the FCX 5-day call and then, if necessary, another 5-day call is sold, the trade would have two opportunities for shares to be called away instead of one.

■ Covered Calls and Dividends

When a company pays a dividend this can have a unique impact on stock and option prices. On the ex-dividend date a stock price will adjust lower by the amount of the dividend. As option holders are not entitled to the dividend option, premiums will also adjust for this price change. When dividends are paid out this also increases the chance that a short-call position will be assigned before expiration. Weekly options actually give traders the flexibility to have a short-call option position in place against long shares and avoid early exercise.

The focus will be on FCX again and the desire to exit shares over 32.00. This time, however, the timing is going to be different and there will be a different piece to the puzzle. FCX is trading at 31.70 and, instead of being a willing seller for just a couple of weeks above 32.00, the trader in this case is a willing seller over the next few weeks. The next FCX expiration date is 30 trading days out so the FCX 30-day 32 call is in the mix as well. Checking out quotes on all the near FCX 32 strike calls that match up to this time frame results in the pricing in Table 10.4.

These three choices match up to have a short call versus a long position in FCX over the next few weeks. As expected over the near term, the FCX 5-day 32 call will give the most return per day as far as time decay goes over

TABLE 10.4	Next Three Expiration FCX 32 Call Bid Prices
Expiration	32 Call Bid
5-Day	0.50
10-Day	0.75
30-Day	1.40

the next five days. The FCX 30-day 32 call appears to have dramatically less time decay benefit than the 10-day option. This is because FCX is expected to pay a dividend of 0.31 in five weeks or before expiration of the FCX 30-day call. When the stock goes ex-dividend the stock price would adjust lower and this lower stock price is anticipated by a lower premium for the option. Because FCX will pay a dividend in five weeks the FCX 30-day 32 call has a little less time value relative to the other two near dated call options. This is due to a slight adjustment being made in the option premiums for the stock price adjustment that will occur in FCX upon payment of the dividend.

■ Index Options and Covered Calls

Some traders and investors may qualify for what is known as *portfolio margin*. There are minimum requirements at each brokerage firm for a client to qualify for portfolio margin. Under portfolio margin an investor may cross margin instruments that have performance based on the same underlying instrument. A good example of this sort of cross margin is the SPDR S&P 500 (SPY) exchange traded fund and S&P 500 Index (SPX) option contracts. The ultimate underlying for both the SPY and SPX options is the S&P 500 Index. Since both derive value from the S&P 500, SPX options may be combined with an SPY position to resemble a covered call.

There has been a consistent 10-to-1 relationship between the S&P 500 and SPY since SPY began trading in January 1993. Figure 10.3 shows the daily closing relationship between the S&P 500 and SPY from January 29, 1993, and June 28, 2013. Note that there are some daily outlier moves that create spikes, but basically the relationship sticks very close to an average of 10.00. The actual average is 9.98. Therefore if a position using SPX options in conjunction with SPY as the underlying were established the result would be selling one SPX call for every 1,000 shares of SPY owned, as opposed to selling 10 SPY call options in conjunction with a holding of 1,000 shares of SPY.

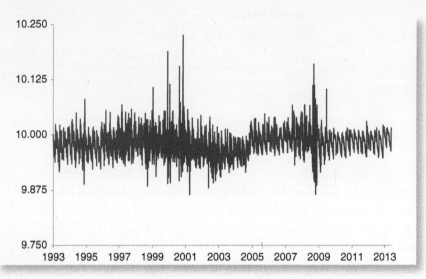

FIGURE 10.3 Ratio of S&P 500 Closes to SPY January 1993 to June 2013

On Wednesday morning SPY was trading at 143.90 and the S&P 500 was at 1,431.50. If an owner of 1,000 shares of SPY felt the market is a bit ahead of itself or that the market may sell off in the near term, they may want to consider selling a call option against their long position. If they qualify for portfolio margin an alternative may be selling an SPX Index call. Checking quotes the trader sees the SPX 2-day 1,435 call with a bid price of 6.00. Seeing this, the trader decides to sell 1 SPX 2-day call at 6.00. The combined position is now:

Long 1,000 SPY at 143.15
Short 1 SPX 2-day 1,435 call at 6.00

This option expires in just two days, which matches up to a short-term outlook for the trader. Selling provides a little room to the upside in the market over the next couple of days and also gives him some income against their holding. Table 10.5 shows the profit and loss for this trade using the assumption that the 10-to-1 relationship between SPX and SPY is in place at expiration of the option.

A payoff diagram may also be constructed, but the assumption of 10-to-1 SPX to SPY is needed for this payout. Figure 10.4 shows a payoff diagram two days after the trade is initiated based on the settlement price of SPX. The difference between using SPY options and SPX options impacts the outcome at expiration. SPX options are cash-settled contracts, so if the S&P

TABLE 10.5   Long 1,000 SPY + Short SPX 1,435 Call Payoff

SPY/SPX	1,000 SPY Profit/Loss	1 SPX 1,435 Call Value	Income	Covered Call Profit/Loss
141.50/1,415	−1,650	0	600	−1,050
142.50/1,425	−650	0	600	−50
143.50/1,435	350	0	600	950
144.50/1,445	1,350	−1,000	600	950
145.50/1,455	2,350	−2,000	600	950

500 were over 1,435 at expiration the transaction would involve the short-call holder paying cash to a long-option holder. Post expiration the position in the SPY ETF would be maintained.

As a recap, there are a few reasons a trader might decide to use an SPX call instead of SPY calls. First, the notional value of an SPX option is very close to 10 times that of the SPY options. Because of the larger notional size only one SPX contact needs to be sold to get the same exposure that 10 SPY contracts would offer. It depends on the broker, but there may be a lower commission paid for selling one SPX as opposed to 10 SPY options. A second reason for using SPX options has to do with taxes. This was covered in Chapter 2 but as a reminder according to the Options Industry Council, short-term gains on ETF option trades do not qualify for the same type of tax treatment as options on broad-based indexes. Using SPX instead of SPY contracts offers a tax benefit. Finally, SPX options are cash settled. This

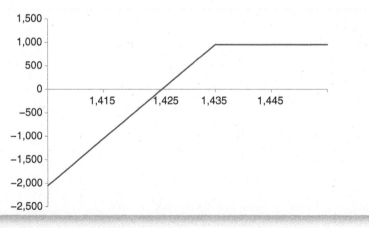

FIGURE 10.4   Long 1,000 SPY + Short SPX 1,435 Call Payoff

means if the trader is wrong and the S&P 500 is over 1,435.00 at expiration their SPY shares will not be called away. The result will be a debit to their account in the amount the market is above 1,435.00 times $100. The higher level of SPY would offset this debit and shares of SPY would continue to be held.

■ CBOE S&P 500 BuyWrite Index

To display the performance of a consistent buy-write strategy CBOE developed the CBOE S&P 500 BuyWrite Index. This index is quoted in real time using the symbol BXM. The BXM replicates the performance of owning a portfolio of stocks indexed to the S&P 500 and selling slightly out-of-the-money call options on the S&P 500 versus this portfolio. The options are sold on the third Friday of each month for the following month standard expiration. Depending on the calendar this option will expire in either four of five weeks from the day it was sold. The benefit of covered call strategies is quantified through BXM versus buy and hold for the S&P 500. The performance of BXM versus a total return investment in the S&P 500 has been fairly impressive on both an absolute and risk adjusted basis.

Figure 10.5 is a direct comparison of the performance of BXM versus the S&P 500 from January 1, 2000 through December 31, 2012. The indexes have been adjusted to begin at 100 on the first day of the year 2000. Another

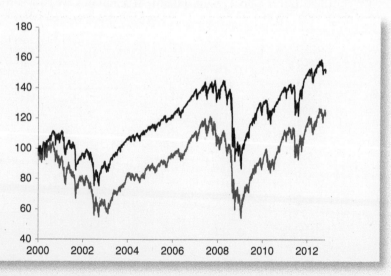

FIGURE 10.5 S&P 500 Total Return versus CBOE BuyWrite Index Return

way to think of this as the performance of $100 invested in the S&P 500 with dividends reinvested over this period versus $100 invested in a fund replicating the strategy quantified by BXM.

An investment of $100 in a portfolio of S&P 500 stocks on the first day of the year 2000 would have resulted in a portfolio worth about $124 at the end of 2012. The lower line on the chart represents this performance. If $100 were invested in a fund following BXM the result would be a portfolio worth just over $152 at the end of 2012, which is depicted by the higher line on this chart. The historical out performance by BXM of the S&P 500 through using covered calls is one of the factors that attract many investors to this strategy.

The stated strategy behind the index involves the option portion of BXM being rolled once a month. The call option that is sold is the closest strike that is higher than the price of the S&P 500. This occurs on the third Friday of each month, which is also the standard expiration date for SPX options. The same basic strategy may also be implemented using Weekly SPX options with the position being rolled every Friday. The weekly options are P.M.-settled so a direct comparison of the BXM using standard SPX options and Weekly SPX options is not possible. However, SPXPM options are P.M.-settled contracts that expire on the third Friday of each month. If the BXM strategy is replicated using SPXPM instead of SPX options the benefit of implementing the basic BXM strategy using weekly options can be demonstrated.

For example, June 21, 2013, was a roll date for the BXM index. On this date the S&P 500 closed at 1,592.43 and the first strike to the upside is 1,595. Based on this closing price for the S&P 500 a trader who is using SPXPM options could have sold 1 SPXPM Jul 19 1,595 call for 27.00. If a trader chose to sell a SPX call that expires the following Friday they would be looking at selling the SPX Jun 28 1,595 call. The option that expires in a week would bring in 14.80, while the option expiring the following month results in a credit of 27.00. This is very typical of pricing for at-the-money options that share a strike price but have different expiration dates.

There are a few advantages to selling a one-week at-the-money call versus a call that expires in a month. The first one should be fairly obvious. Selling the short-dated option contract yields about half the premium, but only has about one-quarter of the holding time. There is the Independence Day market holiday on July fourth, which is between June 21 and July 19, so there are actually only 19 trading days remaining for the July 19 option compared to five trading days for the June 28 option.

First, the obvious advantage for this strategy is the benefit from the time decay differences between the two choices. The weekly call option is going to experience end-of-life time decay, which for at-the-money options is greater for the five-day options than for the five-day option contract. Another less obvious time decay benefit occurs four times a year. Four times a year there are five weeks as opposed to four weeks between standard expiration dates. This offers an extra week of five-day time value versus a long-dated option.

Another advantage is the flexibility offered by implementing this strategy using short-dated options. Each week a trading decision may be made as to whether a trader believes it is a good time to sell at-the-money SPX call options. Maybe the stock market is under pressure and the trader believes the stock market is poised to rally over the near term. BXM actually under-performs the stock market in strong up-trending markets or when the market has a quick bounce to the upside. Using short-dated options allows the trader some flexibility around an index-based covered-call program. Also, with short-dated options there are more opportunities to trade higher or lower strike-call options based on a market outlook.

■ CBOE S&P 500 2 Percent OTM BuyWrite Index

The CBOE S&P 500 2 Percent OTM BuyWrite Index (BXY) is similar to the BXM with the exception of the short-call option having a strike price that is 2 percent out-of-the-money relative to the level of the S&P 500. Through selling a call option that is 2 percent out-of-the-money relative to the S&P 500 there is more allowance for an investor to participate in a move higher for the S&P 500. The tradeoff in this situation is that less premium is taken in when the out-of-the-money call is sold relative to the premium received by selling an at-the-money call.

Figure 10.6 shows the performance of BXY versus the total return of the S&P 500 between January 1, 2000, and December 31, 2012. This chart looks somewhat similar to the previous chart depicting BXM performance versus the S&P 500, but there is a difference between the two.

Again the lower line on this chart shows the S&P 500 total return over this 13-year period. Buying and holding the S&P 500 resulted in a portfolio of $100 growing to $124. BXY did a bit better with $100 applied to consistently selling a 2 percent out-of-the-money SPX call option versus the S&P

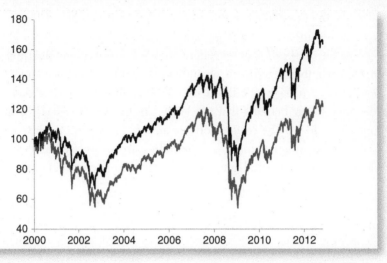

FIGURE 10.6 S&P 500 Total Return versus CBOE 2 Percent OTM BuyWrite Index Return

500 turning a $100 account into just over $166. The higher line on the chart shows this out-performance.

This strategy may also be replicated and possibly enhanced through using short-dated options. As with BXM, June 21, 2013, was a roll date for BXY. Based on the S&P 500 closing level of 1,592.43 the 1,625 calls would be the 2 percent out-of-the-money contracts. Using closing prices that day and P.M.-settled SPX contracts, the SPX Jul 20 1,625 call closed at 12.90. The SPX Jun 28 1,625 call, with only five trading days remaining to expiration, closed at 3.60.

In this case for BXY the near-dated call option provides a little bit of extra relative time decay, but not nearly as significant as the time decay difference between the two options compared in the BXM example. However, the benefit of increased flexibility around choosing strikes as well as whether to actually steer clear of having a short-call position for a short period of time exists with short-dated SPX-related options versus the standard option contracts.

Covered call and buy-write strategies using long-dated options are an effective use of the option markets for a wide variety of traders. With the introduction of short-dated options, there is now more flexibility around taking in premium against either an individual stock or even a portfolio of stocks. This flexibility includes being more dynamic when selling call options along with potentially benefitting from the rapid time decay that goes along with at-the-money options approaching expiration.

The covered call is an excellent method of enhancing portfolio performance whether a trader is an individual with a small account or a large institution managing billions of dollars. Before short-dated options, the time-decay benefits that are gained in the last few days of life for an option could only be realized once a month. Now, with the introduction of short-dated options, these opportunities are more frequent. Finally, the flexibility of short-dated options can result in more chances to take advantage of this strategy.

CHAPTER 11

Hedging with Short-Dated Options

The majority of market participants consider options to be speculative trading vehicles. However, many market participants (mostly professionals) use option contracts as financial risk-management tools. Professional investors approach the financial markets from more of a risk-management perspective, which results in options being considered more of risk-management tools. Purchasing a put option to guard against a loss in a long stock position is the most straightforward of risk management techniques that involve using the option market. The long position may be in a stock or even a portfolio of stocks and may be hedged with a put option on an individual stock or a put on a broad-based index.

This chapter will show how despite their limited life, short-dated options actually are useful as risk-management tools. Short-dated options can offer short-term protection against a potentially adverse move in an underlying security. The limited time left until expiration can be a benefit when considering a short-dated option in this capacity. Due to the limited time until expiration using a short-dated option may result in lower option costs and lower the cost of hedging.

■ Protective Put

A protective put combines a long stock position with a long put position. The long put is purchased to guard against a potential downside move while allowing the stock's owner the ability to continue to profit from ownership of shares. This benefit may include upside price appreciation or receiving dividends paid to shareholders.

Consider a trader who is long 100 shares of XYZ and is concerned that XYZ may drop 10 to 20 percent over the next two months. With XYZ trading at 51.00 this would mean a price drop of 5.10 to 10.20. At this time August expiration is two months into the future and an XYZ Aug 50 put could be purchased for 2.00. In order to gain some downside protection the put is purchased and the combined position is:

Long 100 XYZ at 51.00
Long 1 XYZ Aug 50 put at 2.00

There are four potential outcomes for the protective put position:

1. The first outcome involves selling out of the long put position before August expiration. If the stock price drops dramatically, with the worst-case scenario of a 20 percent loss in the stock price, the put option may be sold for a profit. This profit would be used to offset the unrealized loss in the stock. After selling the put there would still be long exposure to the stock; if that is no longer desirable the stock may be sold as well. If the stock is a good value at this point and there is an expectation it will move higher over time then the shares do not necessarily have to be sold.

2. The second outcome also involves selling the option, but not at a profit. If expiration approaches and the stock price did not drop, it may be prudent to salvage some of the premium spent for protection against the stock price going lower through selling the option. When the put was purchased it was done so as a sort of insurance policy against a lower stock price. Once this concern has passed, the need no longer exists for the long put position and it should be sold.

3. Third, if the stock moves lower and expiration approaches the option may be held through expiration. The August 50 put would be exercised and shares sold at 50.00. This is an attractive alternative if the stock price is much lower than 50.00 and there are not expectations for a recovery in the share price.

4. Finally, if the stock price rallies up to much higher levels, there may not be a willing buyer of the XYZ Aug 50 put in the market. If this is the case

TABLE 11.1	Long XYZ + Long XYZ Aug 50 Put Payoff			
XYZ	XYZ Profit/Loss	XYZ 50 Put Value	Option Cost	Covered Call Profit/Loss
46.00	−5.00	4.00	−2.00	−3.00
48.00	−3.00	2.00	−2.00	−3.00
50.00	−1.00	0.00	−2.00	−3.00
52.00	1.00	0.00	−2.00	−1.00
54.00	3.00	0.00	−2.00	1.00
56.00	5.00	0.00	−2.00	3.00

then the option may be held through expiration and expire out of the money with no value. The premium that was paid is a loss on this option. What was purchased was peace of mind in place for a two-month period regarding a potential loss of the stock.

Table 11.1 summarizes the result for the combination of holding 100 shares of XYZ combined with a long position in the XYZ Aug 50 put. Note that as the stock price moves below 50.00 the long put position begins to offset any losses that are incurred from being long the stock. Also as the stock price moves higher the position does benefit from long stock exposure, but is held back a little by the premium paid for protection against a lower stock price.

A payout diagram for this trade, with the same assumption that the put option is held to expiration appears in Figure 11.1. Note to the left of the option strike price of 50.00 the losses are limited to 3.00. Over 50.00 the line moves higher on a one-for-one basis, profiting from the performance of

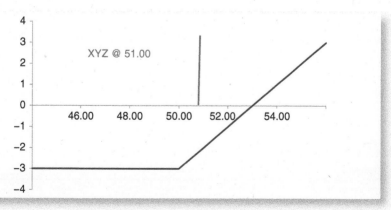

FIGURE 11.1   Long XYZ + Long XYZ Aug 50 Put Payoff

the stock. A benefit of using a protective put is that the potential for upside still exists when a put is purchased for protection against a loss.

Take note of where XYZ is trading on this payout diagram. Due to the premium paid for the put option a loss of 2.00 would occur if the stock is unchanged at expiration. This is a way to visualize the cost of peace of mind or the cost of hedging this position.

When a put option is purchased to protect against a loss in a stock there is usually some time value to overcome before the protection cushions the loss in a stock. Short-dated options often have very little time value and offer protection against short-term concerns regarding a stock position. The trading examples show how this lack of time value results in fairly inexpensive short-term protection.

■ Protective Put Trading Example

A common reason for a trader to want a short-term hedge against a drop in the price of a stock may be an earnings release. On a quarterly basis companies will issue a press release that includes a wide variety of financial information regarding business activity in the previous quarter. A majority of companies will schedule their earnings release dates a couple of weeks after the end of a calendar quarter. Typically the price change for a stock is much greater on the first trading session after a company has reported their earnings.

On a Friday afternoon an investor notes that Yum Brands (YUM) will be reporting their quarterly earnings on Wednesday of the following week. At the time, the stock is trading at 71.65 and the investor holds 100 shares of YUM. The growth for YUM comes primarily from the Chinese market and it appears there has been some recent slowing in that economy. The investor wants to be a holder of shares of YUM over the long term, but has short-term concerns. Due to these concerns the investor decides to buy a 5-day put option on YUM that expires the following Friday.

The two most logical put option choices for protection against a drop in the share price of YUM appear in Table 11.2. Weighing the two option

TABLE 11.2	YUM 5-day Put Option Quotes	
Option	Bid	Ask
67.50 Put	0.40	0.45
70.00 Put	1.00	1.05

YUM	YUM Profit/Loss	YUM 70 Put Value*	Option Cost	Protective Put Profit/Loss
65.00	−6.65	5.00	−1.05	−2.70
67.50	−4.15	2.65	−1.05	−2.55
70.00	−1.65	0.95	−1.05	−1.75
71.65	0.00	0.35	−1.05	−0.70
72.50	0.85	0.20	−1.05	0.00
75.00	3.15	0.00	−1.05	2.10

premiums, strike prices of the two options and level of concern about how the stock may react to the earnings announcement the investor decides to buy 1 YUM 70.00 put for 1.05 to protect against a loss in the share price when the earnings results are released the following week. The combined protected-put position consists of:

Long 100 YUM at 71.65
Long 1 YUM 70.00 put at 1.05

The exit for this trade will be dependent on the news from the earnings release. If the news is particularly bad and the stock price drops dramatically the investor may choose to sell the stock and sell the put option with profits from the put offsetting a portion of the losses in the stock. If the news pushes the stock to lower prices, but the investor wants to maintain a long-term position in YUM, they may decide to sell the put option, with profits offsetting the unrealized losses in the stock. They would also still have a long position in the stock, which matches up with the long-term positive outlook for YUM. Finally, if the news is positive and the stock moves higher, the investor should sell the put option to recoup some of the cost of the put. Table 11.3 shows the expected profit and loss for this protective put combination with two days remaining until expiration.

Note that at all prices on the payoff table, with the exception of 75.00, there is some value for the 70 put. Post earnings, even if the stock moves higher, the 70 put may be sold to get some value back out of the position. This is a function of there being two days remaining until expiration. With YUM at 75.00 there would be very little value left for the put option so the assumption is that there may be no bid price or that the bid price would not make selling the option worthwhile when commissions are

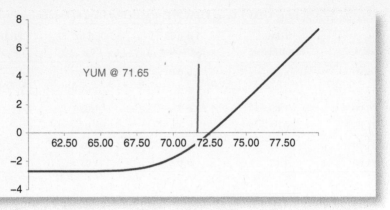

FIGURE 11.2 Long YUM + Long YUM 5-Day 70 Put Payoff

figured in. The payout diagram for this protective put position appears in Figure 11.2.

The payout diagram for this YUM position has curved lines as it assumes that the trade will be exited with a couple of days remaining until expiration for the put option. Again, the put option is purchased in order to hedge against a potential drop based on an event (earnings). Once the event has passed the option position should be exited.

The price for YUM when the hedges were put on is highlighted on the diagram. The payoff value at this price may be considered the anticipated cost of hedging. In this example the cost would be about 0.70, which is the anticipated loss if YUM is unchanged from current levels after their earnings report. Sometimes the cost of hedging is considered unreasonably high in dollar terms. When this occurs there are alternatives—the next section discusses one of the most common.

■ The Collar

Many times an investor may be concerned with neat term *downside* in a holding and be discouraged by the cost of protection due to a high price of an available put option. In order to offset the cost of an expensive put option, some premium may be taken in through selling a call option. The result is a strategy that combines a protective put with a covered call.

Revisiting the XYZ example from earlier in this chapter, again consider XYZ trading at 51.00. Again, the trader who is long 100 shares of XYZ is concerned that XYZ may drop 10 to 20 percent over the next two months. The trader then checks his quotes and notices that hedging this position for two months would again cost 2.00 for the XYZ Aug 50 put. He decides this is too costly for the protection against a drop he is concerned about. However, he also would be a willing seller of his shares a point higher or he feels that the stock will not move higher over the next couple of months. In either of these situations he would look to sell a call in conjunction with the long put to create a *collar*.

The trader notes that the XYZ Aug 52 call may be sold for 2.00. The result is selling a XYZ Aug 52 call for 2.00, buying a XYZ Aug 50 put for 2.00 with the cost being equal to whatever commission is charged by the brokerage firm. The combined positions that create a collar are:

Long 100 XYZ at 51.00
Long 1 XYZ Aug 50 put at 2.00
Short 1 XYZ Aug 52 call at 2.00

There are three potential outcomes for this trade if held through expiration:

1. First, if the stock closes between 50.00 and 52.00, then both options will expire with no value and the shares will still be hold. There had been protection against a big loss in XYZ that was funded by giving up upside potential when the call was sold. This protection against a large drop in the price of shares was not needed. Also in this case the profit or loss of this trade is equal to the move higher or lower in XYZ stock.
2. The second outcome involves the stock losing value and trading under 50.00 at expiration. If held through expiration the shares would be called away at 50.00. If the trader wants to hold the stock long term then they should sell the put option. The proceeds from that sale will offset any of the value lost in XYZ beyond 50.00 a share.
3. Finally, if the price of XYZ is over 52.00 at expiration, shares should expect to be called away at 52.00. If the trader would like to continue to hold XYZ beyond expiration, he would need to repurchase the short position in the XYZ 52 call. There would be a loss associated with this part of the collar that would be offset by profits in XYZ stock above 52.00. Table 11.4 shows the net profit or loss for this collar position at August expiration.

Note between 50.00 and 52.00 the profit and loss of this position is the same as the performance of the stock. Above 52.00 and below 50.00 the performance hits a wall, which could be considered a positive if the stock trades lower. Conversely, it may be a bit of a disappointment if the stock

TABLE 11.4   Long XYZ + Long XYZ 50 Put + Short XYZ 52 Call Payoff

XYZ	XYZ Profit/Loss	XYZ 50 Put Value	XYZ 52 Call Value	Combined Collar P/L
46.00	−5.00	4.00	0.00	−1.00
48.00	−3.00	2.00	0.00	−1.00
50.00	−1.00	0.00	0.00	−1.00
51.00	0.00	0.00	0.00	0.00
52.00	1.00	0.00	0.00	1.00
54.00	3.00	0.00	−2.00	1.00
56.00	5.00	0.00	−4.00	1.00

trades dramatically higher, but remember the trader in this case was a willing seller of his shares at 52.00.

Figure 11.3 is a payoff diagram showing the result of this collar at expiration. The middle of this diagram would mirror the profit or loss of the underlying stock. On both sides the protection received through the long put and obligation taken on by the short call are both very apparent. Note the price of XYZ falls right on the breakeven point for this collar. This is a rare occurrence in the markets, but the cost of hedging may be very low on a dollar basis when a collar is implemented.

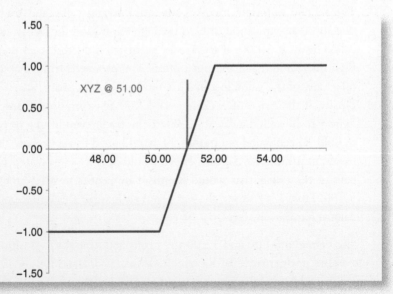

FIGURE 11.3   Long XYZ + Long XYZ 50 Put + Short XYZ 52 Call Payoff

■ Trading Example Using the Collar

The trading example for using short-dated options for a collar revisits the situation using the protective put. The Friday before the week where YUM reports earnings a holder of YUM stock is concerned about a short-term drop in the price of the stock that may occur when earnings are announced the following Wednesday. The investor who is concerned about the share price of YUM in reaction to the earnings report may consider using a collar instead of the protective put. This may prove more appropriate when the investor would be willing to sell shares at a higher price or does not think there is a good chance the stock is going to move higher based on the earnings announcement.

Two potential collar scenarios will be investigated using both the 72.50 call and the 75.00 call (Table 11.5). If the investor believes there is very limited upside for YUM over the near term then they would want to sell a 5-day YUM 72.50 call and take in 1.00 of premium. As in the protective put example, to guard against a drop in YUM's stock price a 5-day YUM 70.00 put would be purchased. The net result would be the following positions related to YUM:

Long 100 YUM at 71.65
Long 1 YUM 70.00 put at 1.05
Short 1 YUM 72.50 call at 1.00

The first alternative involves paying just 0.05 for the collar which results in limited upside and protection from a big downside move into the earnings release. Table 11.6 is a payoff table based on assumed option pricing at various levels the trading day after YUM has released their earnings.

At many price levels for YUM both the put and call options that make up the collar will have some sort of value. Notice if YUM moves down to 67.50 there is no expected market value for the 72.50 call and with YUM up at

TABLE 11.5	YUM 5-Day Call Option Quotes	
Option	Bid	Ask
72.50 Call	1.00	1.05
75.00 Call	0.30	0.35

TABLE 11.6

TABLE 11.6	**Long YUM + Long YUM 70.00 Put + Short YUM 72.50 Call Payoff**				
YUM	**YUM Profit/Loss**	**YUM 70.00 Put Value**	**YUM 72.50 Call Value**	**Collar Cost**	**Combined Collar P/L**
67.50	–4.15	2.65	0.00	–0.05	–1.55
70.00	–1.65	0.95	–0.15	–0.05	–0.90
71.65	0.00	0.35	–0.55	–0.05	–0.25
72.50	0.85	0.20	–0.90	–0.05	0.10
75.00	3.35	0.00	–2.65	–0.05	0.65

75.00 there is no expectation of any value for the 70.00 put. The time-value component does have an impact to the value of this collar if the trade is exited with two days left until expiration. Even with two days remaining until expiration, many options will still have some value.

Figure 11.4 shows a payoff diagram based on the assumption that the collar may be unwound before expiration. The remaining time value results in a curved diagram as opposed to the linear type of payout that occurs at expiration. The price of YUM stock is highlighted on the payoff diagram. Do note, due to the different rates of time decay there is a slight loss for this trade if YUM is unchanged after earnings.

The other potential collar would allow for some upside in shares of YUM, but also be a little more costly. Instead of selling the YUM 72.50 call the 75.00 call would be sold for 0.30. The result on the call side of this collar is an obligation to sell shares at 75.00 as opposed to 72.50.

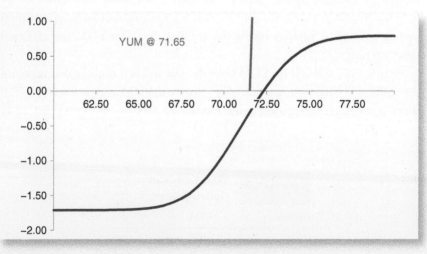

FIGURE 11.4   YUM 70.00/72.50 Collar Payoff

(See Figure 11.5.) The result is more premium being paid as the short call would cover some of the cost of the put, but not a substantial amount. Since less of the premium would be covered, it would probably only make sense to sell the 75.00 call if the investor would be a willing seller of YUM above 75.00 the following week. (See Table 11.7.) When the 72.50 call was sold the outlook for YUM was that the stock would probably not trade over that price the following week. Selling the 75.00 call should be motivated by the idea that if YUM trades up to that price the investor would be a willing seller of their shares since they are only getting 0.30 of benefit from taking on this obligation. The net result of selling this call would be the following positions:

Long 100 YUM at 71.65
Long 1 YUM 70.00 put at 1.05
Short 1 YUM 75.00 call at 0.30

The maximum potential loss for the 70.00 to 75.00 collar is higher than the maximum loss for the 70.00 to 72.50 collar. This is a function of more premium being paid out to implement this strategy. Of course the benefit of selling a higher strike call is that that there is more potential upside that exists in the case of a rally in the shares.

Low cost short-term protection can come in the form of a protective put or a lower-cost collar. Protection from a downside move over a longer period of time can be had as well using a collar. The collar may be modified a little with a long put and short call with different expiration dates being

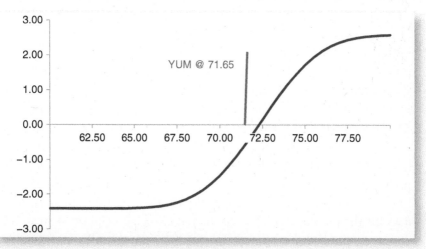

FIGURE 11.5   YUM 70.00/75.00 Collar Payoff

TABLE 11.7   Long YUM + Long YUM 70.00 Put + Short YUM 75.00 Call Payoff

YUM	YUM Profit/Loss	YUM 70.00 Put Value	YUM 75.00 Call Value	Collar Cost	Combined Collar P/L
67.50	−4.15	2.65	0.00	−0.75	−2.25
70.00	−1.65	0.95	0.00	−0.75	−1.45
71.65	0.00	0.35	−0.05	−0.75	−0.45
72.50	0.85	0.20	−0.15	−0.75	0.15
75.00	3.35	0.00	−0.90	−0.75	1.70
77.50	5.85	0.00	−2.65	−0.75	2.45

combined to offer downside protection funded by a short call option. The short position of the shorter-term option contract will offer a time decay advantage over the long position in a longer-dated put option.

■ The Modified Collar

There is another approach to the collar that is a bit more dynamic and takes advantage of the benefit of short-dated options. This involves combining a long put with a short call option where the two contracts have different expiration dates. A longer dated put will be purchased to protect against loss in the underlying stock and a shorter-dated call option may be sold to cover some of the cost of the put option. Weekly calls may be sold opportunistically based on a short-term outlook for the stock while the longer-dated put option will be consistently held.

If XYZ is trading at 51.00 in late June, just a little under three months of protection against a loss in XYZ may be purchased using September options. An XYZ Sep 50 put with 60 trading days remaining until expiration may be purchased for 1.95. After purchasing this put option, short-dated call options may be sold in order to offset some of the premium that was paid for the put. For example, a short-dated XYZ 5-day 52 call may be sold for 0.35. If XYZ is a stock that has serial options available, a 10-day 52 call may be sold for 0.60. In both cases if XYZ is below 52.00 then the premium received will be a realized short-term profit. If this exercise is effectively repeated a few more times the cost of protection may be reduced. Table 11.8 shows the outcome in five days for the modified collar constructed using a long position in an XYZ 60-day 50 put and short position in a XYZ 5-day 52 call which would be initiated for a cost of 1.60.

		TABLE 11.8	Long XYZ + Long 60-Day 50 Put + Short 5-Day XYZ 52 Call Payoff		
XYZ	XYZ Profit/Loss	60-Day 50.00 Put Value	5-Day 52.00 Call Value	Initial Cost	Combined Unrealized P/L
46.00	−5.00	4.70	0.00	−1.60	−1.90
48.00	−3.00	3.35	0.00	−1.60	−1.25
50.00	−1.00	2.30	0.00	−1.60	−0.30
51.00	0.00	1.85	0.00	−1.60	0.25
52.00	1.00	1.45	0.00	−1.60	0.80
54.00	3.00	0.90	−2.00	−1.60	0.30
56.00	5.00	0.50	−4.00	−1.60	−0.10

Note in Table 11.8 that if XYZ climbs about 10 percent to 56.00 over the course of just a few days it is actually possible that the hedge could turn into a losing prospect. Combining the cost of initiating the collar with the amount of value that exists in the short-call option along with the value coming out of the long put results in a small loss occurring. The payout diagram in Figure 11.6 illustrates this risk as well.

The 50 strike put option is a near at-the-money option so there is some dramatic time decay toward the last couple of weeks until expiration, but over the first half of the time covered on the time decay chart in Figure 0.70 comes out of the value of the option. As a perspective, that is the equivalent

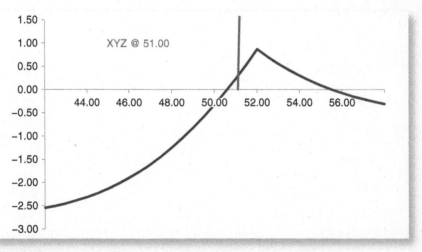

FIGURE 11.6 Long XYZ + Long 60-Day 50 Put + Short 5-Day XYZ 52 Call Payoff

of selling two XYZ 5-day 52 call options at 0.35. Also notice there is pretty good protection almost immediately to the downside of where XYZ is marked on this payoff diagram. This occurs through lowering the cost of the put with the near dated call.

■ The Modified Collar Trading Example

On a Friday in mid-July shares of Federal Express (FDX) were trading at 102.30. The S&P 500 was making new highs and shares of FDX were bordering on all-time high levels as well. There were some fundamental concerns and it appears support on a chart was around 95.00. If that support level was broken lower prices may be on the horizon. Resistance was around 104.00 based on previous highs and recent stock-trading action. Based on longer-term concern about the potential for lower prices a FDX Oct 95.00 put was purchased for 2.60. The October contract had 69 trading days remaining until expiration. Figure 11.7 is a daily price chart of FDX stock with lines indicating the support and resistance levels.

Since 104.00 is considered a resistance level, pricing on the shorter-dated FDX 5-day 104.00 calls are checked and these calls may be sold at 0.90. This short-call position combined with the longer-dated long puts results in the following positions that comprise a modified collar:

Long 100 FDX at 102.30
Long 1 FDX Oct 95.00 put at 2.60
Short 1 FDX 5-day 104.00 call at 0.90

FIGURE 11.7 Daily Price Chart for FDX

TABLE 11.9	Long FDX + Long Oct 95 Put + Short FDX 5-Day 104 Call Payoff				
FDX	XYZ Profit/Loss	Oct 95 Put Value	5 Day 104 Call Value	Initial Cost	Combined Unrealized P/L
90.00	−12.30	7.80	0.00	−1.70	−6.20
95.00	−7.30	5.05	0.00	−1.70	−3.95
100.00	−2.30	3.10	0.00	−1.70	−0.90
102.30	0.00	2.45	0.00	−1.70	0.75
105.00	2.70	1.80	−1.00	−1.70	1.80
110.00	7.70	1.00	−6.00	−1.70	1.00

There are two time decay advantages for this example. The call option expires in only five days while the long put option has months until expiration. Also, the call strike price is much closer to where FDX is trading than the put option so the advantage of at-the-money time decay is present as well. Table 11.9 runs through the unrealized profit or loss of this modified collar upon expiration of the short-dated call option.

A good portion of upside is capped over the near term based on the short position in the 104 call. A feeling that FDX is not going much higher over the near term should accompany this spread trade. However, the longer amount of time remaining for the FDX 95 put allows this option to retain some value even if FDX trades up to 110.00 a share.

Figure 11.8 is a payoff diagram for this collar at expiration of the short-dated call option. Note there is some upside from where FDX was trading but then

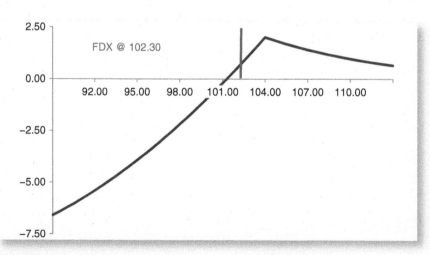

FIGURE 11.8 FDX Payoff Diagram at 5-Day Call Expiration

the loss of value of the long put begins to tail off. Looking in the other direction, the put option does retain time value and begins to experience some intrinsic value at well below 95.00. As the stock moves even lower the maximum loss is 9.00, which is the loss in FDX down to 95.00 from 102.30 combined with the 1.70 cost associated with the initial implementation of the collar.

Finally, remember that the long put still has several weeks remaining until expiration. More short-dated calls can opportunistically be sold to bring in more income. This income could be a method of eventually funding the cost of hedging.

Options are just as much speculative tools as risk-management tools. This chapter has discussed the role that short-dated options may take in a risk-management capacity. A put option with just a few days remaining to expiration may be purchased for short-term protection. If the cost of options is too high for comfort then a call option may be sold in order to fund this cost. The result will be sacrificing some upside in the underlying market or stock as a method of paying for this protection. Finally, long-term protection against a loss in a stock may always be purchased with longer-dated put options. A method of covering this cost could be opportunistically selling near dated call options.

CHAPTER 12

Bullish Spread Trading

A bullish vertical spread is probably one of the best uses of the option market. The spread involves taking a combination of a long and short position in the same type of option. The result is a reduction in exposure to time decay and potentially a lower dollar cost when comparing the spread trade to buying a call option when having a bullish outlook. These spreads are very practical in that they allow a trader to benefit from an outlook for a stock or market where there is a target price involved. One of the reasons many traders will shy away from using a vertical spread relates to time decay. In order to realize the full profit expected from a bullish vertical spread the trade will need to be held until there is very little time left until expiration. However, now that short-dated options are available and there are options that expire every Friday, when a trader has a bullish outlook for an underlying market, they should give a strong consideration to putting on a vertical spread.

■ Bullish Vertical Spread

A bullish vertical spread may be initiated using either call or put options. Despite which type of option is used, the trade will be constructed through buying a lower strike option and purchasing a higher strike option. A call with a lower strike will cost more than a call sharing an expiration date with a higher strike so a bullish spread created with call options would be created

TABLE 12.1	Option Quotes Used to Create 30-Day Bull Call and Bull Put Spreads			
Call Bid	Call Ask	Strike	Put Bid	Put Ask
3.55	3.60	45	0.50	0.55
0.85	0.90	50	2.80	2.85

by incurring an account debit or cost. A put option with a higher strike price will have a higher premium than a put with a lower strike price that shares an expiration date. When creating this spread with put options the higher strike option would be sold for a higher premium than is paid for the lower strike option. So a bullish spread created with put options would be done, with the result being income taken in. The option quotes in Table 12.1 will be used to demonstrate bullish spreads created with both call options and put options.

A bullish call spread would be entered into through buying the 45 call for 3.60 and selling the 50 call for 0.85. This would result in a net cost of 2.75 with the best possible outcome being that the underlying stock is at or above 50.00 at expiration. At any price above 50.00, the long 45 call is worth 5.00 more than the short position in the 50 call. With the long position worth 5.00 more than the short-call option the result would be a profit of 2.25. A payoff table that shows the profit and loss for this bull call spread appears in Table 12.2.

Using the same market prices a bullish-put spread would be entered into by selling the 50 put for 2.80 and purchasing the XYZ 45 put for 0.55. This would result in a credit or net income of 2.25 which is the net result of paying out 0.55 and taking in 2.80. The credit received of 2.25 is also the best possible outcome for this trade. With the stock at or above 50.00 at expiration then both put options will expire with no value. The profit and loss for the XYZ 45/50 Bull put spread appears in Table 12.3.

TABLE 12.2	Payoff Table for XYZ 45/50 Bull Call Spread at Expiration			
XYZ	XYZ 45 Call	XYZ 50 Call	Cost	P/L
40.00	0.00	0.00	−2.75	−2.75
45.00	0.00	0.00	−2.75	−2.75
50.00	5.00	0.00	−2.75	2.25
55.00	10.00	−5.00	−2.75	2.25

TABLE 12.3	Payoff Table for XYZ 45/50 Bull Put Spread at Expiration			
XYZ	XYZ 45 Put	XYZ 50 Put	Income	P/L
40.00	5.00	−10.00	2.25	−2.75
45.00	0.00	−5.00	2.25	−2.75
50.00	0.00	0.00	2.25	2.25
55.00	0.00	0.00	2.25	2.25

Both the bull call spread and the bull put spread would realize the maximum profit from the trade if the underlying stock is at or above 50.00 at expiration. In the case of the spread created with put options both options would expire with no value and the profit of 2.25 which is equal to the credit received when the trade was initiated. Despite being created in two different manners, both spreads have the same ultimate profit or loss at expiration. Figure 12.1 illustrates the payout for these two spreads.

The payout in Figure 12.1 applies to both the bull call and bull put spreads. Both spreads have the same risk, reward, and breakeven levels. Despite the potential profit and loss for both spreads being the same, most traders prefer using put options when creating a bullish spread for a couple of reasons. First, many traders like the idea of getting paid to initiate a trade. There may be some logic to this, but not too much since the net result of the trade is basically the same whether it involves the margin requirement or paying up front to put on the trade. The second reason that many traders prefer creating bullish spreads with put options has to do with the mechanics at expiration.

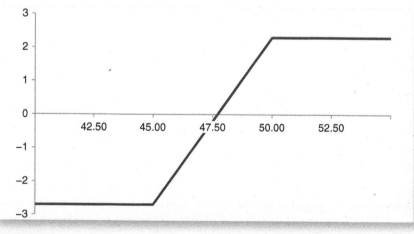

FIGURE 12.1 Bullish Vertical Spread Payout at Expiration

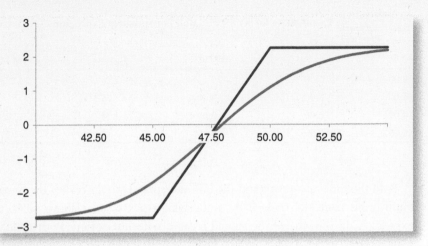

FIGURE 12.2 Bullish Vertical Spread Payout at Expiration and with 15 Days to Expiration

This second point is worth illustrating a bit. The maximum profitability of the bull put spread would occur if both the 45 strike and 50 strike put options expire with no value or out of the money. That is the reason for a preference to use put option in this case—if the options expire with no value then the trader does not need to take any action at expiration. On expiration Friday the two options are in their account, on Monday morning after expiration the options are no longer in their account, and they have realized profit equity to the credit received when they put the trade on.

A big advantage of using short-dated options to trade vertical spreads is that the full amount of profit may be realized in a shorter amount of time. Using the same example with the 45.00/50.00 bullish spread, consider if this trade involves using options that expire in 30 calendar days. The trader puts on this trade thinking that the underlying stock will trade to 50.00 over the next month. The payoff diagram in Figure 12.2 shows the payout at expiration compared to the payout on this trade with 15 days remaining to expiration.

The curved payout represents the profit or loss for this trade based on the underlying market at a variety of prices half way to expiration. Note at 50.00 about half the profit would be realized if the trade were exited. If exited the profit would be close to 1.05 which is just under half of the potential maximum profit or 2.25 for this trade. As the time to expiration approaches, the payoff of the spread also approaches the payoff at expiration, but not quite at a linear rate. Figure 12.3 compares the payoff at expiration to the payoff if the trade is exited five days before expiration.

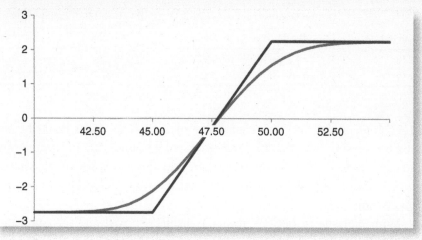

FIGURE 12.3 Bullish Vertical Spread Payout at Expiration versus Five Days to Expiration

In this payoff diagram the curved line is closer to the rigid payoff at expiration, but there is still a gap between the payoff with five days remaining and the payoff at expiration. If the underlying market is at 50.00 with five days to go it appears the trade can be exited with a profit of about 1.50. This is two-thirds of the expected payout of 2.25 with the underlying at the target price of 50.00 at expiration. Of course if the stock has greatly overshot the target the trade can be exited with a profit that is within pennies of the maximum expectation. Table 12.4 breaks down the daily profit or loss for the bullish XYZ 45/50 spread at a variety of times left to expiration.

It is interesting that even if the stock trades up to 52.50 immediately after the trade is initiated the profit that may be realized is only

TABLE 12.4	XYX 45/50 Bull Spread Payoff for Different Prices and Times to Expiration				
	42.50	45.00	47.50	50.00	52.50
30	−2.20	−1.40	−0.30	0.75	1.55
25	−2.30	−1.50	−0.30	0.85	1.65
20	−2.40	−1.55	−0.30	0.95	1.75
15	−2.50	−1.70	−0.28	1.05	1.85
10	−2.60	−1.85	−0.27	1.25	2.05
5	−2.70	−2.10	−0.26	1.50	2.20
0	−2.75	−2.75	−0.25	2.25	2.25

TABLE 12.5	Option Quotes Used to Create 5-Day Bull Call and Bull Put Spreads			
Call Bid	Call Ask	Strike	Put Bid	Put Ask
3.10	3.15	45	0.15	0.20
0.35	0.40	50	2.40	2.45

1.55 compared to the targeted profit of 2.25. The result could be the stock reversing over the 30-day period and a winning trade turning into a losing trade. Of course the maximum gain also works for the maximum loss. If the stock quickly drops to 45.00 the trade could be exited for a loss of only 1.40.

With short-dated options always available, the wait-and-see game that used to be in place for a bullish spread is not as long as it has to be. The same pricing that was used to create the 30-day examples was used to determine 5-day option premiums. The quotes for those 5-day 45 and 50 strike options appear in Table 12.5.

Based on these quotes a 5-day bullish call spread would be entered into through purchasing the 45 call at 3.15 and selling a 50 call for 0.35. This would result in a net cost of 2.80 and a maximum reward on this trade of 2.20 if the underlying trades up to or over 50.00 at expiration. Like the long-dated example, at a price from 50.00 and higher the 45 call will be worth 5.00 more than the 50.00 call.

A bullish spread created with put options would bring in 2.20. The 50 put would be sold for 2.40 and the 45 put would be purchased for 0.20 for a net credit of 2.20. The goal is for the market to be over 50.00 at expiration and both of these put options expire out-of-the-money. Table 12.6 shows the payout at expiration for this 5-day bull put spread.

The risk versus reward of this 5-day trade is very close to the risk versus reward for the 30-day trade. Of course, the stock needs to trade up to 50.00 more quickly than in the case of the trade with the 30-day options.

TABLE 12.6	Payoff Table for XYZ 45/50 Bull Put Spread at Expiration			
XYZ	XYZ 45 Put	XYZ 50 Put	Income	P/L
40.00	5.00	−10.00	2.20	−2.80
45.00	0.00	−5.00	2.20	−2.80
50.00	0.00	0.00	2.20	2.20
55.00	0.00	0.00	2.20	2.20

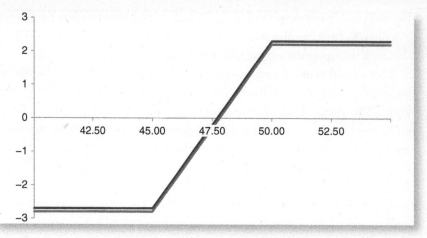

FIGURE 12.4 5-Day and 30-Day Bullish Spread Payoffs at Expiration

Figure 12.4 compares the payout at expiration for both the 30-day and 5-day bullish spreads. Notice there is very little difference between the two.

This may actually be looked at as either a positive or a negative. If you have a short-term outlook for the underlying market and expect the target to be reached quickly, the short-dated options give you an alternative that may match up to your outlook. The other side of this argument would be that with a long-term outlook it is possible the trade may be early, but in that case a position may always be rolled out to the next weekly expiration.

■ Bullish Spread Trading Examples

There are basically three types of short term bullish trades that would be based on technical analysis. A bullish trade may:

1. Follow an established trend.
2. Result from trying to buy a stock when it has fallen too much.
3. Be based on a breakout to the upside.

All three of these types of scenarios may be taken advantage of with the use of a bullish vertical spread.

The first type of trade, following a trend, is a very common approach that many traders follow for longer holding periods. The old Wall Street saying, "The trend is your friend" caught on for a reason. Being on the right side of a trend is one of the most pleasant trading experiences around. Determining what the trend is may always be a bit subjective or quantitative. Despite the analysis behind determining the direction of a trend, when a stock is in a defined uptrend a valid strategy is a bullish spread based on a target price that matches up to the magnitude of a trend.

The second type of short-term, bullish trading involves trying to buy on weakness. There in another Wall Street saying, "Trying to catch a falling knife." The visual should be fairly obvious as attempting to catch a falling knife would be a pretty dangerous endeavor where one might sustain an injury or even lose a finger. A more technical term for this sort of trading is counter-trend trading. Buying when a stock or market appears to be in a free fall can be a pretty risky move. The known risk and reward associated with a bullish spread is a method that offers the opportunity to buy on weakness, but not get to hurt if the trade does not go your way.

Finally, buying when a stock or market is making a new high is a bullish strategy that is utilized by many levels of traders. Admittedly, it can be emotionally difficult to buy a stock when it is making a new high, but doing just that can be the basis of successful trades. Many successful traders have made a career from buying breakouts to the upside.

Bullish-Trend Trade

There are multiple methods of defining a trend. Many trend-following traders will define an uptrend as a stock trading above a certain moving average. Others traders may use a relative strength index (RSI) or average directional index (ADX) to define a trend. Another less quantifiable method of defining a trend is through use of a trend line. Regardless of the method used to determine a trend, a short-term vertical spread can always be a good method of taking advantage of a bullish trend.

For example, on a Monday afternoon shares of 3D Systems Corporation (DDD) were trading at 32.50 after trading below and then recovering to above an uptrend line that has been in place for a few weeks. Projecting the trend line out a few days it appears that DDD could trade to 34.00 or higher by the end of the week. Figure 12.5 is a daily chart of DDD showing the chart analysis that leads to this outlook.

With an end-of-week target price of 34.00 for shares of DDD a bull put spread is considering selling the 34 strike and buying a lower strike to complete a bull put spread. The quotes for DDD options that expire at the end of the week appear in Table 12.7. A short position in the DDD 34 put may be combined with a long position in the lower strike puts. Each combination will have different risk, reward, and breakeven levels.

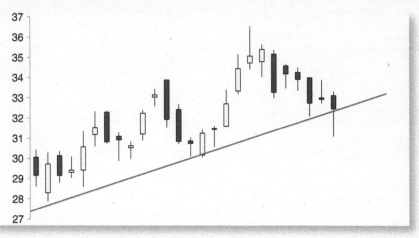

FIGURE 12.5 DDD Daily Chart with Uptrend Line

With the target price at 34.00 at expiration the logical short option in the bull put spread will be the 34 put, which may be sold at 1.85. The other options that are long candidates to complete the bull put spread stretch from 33 down to 30. A comparison of the various spreads that may be created appears in Table 12.8.

The spread that stands out on this table appears to be the 32/34 bull put spread. The credit received is greater than the maximum potential loss and the breakeven price for the spread is just 0.15 higher than where the stock is trading at the moment. Based on those two factors, along with expectations that DDD will trade to 34.00 by the end of the week, a DDD 34 put would be sold for 1.85 and the DDD 32 put would be purchased for 0.70 resulting in a net credit of 1.15.

Table 12.9 covers the potential gain and loss for this bullish spread for a variety of prices. At or below 32.00 the maximum loss for this trade

TABLE 12.7	DDD Option Quotes with Four Days to Expiration	
Option	Bid	Ask
30 Put	0.10	0.15
31 Put	0.30	0.35
32 Put	0.65	0.70
33 Put	1.30	1.35
34 Put	1.85	1.90

TABLE 12.8 DDD Bull Put Spread Comparison

Spread	Credit	Max Loss	Breakeven
30/34	1.75	−2.25	32.25
31/34	1.50	−1.50	32.50
32/34	1.15	−0.85	32.85
33/34	0.50	−0.50	33.50

TABLE 12.9 DDD 32/34 Bull Put Spread Payoff at Expiration

DDD	DDD 32 Put	DDD 34 Put	Income	P/L
30.00	2.00	−4.00	1.15	−0.85
32.00	0.00	−2.00	1.15	−0.85
34.00	0.00	0.00	1.15	1.15
36.00	0.00	0.00	1.15	1.15

comes in at −0.85. If the stock gets up to 34.00 or higher the net result is a gain of 1.15 as both options expire with no value. The payout diagram in Figure 12.6 displays this payout along with the price for DDD when the trade was initiated.

If DDD does not move at all and closes at 32.50 at expiration the net result is a loss of 0.65 or a partial loss. There is very little room between DDD's price of 32.50 and the breakeven price of 32.85 at expiration. DDD only has to move 0.35 higher to reach the point where the trade turns from a loss to a gain.

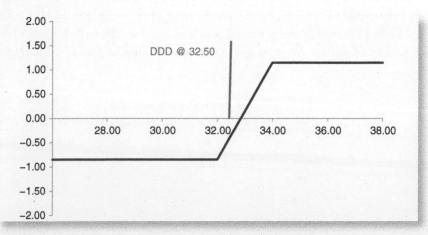

FIGURE 12.6 DDD 32/34 Bull Put Spread Payoff at Expiration

The goal of the DDD trade is to ride the trend that is currently in place. The next trading example can be a bit more risky as in involves taking the other side of a trend.

Bullish Reversal Trade

A reversal trade is a risky proposition. Also, many traders shy away from option trading because of the perception that option trading is too risky. It is interesting that a trader can combine the perceived riskiness of option trading with what is a high-risk trading strategy and actually end up with a trade that has a defined outcome. The defined outcome means that the potential maximum risk and potential maximum reward are known when the trade is initiated.

On a Thursday the SPDR Gold Shares ETF (GLD) comes under some pressure making new multiyear lows closing just under 116.00. The chart in Figure 12.7 shows this price action. If a trader feels this move is overdone and that the price of gold will begin to develop support at the 115.00 level a bullish put spread would be an appropriate trade.

Table 12.10 shows the market prices for GLD put options that expire on the following Friday. GLD options offer some great flexibility as there are dollar strikes despite the high notional level of GLD quotes. If the expectation is that GLD would begin to trade higher the 116 put would be a good candidate to sell. This would bring in 2.45.

Table 12.10 shows the market prices for GLD put options that expire on the following Friday. GLD options offer some great flexibility as there are

FIGURE 12.7   GLD Daily Price Chart

TABLE 12.10	GLD 6-Day Put Option Quotes Spread Comparison	
Option	Bid	Ask
110 Put	0.65	0.70
111 Put	0.85	0.90
112 Put	1.10	1.15
113 Put	1.35	1.40
114 Put	1.65	1.70
115 Put	2.00	2.05
116 Put	2.45	2.50

dollar strikes despite the high notional level of GLD quotes. If the expectation were that GLD would begin to trade higher, the 116 put would be a good candidate to sell. This would bring in 2.45.

Table 12.11 combines the short 116 put with buying each strike between 110 and 115. The maximum loss relative to the credit received, along with breakeven level for each spread is shown in the table. When choosing the final spread a combination of risk versus reward and breakeven pricing should be considered.

Considering the credit received versus the maximum loss along the breakeven level for the trade results in choosing the GLD 113/116 bull put spread. A credit of 1.05 is received for the trade and if GLD makes another leg to the downside the maximum loss would be 1.95. Also, the breakeven price is 114.95, well below the lowest price on the day that GLD was making new lows. (See Table 12.12.)

Figure 12.8 shows the payoff at expiration for the GLD 113/116 bull put spread that took in a credit 1.05. Note that the price of GLD is just 0.05 below the maximum payoff level for this trade of 116.00. The risk of

TABLE 12.11	GLD Bull Put Spread Comparison		
Spread	Credit	Max Loss	Breakeven
110/116	1.75	−4.25	114.25
111/116	1.55	−3.45	114.45
112/116	1.30	−2.70	114.70
113/116	1.05	−1.95	114.95
114/116	0.75	−1.25	115.25
115/116	0.40	−0.60	115.60

TABLE 12.12 GLD 113/116 Bull Put Spread Payoff at Expiration

GLD	DDD 113 Put	DDD 116 Put	Income	P/L
110	3.00	−6.00	1.05	−1.95
113	0.00	−3.00	1.05	−1.95
116	0.00	0.00	1.05	1.05
119	0.00	0.00	1.05	1.05

1.95 relative to the reward of 1.05 is a result of the exchange-traded fund barely having to trade higher for the maximum profit to be realized.

Trying to take the other side of a market that is making new lows is often a dangerous trade. With a vertical spread the risk is limited and known when the trade is initiated. The defined risk and reward of a vertical spread makes taking the other side of a market that is dropping a little less risky than directly buying the underlying market.

Bullish Breakout Trade

A common description for a stock that is making new highs would be that the stock is breaking out. Although emotionally difficult for many traders to execute, buying a stock making new highs may result in a very profitable outcome. The issue that many traders have with buying stock that is making new highs may be rooted in the thought that they should try to buy low and

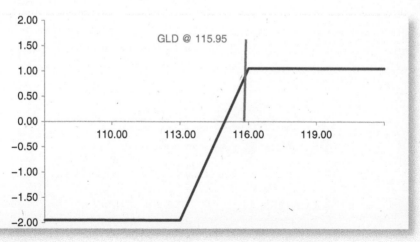

FIGURE 12.8 GLD 113/116 Bull Put Spread Payoff at Expiration

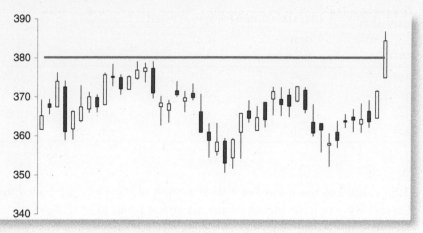

FIGURE 12.9 CMG Daily Price Chart

sell high. There is absolutely nothing wrong with buying high with the intent of selling higher. In fact it works for many successful traders.

On a Thursday afternoon shares of Chipotle Mexican Grill (CMG) were making new highs and trading at 384.50. Figure 12.9 shows this price action, which is very representative of a textbook breakout.

The line on the chart represents what had been long-term resistance at 380.00 that was finally overcome. Technically when a resistance level is overcome it becomes a support level. A trader that trades breakouts would consider this a long trading signal and would consider some sort of bullish strategy. As buying a breakout is not for the faint of heart, the known risk reward of a vertical spread would be a good method of becoming comfortable with this sort of trading without risking a sudden reversal in the stock price. Taking this approach, 6-day CMG option contract prices were taken into consideration. A couple of approaches to trading this breakout are going to be demonstrated with the option pricing in Table 12.13.

TABLE 12.13	CMG 6-Day Put Option Quotes Spread Comparison	
Option	Bid	Ask
370 Put	1.15	1.20
375 Put	2.05	2.10
380 Put	3.40	3.50
385 Put	5.60	5.70

TABLE 12.14 **CMG 375/380 Bull Put Spread Payoff at Expiration**

GLD	CMG 375 Put	CMG 380 Put	Income	P/L
370	5.00	−10.00	1.30	−3.70
375	0.00	−5.00	1.30	−3.70
380	0.00	0.00	1.30	1.30
385	0.00	0.00	1.30	1.30

A less aggressive approach would involve selling a CMG 6-day 380 put for 3.40 and buying a CMG 6-day 375 put for 2.10. The net credit for this trade would be 1.30 with the maximum potential loss at 3.70 if the stock takes a sudden turn to the down side. Table 12.14 shows the payout for this trade at a variety of price levels for CMG at expiration in six days.

This not a terribly aggressive approach to trading this breakout as the breakeven point for this trade is 378.70. The breakout might actually fail and CMG can trade off by a couple of points and the result may still be a profit. The diagram in Figure 12.10 demonstrates this fairly well.

A more aggressive trading approach may be warranted if the expectation is that CMG will follow through this breakout and continue to trade higher. This more aggressive approach would entail selling the CMG 6-day 385 put for 5.60 and buying the CMG 6-day 380 put for 3.50. This would bring in a net credit of 2.10. The credit is greater than the 1.30 brought in for the

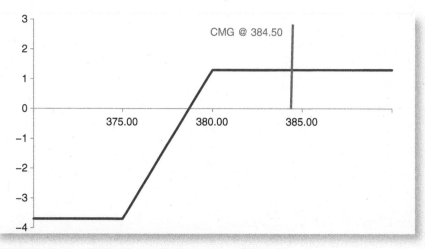

FIGURE 12.10 **CMG 375/380 Bull Put Spread Payoff**

TABLE 12.15	CMG 380/385 Bull Put Spread Payoff at Expiration			
GLD	CMG 380 Put	CMG 385 Put	Income	P/L
375	5.00	−10.00	2.10	−2.90
380	0.00	−5.00	2.10	−2.90
385	0.00	0.00	2.10	2.10
390	0.00	0.00	2.10	2.10

spread using the 375 and 380 put options, but the risk of the trade not resulting in a profit is higher as well.

Table 12.15 runs through the profit or loss for this bullish spread. The target price or price of maximum profitability is 385.00. At 385.00 or higher at expiration, both options expire and the credit is the resulting profit. This is just a bit higher than where the stock is trading when the spread was initiated. Figure 12.11 highlights the price of CMG in addition to the payout for this 380/385 bullish spread.

Note there is a little less cushion for being wrong using the more aggressive 380/385 spread versus the 375/380 spread. This is the reason more income is taken in when trading the 380/385 spread. The trader will receive more income, but there is actually more risk that the trade will not be successful. A direct comparison of the key levels of the two trades appears in Table 12.16.

The breakeven level for the 375/380 spread is just over four points lower than the breakeven for the 380/385 spread. The spread using lower strike

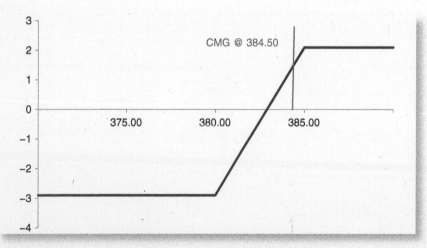

FIGURE 12.11 CMG 380/385 Bull Put Spread at Expiration

TABLE 12.16	CMG 375/380 Bull Put Spread versus CMG 380/385 Bull Put Spread		
Spread	Credit	Max Loss	Breakeven
375/380	1.30	−3.70	378.70
380/385	2.10	−2.90	382.90

options gives a trade the ability to be wrong by four points and still make a profit. In addition to this extra cushion for being wrong there is another advantage of the spread using lower strike prices. This advantage relates to managing the trade if it appears the stock is not going to follow through after breakout over 380.00.

The 380.00 price level is a fairly significant price for the success of this trade. It was considered resistance before CMG traded through that level and when a resistance price is broken through it becomes a support level. The success of this breakout by CMG will be judged by whether the stock continues to trade above 380.00. As this trade is based on the CMG breakout, an exit or stop-loss trade would occur if this support level is broken. Table 12.17 shows some results for this trade if CMG trades down to 379.00 before expiration.

The table estimating the profit or loss for this CMG was constructed with the assumption that CMG stock trades down to 379.00, a significant breach of the 380.00 support level and that there is not any change in the implied volatility of the respective options. The two spread-value columns are based on having to sell the lower strike option and buy back the higher strike option. The Profit–Loss columns take the sum of the credit received when the trade was initiated versus the debit incurred when the trade is exited.

TABLE 12.17	CMG 375/380 Bull Put Spread versus CMG 380/385 Bull Put Spread Losses at 379.00 with Different Times to Expiration						
Days	375 Put	380 Put	385 Put	375/380 Spread	375/380 Profit–Loss	380/385 Spread	380/385 Profit–Loss
6	3.65	6.00	9.00	2.35	−1.05	3.00	−0.90
5	3.20	5.50	8.55	2.30	−1.00	3.05	−0.95
4	2.70	5.00	8.10	2.30	−1.00	3.10	−1.00
3	2.15	4.40	7.60	2.25	−0.95	3.20	−1.10
2	1.55	3.70	7.00	2.15	−0.85	3.30	−1.20
1	0.80	2.75	6.40	1.95	−0.65	3.65	−1.55
0	0.00	1.00	6.00	1.00	0.30	5.00	−2.90

The maximum gain for the 375/380 spread was 1.30. If the stock trades down to 379.00 right after the trade was initiated a loss of 1.05 would be taken if the spread is exited. A similar situation for the 380/385 spread would result in a loss of 0.90. In fact the loss relative to the potential gain favors the 380/385 spread over the first few days of holding the position. It is possible for a more dynamic approach to be considered when trading a vertical spread. If there is a stop price where the trade will be exited early such as the stock trading below the 380.00 level, the 380/385 spread may actually come across as the less risky of the two spreads.

Bullish spreads are a good use of the options market as they reduce exposure to time decay and cost relative to purely long option trades. The benefit of these defined spread trades is they, by default, control risk as there is a maximum potential loss known when the trade is initiated.

CHAPTER 13

Bearish Spread Trading

L ike the bullish vertical spread, a bearish spread is one of the best ways offered in the option market to benefit from a bearish outlook. With a downside target in mind, a bearish spread may be the preferred method of taking a position based on that outlook. Typically a bearish spread must be held until close to or even through expiration in order to realize the full potential profit of the trade. Historically this timing component of a vertical spread meant that a bearish forecast would need to be very accurate with respect to both price target and timing. With short-dated options consistently available, bearish vertical spreads may be appropriate for several types of short term trading scenarios.

■ Bearish Vertical Spread

A bearish vertical spread may be initiated using either put or call options. Often put options are automatically associated with a bearish outlook, but the correct combination of call positions may be bearish as well. Despite which type of option is used, the trade will involve buying a higher strike option and selling a lower strike option. A put option with a higher strike price will have a higher premium than a put option that shares an expiration date but has a lower strike price. So when a bearish spread is created with puts there will be a debit or cost involved. Consider the option quotes in Table 13.1.

TABLE 13.1	Option Quotes Used to Create 30-Day Bear Put and Bear Call Spreads			
Call Bid	Call Ask	Strike	Put Bid	Put Ask
3.55	3.60	45	0.50	0.55
0.85	0.90	50	2.80	2.85

A bearish put spread would be entered into through buying the 50 put for 2.85 and selling the 50 put for 0.50. This would result in a net cost of 2.35. The best possible outcome for this trade will be that the underlying stock is at or below 45.00 at expiration. With the underlying below 45.00 the long position in the 45 put is worth 5.00 more than the short position in the 50 put. With the long position worth 5.00 more than the short put option the result would be a profit of 2.65. A trader paid 2.35 for a spread that is worth 5.00. A summary of payouts at expiration appears in Table 13.2.

Using the same market prices, a bearish call spread would be entered into by selling the 45 call for 3.55 and purchasing the 50 call for 0.90. This would result in net income 2.65. This net credit is the result of 3.55 being taken in for a credit and 0.90 being paid out. The credit received of 2.65 is also the best possible outcome for this trade. If the underlying is at or below 45.00 at expiration both put options expire with no value and the credit of 2.65 is a realized profit. Regardless of the structure of the trade, using calls or puts, the goal is for the underlying instrument to be at or below 45.00 at expiration. The outcome for this bear spread using call options appears in Table 13.3.

The payout in Figure 13.1 applies to both the bearish call and put spreads as they both have the same risk and reward profiles. The profit and loss or risk and reward for either spread are the same despite the two spreads being created with different options.

The majority of traders prefer using call options when creating a bearish spread for a couple of reasons. First many traders like the idea of taking in a

TABLE 13.2	Payoff Table for XYZ 45/50 Bear Put Spread at Expiration			
XYZ	XYZ 45 Put	XYZ 50 Put	Cost	P/L
40.00	−5.00	10.00	−2.35	2.65
45.00	0.00	5.00	−2.35	2.65
50.00	0.00	0.00	−2.35	−2.35
55.00	0.00	0.00	−2.35	−2.35

TABLE 13.3 **Payoff Table for XYZ 45/50 Bear Put Spread at Expiration**

XYZ	XYZ 45 Call	XYZ 50 Call	Income	P/L
40.00	0.00	0.00	2.65	2.65
45.00	0.00	0.00	2.65	2.65
50.00	−5.00	0.00	2.65	−2.35
55.00	−10.00	5.00	2.65	−2.35

credit and being paid to initiate a trade. There may be some logic to this, but not too much since the net result of the trade is basically the same whether it involves the margin requirement or paying up front to put on the trade. The alternate reason to prefer using calls to create a bearish spread relates to the outcome at expiration.

At expiration a bearish spread created with put options means that both options will be in-the-money and be exercised. If they are both in-the-money then a trader should expect them to both go through the exercise and assignment process. There will be no position in the underlying stock after this process, but there may be a brokerage charge incurred. To avoid ticket charges associated with exercise and assignment both option positions should be closed out near expiration. This also results in charges in the form of commissions.

The best-case scenario for a bearish call spread is that both options will be out-of-the-money at expiration. This would result in the two contracts expiring and no longer being in a trader's account on the Monday

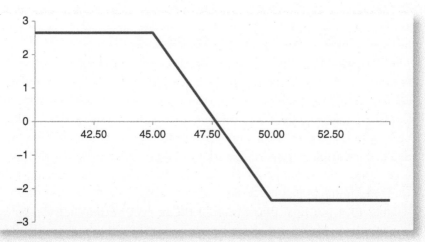

FIGURE 13.1 Bearish Vertical Spread Payout at Expiration

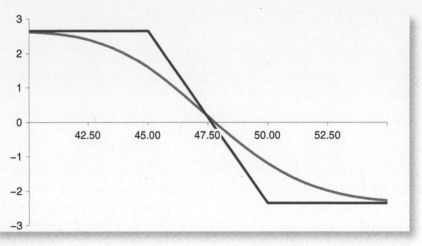

FIGURE 13.2 Bearish Vertical Spread Payout at Expiration and with 15 Days to Expiration

following expiration. Instead of having to pay some sort of commission, the options will just expire and there will be no extra costs associated with this trade.

The curved payout represents the profit or loss for this trade based on the underlying market at a variety of prices halfway to expiration. (See Figure 13.2.) Note that if the underlying has traded down to the target price of 45.00 then only about half the profit would be realized if the trade were exited. At 45.00 with 15 days remaining to expiration the profit would be close to 1.60, which is over 1.00 less than the potential profit for this trade. As the time to expiration approaches, the payoff of the spread also approaches the payoff at expiration, but not quite at a linear rate. Figure 13.3 compares the payoff at expiration to the payoff if the trade is exited five days before expiration.

In this payoff diagram the curved line is closer to the rigid payoff at expiration, but there is still a gap between the payoff with five days remaining and the payoff at expiration. If the underlying market is at 45.00 with five days to go it appears the trade can be exited with a profit of about 2.00 or 0.65 shy of the expected maximum payout for this trade at expiration. Also note that if the underlying has lost a lot of value and is well below the target price of 45.00 it would be possible to exit the trade and realize almost the whole maximum hoped-for profit.

Table 13.4 is a final illustration of the impact of time left to expiration and the gain or loss for this bear spread. The column down the left-hand side indicates days left to expiration with the figures across the top

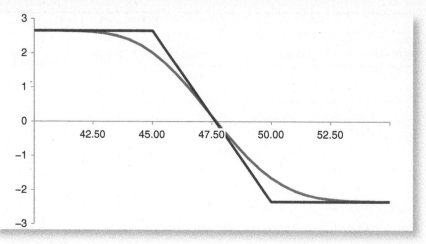

FIGURE 13.3 Bearish Vertical Spread Payout at Expiration versus Five Days to Expiration

representing different prices for XYZ. Note that extreme price moves, higher or lower, result in a good portion of the maximum loss or gain being unrealized. For the target price of 45.00 the options do need to be very close to expiration, less than five days, for the maximum profit to be realized.

With short-dated options always available, the wait-and-see game that used to be in place for a bullish spread is not as long as it has to be. The same pricing that was used to create the 30-day examples was used to determine 5-day option premiums. The quotes for those 5-day 45 and 50 strike options appear in Table 13.5.

TABLE 13.4 XYX 45/50 Bear Spread Payoff for Different Prices and Times to Expiration

	42.50	45.00	47.50	50.00	52.50
30	2.10	1.30	0.20	−0.85	−1.65
25	2.20	1.40	0.20	−0.95	−1.75
20	2.30	1.50	0.18	−1.05	−1.85
15	2.40	1.60	0.18	−1.20	−2.00
10	2.50	1.75	0.17	−1.40	−2.15
5	2.60	2.00	0.16	−1.65	−2.30
0	2.65	2.65	0.15	−2.35	−2.35

TABLE 13.5	Option Quotes Used to Create 5-Day Bear Call and Bear Put Spreads			
Call Bid	Call Ask	Strike	Put Bid	Put Ask
3.10	3.15	45	0.15	0.20
0.35	0.40	50	2.40	2.45

A bear spread using put options would purchase a 50 put for 2.45 and sell the 45 put for 0.15 and a net cost of 2.30. The maximum gain would be 2.70. The more popular version of creating this spread, which would use call options, would sell the 45 call for 3.10 and buy a 50 call for 0.40 and net income of 2.70. This is actually a 0.05 more than the income that would result from using the 30-day options.

Note the payout diagram in Figure 13.4 shows very little difference between the higher line representing the 5-day spread and the lower line representing the 30-day spread. The reason the 5-day spread pays just a little more is because the underlying stock, XYZ, is priced at 47.65 for this example. Because the stock is a little closer to the higher strike than the lower strike price, a 5-day spread may actually have what appears to be a more favorable profit-and-loss profile. Do remember that the stock would need to trade down to 45.00 over just five days for the maximum profit to be realized, but if that is a trader's outlook it would make sense to consider a shorter-term spread trade.

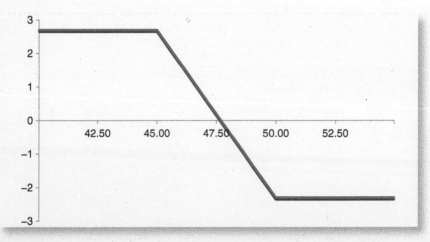

FIGURE 13.4 5-Day and 30-Day Bearish Spread Payoffs at Expiration

■ Bearish Spread Trading Examples

Utilizing technical analysis there are three general types of bearish trades:

1. A bearish trade may be initiated when a stock or market is in a defined downtrend.
2. If a stock or market has traded too high too quickly, then a bearish trade may be initiated with the assumption that this instrument will reverse.
3. If a stock or market is making new lows, which is referred to as a bearish breakout, a bearish position may be taken with the belief that lower prices are on the horizon.

Trying to catch and stick with a trend in the markets is one of the oldest methods of trading. Anyone who has been on the correct side of a trend will happily recount their success. A downtrend in the market can be just as profitable to a nimble trader as an uptrend, but may also be a dangerous trade if the trend takes a bullish turn. A bearish vertical spread that targets where the trend should take the underlying market by expiration is a great way to take advantage of this market condition with a defined maximum risk and reward in place.

The second potential type of bearish trade involves taking the other side of a bullish move in an underlying market. The most common method of taking the other side of a bullish move would involve selling short the underlying stock or market. Academically this is fraught with risk as a stock can theoretically go to infinity. Selling short is a tough method of trading and taking the other side of a big upside move can be a difficult prospect, but with a vertical spread the worst case result is known, even if the stock goes to infinity.

When bad news hits the stock market or an individual stock it can set off a stampede of traders trying to get out as quickly as possible. This rapid selling pressure often results in a series of new lows being made until some sort of support level is found. Selling short a stock that is making a new low is difficult for a trader as they often do not want to be selling the lowest price before a reversal. However, shorting a market that is breaking downside support can be a very rewarding prospect as well.

Bearish Trend Trade

A bearish trend can be determined through some sort of technical indicator or through noting on a chart that a stock is making lower lows. Visually all that would need to be done is draw a trend line that indicates the current and hopefully future direction of the stock. That is the method used here for

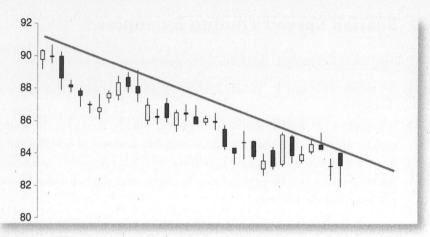

FIGURE 13.5 CAT Stock in a Defined Downtrend

the first trading example, but any bearish trend signal could be traded in the same manner.

The first bearish trading example uses a chart on Caterpillar (CAT) when the stock is trading at 83.25. Figure 13.5 is a daily chart of CAT with a well-defined downtrend in place. The closing price on this chart is also on a Thursday afternoon so options with six days remaining until expiration may be used to benefit from this downtrend if it continues.

Projecting the trend forward for six trading days results in a reasonable price target of 82.50 for CAT. With a time frame of six trading days and a price target of 82.50 the option contracts that are in Table 13.6, it stands to reason that the 82.50 call would be sold for 1.55 as the stock is expected to be at that price level upon expiration. On the long side of the bear call spread either the 85.00 call or 87.50 call may be purchased to complete the spread.

Projecting the trend forward for six trading days will result in a reasonable price target of 82.50 for CAT. With a time frame of six trading days and a price target of 82.50 the option contracts that are in Table 13.6. It stands to reason that the 82.50 call would be sold for 1.55 as the stock is

TABLE 13.6	Six-Day CAT Call Option Quotes Downtrend	
Option	Bid	Ask
82.50 Call	1.55	1.60
85.00 Call	0.25	0.30
87.50 Call	0.03	0.05

TABLE 13.7 CAT 82.50/85.00 Bear Call Spread Payoff at Expiration

Days to Expiration	Stop Price	Cost to Cover	Profit/Loss
5	84.25	1.65	−0.40
4	84.00	1.50	−0.25
3	83.75	1.35	−0.10
2	83.50	1.20	0.05
1	83.25	0.90	0.35

expected to be at that price level upon expiration. On the long side of the bear call spread either the 85.00 call or 87.50 call may be purchased to complete the spread.

Purchasing the 85.00 call for 0.30 would result in a maximum profit of 1.25 and a maximum risk of 1.25 as well. Moving up to the higher strike 87.50 call this option may be bought for only 0.05 which would improve the maximum profitability to 1.50, but the maximum potential loss would rise up to 3.50. In this case the trader is going with the lower strike CAT 85.00 call. The bear call spread trade results in selling the CAT 82.50 call at 1.55 and buying the CAT 85.00 call at 0.30 for a net credit of 1.25.

Table 13.7 shows the maximum profit at loss for the CAT 82.50/85.00 bear call spread at expiration. This is an interesting trade as the risk and reward come to either a gain or loss of 1.25. Also, as highlighted in the payoff diagram in Figure 13.6, CAT is currently trading at a price where the trade would result in a profit if it were not to be unchanged at expiration.

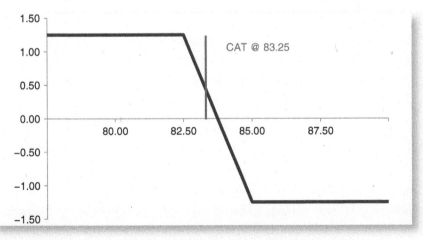

FIGURE 13.6 Six-Day CAT Bear Call Spread Payoff at Expiration

TABLE 13.8	CAT 82.50/85.00 Bear Call Spread Payoffs When Stopped Out before Expiration		
Days to Expiration	Stop Price	Cost to Cover	Profit/Loss
5	84.25	1.65	−0.40
4	84.00	1.50	−0.25
3	83.75	1.35	−0.10
2	83.50	1.20	0.05
1	83.25	0.90	0.35

Checking out the payout diagram shows that CAT is at a price where if the stock is unchanged at expiration the trade would result in a small profit. Of course the goal is for the stock to trade down to 82.50 or lower, but having the ability to be slightly wrong and still make a profit is a positive.

The exit strategy does not necessarily have to be holding the trade through expiration. If it appears the stock is not continuing on the downtrend as expected through the charting analysis the trade may be exited early. A stop price where the downtrend is broken might be a sensible method for exiting the stock early. As the line is continuously moving lower, the stop loss or stop price to get out if the stock is moving in the wrong direction will change from day to day. Table 13.8 is a rough estimate of a closing price slightly above the downtrend line combined with days to expiration. The final column is the estimated profit or loss on the spread if the trade is closed out based on this break of the downtrend.

The table showing the profit or loss based on being stopped out is based on a few assumptions. The first assumption is that there is no change in the implied volatility of either option contract used to create the spread. Also, the prices are estimates of CAT closing slightly above the downtrend line. The estimate is for CAT to be closing about 0.15 to 0.25 above the line; that would indicate a clear breach of the downtrend. Finally, the pricing is just slightly above the downtrend line. If the stock were to gap higher it is very possible that the trade may be closed out for a greater loss.

One thing to note on this table is that with one day to go the stock price that indicates the downtrend has been broken is actually the price where CAT was trading when the spread was initiated. An unchanged stock price may result in a break of the downtrend as well as the stock moving higher.

Trading with a trend is one method of taking a bearish position. It is a comfortable type of trade because you are trading in line with the rest of the crowd. The next type of trade—counter-trend trading or selling when a market is making new highs—results in going against the crowd, but if it works it is a profitable type of trading.

Bearish Reversal Trade

A bearish reversal trade involves taking the other side of a stock or other market that is making a new high. It is a little bit safer method of trying to get short exposure to a stock that has had a run to the upside. Stocks rarely turn on a dime and although there is always the urge to try to sell the top, it may be worthwhile to wait a day or two to make sure the run to the upside is out of momentum. The example in this section approaches trading a reversal in that manner.

Figure 13.7 is a chart of FedEx Corporation (FDX). The line at the high end of the price action indicates the highest price FDX stock had reached over a few months. After trading slightly above 102.00 the stock started to drift between 100.00 and 102.00 for a few days. It does appear that for the near term the upside momentum has stalled out.

The last day shown on this chart is a Thursday afternoon with FDX closing at 100.05. FDX options strike prices are offered at 2.50 intervals below 100 and intervals of 5 points above 100. The three call options with the closest 6-day options appear in Table 13.9.

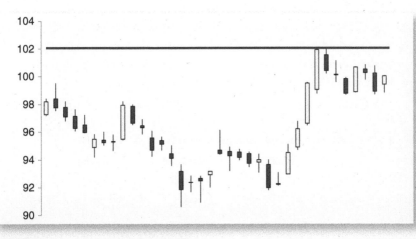

FIGURE 13.7   FDX Stock Reversal

TABLE 13.9	Six-Day FDX Call Option Quotes	
Option	Bid	Ask
97.50 Call	2.75	2.80
100.00 Call	1.25	1.30
105.00 Call	0.05	0.10

The choice of which spread to initiate will be based on how aggressive a trader wants to be regarding the near-term direction of FDX stock. If he feels that the stock is going to drop dramatically then he may choose to sell an FDX 97.50 call and buy either the 100 strike or 105 strike call option. This is a fairly aggressive trading idea for a short-term trade, especially one where the stock would need to reverse course and break support that seems to be showing up in the 99.00 to 100.00 range.

A less aggressive trade involves selling an FDX 100.00 call at 1.25 and buying the FDX 105.00 call for 0.10. The FDX 100.00/105.00 bear call spread is in place for a credit of 1.15. Table 13.10 shows the profit and loss for this trade based on the stock at a few price levels at expiration.

A less aggressive trade involves selling a FDX 100.00 call at 1.25 and buying the FDX 105.00 call for 0.10. The FDX 100.00/105.00 bear call spread is in place for a credit of 1.15. Table 13.10 shows the profit and loss for this trade based on the stock at a few price levels at expiration. Figure 13.8 shows the payout at expiration for the FDX 100.00/105.00 Bear call spread.

FDX at 100.00 or lower at expiration results in a gain of 1.15. If the stock begins to make new highs and closes at or above 105.00 at expiration the result would be a loss of 3.85. This dollar risk–reward may appear to be somewhat unattractive, but if the stock begins to make new highs it would probably be advisable to exit the trade before expiration.

TABLE 13.10	FDX 100/105 Bear Call Spread Payoff at Expiration			
FDX	FDX 100 Call	FDX 105 Call	Income	P/L
95.00	0.00	0.00	1.15	1.15
100.00	0.00	0.00	1.15	1.15
105.00	−5.00	0.00	1.15	−3.85
110.00	−10.00	5.00	1.15	−3.85

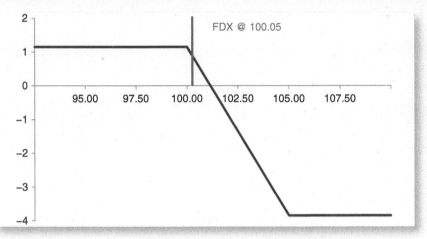

FIGURE 13.8 Six-Day FDX 100.00/105.00 Bear Call Spread Payoff at Expiration

A reasonable stop loss for this trade would be at a price above 102.00. To illustrate the profit or loss of this trade based on getting stopped out before expiration at a price of 102.25 for FDX is used to create the outcomes in Table 13.11.

If FDX closes at 102.25 any day up to expiration and the spread is exited the loss would be somewhere between 1.10 and 1.20 or very close to equal to the income of 1.15 that was taken in to initiate the bear spread. From a risk–reward standpoint this is a little more reasonable than the maximum loss of 3.85 at expiration.

The final type of trade that could prompt a bearish spread is a breakout to the downside. This type of trade is basically the opposite of the idea behind a short position that has recently made a new high. In the case here support is broken and a short position is taken with the expectation of lower prices to come.

TABLE 13.11 FDX 100.00/105.00 Bear Call Spread Payoffs When Stopped Out before Expiration

Days to Expiration	Stop Price	Cost to Cover	Profit/Loss
5	102.25	2.35	−1.20
4	102.25	2.30	−1.15
3	102.25	2.30	−1.15
2	102.25	2.30	−1.15
1	102.25	2.25	−1.10

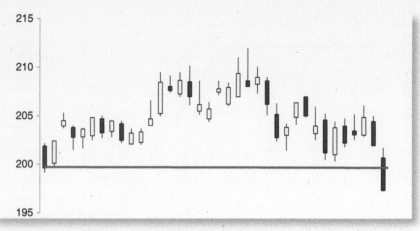

FIGURE 13.9 IBM Stock Downside Breakout

Bearish Breakout Trade

When bad news pushes a stock lower it can hit the stock price in a blink of an eye. Often when key support is broken the price continues to follow through, making several consecutive new lows. Although selling short when a stock or market is at lower prices than have been seen in some time may not be an emotionally easy trade to execute, it can be a profitable one.

The chart in Figure 13.9 is an example of a breakdown in shares of International Business Machines (IBM) on a Thursday afternoon. The stock had been testing support at the 200.00 level and finally broke through this level. Based on this breakdown in price a position with a short bias is considered.

IBM closed at 197.35 so the two closest 6-day option contracts are the 195 and 200 strike calls. Those quotes are checked out along with the IBM 205 call that would be purchased if the decision were made to short the IBM 200 call. These quotes show up in Table 13.12.

A more aggressive trade would be shorting an IBM 195 call and purchasing the 200 call for a net credit of 2.55. As IBM is a blue chip company with

TABLE 13.12	6-Day IBM Call Option Quotes	
Option	Bid	Ask
195 Call	3.90	4.00
200 Call	1.30	1.35
205 Call	0.15	0.20

TABLE 13.13 **IBM 200/205 Bear Call Spread Payoff at Expiration**

IBM	IBM 200 Call	IBM 205 Call	Income	P/L
195	0.00	0.00	1.10	1.10
200	0.00	0.00	1.10	1.10
205	−5.00	0.00	1.10	−3.90
210	−10.00	5.00	1.10	−3.90

great long-term prospects and also one of Warren Buffett's top holdings, maybe a more cautious approach is warranted.

Selling the IBM 200 call at 1.30 and then buying an IBM 205 call for 0.20 that results in net income of 1.10 would be a less aggressive approach to getting short-term short exposure to IBM.

Table 13.13 is an overview of this trade if held for six days through expiration. The maximum gain and loss are 1.10 and 3.90, respectively. Like the trade in FDX this dollar risk versus dollar reward does not look particularly favorable, but this trade is based on IBM staying under 200.00, a price level that was support and now should be resistance. The payout diagram in Figure 13.10 shows the trade if held through expiration, but there should be an exit plan in place if IBM trades over 200.00 before expiration.

If a stop price is set based on the performance of IBM stock and the trade is exited with IBM trading over 200.00 then the loss may be a fraction of 3.90 that appears in the payoff diagram. Table 13.14 assumes the implied

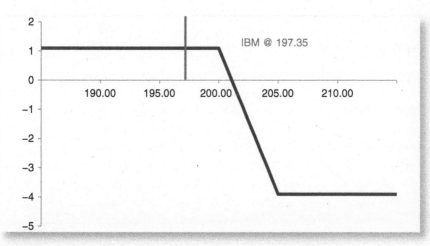

FIGURE 13.10 Six-Day IBM Bear Call Spread Payoff at Expiration

TABLE 13.14	IBM 200/205 Bear Call Spread Payoffs When Stopped Out before Expiration		
Days to Expiration	Stop Price	Cost to Cover	Profit/Loss
5	200.25	1.70	−0.60
4	200.25	1.65	−0.55
3	200.25	1.55	−0.45
2	200.25	1.35	−0.25
1	200.25	1.10	0.00

volatility levels that figure into the value of the IBM 6-day 200 call and IBM 6-day 205 call are fairly consistent over time. The only things that change are the price of IBM moving up to 200.25 and the number of days remaining to expiration.

Using 200.25 as a stop price, the potential loss on this trade goes down tremendously. Of course, executing the spread when this price level is hit, along with there being no gap opening to the upside in IBM, are key to exiting the trade with a smaller loss than if held to expiration and shares trading at 205.00. A rally to 200.25 the day after this trade is initiated could result in exiting with a loss of 0.60. As the days pass leading up to expiration the loss with IBM at 200.25 inches lower to actually breaking even on the trade if exited one day before expiration.

Bearish spreads are a good use of the options market as they reduce exposure to time decay and cost relative to purely long option trades. The benefit of these defined spread trades is they by default control risk as there is a maximum potential loss known when the trade is initiated. Using risk control measures that involve exiting the trade early can result in a loss that is just a fraction of the maximum potential loss.

CHAPTER 14

Neutral Spread Trading

Most trading involves picking a direction for a stock or underlying market. A trader makes a decision that they believe a stock is going to move up in price and they take some sort of position to attempt to benefit from this rise in price. With option contracts a trader may actually profit from a position that anticipates a stock will not change much in price. The most common of these spreads are iron butterflies and iron condors.

■ Iron Butterfly

An iron butterfly is created through a combination of four different option contracts. All of these options share an expiration date and underlying security. Two of the options are calls and two of the options are puts. One long and one short position are taken in each of these contracts. Lower-priced call and put options are purchased while a call and put with higher premiums are sold. The net result is a trade that is done for a credit. With XYZ trading at 50.00 a basic example of an iron butterfly may be constructed in the following way:

Buy 1 XYZ 45 put at 0.25
Sell 1 XYZ 50 put at 1.70
Sell 1 XYZ 50 call at 1.75
Buy 1 XYZ 55 call at 0.30

TABLE 14.1	Payoff at Expiration for a 30-Day 45/50/55 Iron Butterfly					
XYZ	45 Put	50 Put	50 Call	55 Call	Income	Profit/Loss
40.00	5.00	−10.00	0.00	0.00	2.90	−2.10
45.00	0.00	−5.00	0.00	0.00	2.90	−2.10
50.00	0.00	0.00	0.00	0.00	2.90	2.90
55.00	0.00	0.00	−5.00	0.00	2.90	−2.10
60.00	0.00	0.00	−10.00	5.00	2.90	−2.10

The net income received from creating this trade would be 2.90 that results from taking in 3.45 from selling the 50 put and 50 call and then paying out 0.55 through purchasing the 45 put and 55 call. The best result for this trade would be XYZ closing at 50.00 at expiration. Table 14.1 demonstrates the payout for this spread if held to expiration.

Note at 50.00 the maximum profit is 2.90, which was the income taken in from selling this contract. If XYZ settles right at 50.00 at expiration then all four of the option contracts used to construct this iron butterfly will expire with no value. This is highly unlikely and a more realistic goal will consist of forecasting a price in a narrow range as opposed to pinpointing a specific price. Figure 14.1 does a good job of illustrating the payoff at expiration for this XYZ 45/50/55 iron butterfly.

As the underlying stock price moves higher or lower the potential profitability of this spread begins to decrease. This loss is capped to the upside

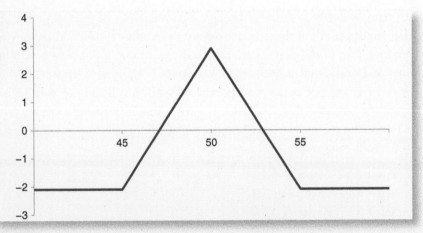

FIGURE 14.1 Payoff Diagram at Expiration for a 30-Day 45/ 50/55 Iron Butterfly

through the long call and on the downside through the long put. On the diagram the flat lines continuing out in both directions represent the maximum potential loss for these spreads.

The goal of an iron butterfly is either for the stock to be very close to the middle strike price or possibly benefit from a day or two of time decay. The time decay for the short options will be higher than that of the out-of-the-money options, so an iron butterfly may be traded with the intent of taking advantage of just a day or two of time decay. As time decay accelerates near expiration an iron butterfly that has strike prices very close to where the underlying market is trading is an excellent use of this neutral spread.

Instead of a 30-day iron butterfly, consider one with just three days to expiration. Using the same pricing conditions that were used to put together the 30-day example results in the following trades being used to create a 3-day iron butterfly:

Buy 1 XYZ 45 put at 0.05
Sell 1 XYZ 50 put at 0.55
Sell 1 XYZ 50 call at 0.55
Buy 1 XYZ 55 call at 0.05

The result of this trade would be a credit of 1.00 after 1.10 is taken in for selling the two at-the-money options and then buying a 45 put and a 55 call for 0.05 each. If XYZ is at 50.00 at expiration this trade results in a profit of 1.00. However, this trade may be initiated to take advantage of just a day or two of time decay. Table 14.2 shows the profit or loss for this 3-day iron butterfly at a variety of prices and number of days left to expiration.

The hope the trade has when putting on this 3-day iron butterfly is for the stock to stay very close to 50.00 over the next few days. The middle column shows the running profit for this spread based on the stock not changing in price at all. The profit accelerates in a similar manner to the increase in time decay for at-the-money options. If the stock price moves a point higher or lower the spread has reached the breakeven price points at expiration.

TABLE 14.2 **Payoff at Different Stock Prices and Times Left to Expiration for a 3-Day 45/50/55 Iron Butterfly**

	48.00	49.00	50.00	51.00	52.00
2	−1.00	−0.10	0.10	−0.10	−1.00
1	−1.00	0.00	0.35	0.00	−1.00
0	−1.00	0.00	1.00	0.00	−1.00

This may also work as a stop-loss point for the trade. If XYZ trades below 49.00 or trades above 51.00 by 0.10 or 0.25, maybe the trade is exited at that time for a small loss.

■ Iron Butterfly Trading Examples

The first iron butterfly example is going to be based on a short-term outlook for the SPDR Gold Shares ETF (GLD). Figure 14.2 shows price action for GLD, and it appears it has stalled out in the mid-120s after dropping and then recovering quickly. An iron butterfly is a very appropriate trade if the expectation is for very little movement in GLD over the next few days.

Figure 14.2 ends on a Tuesday with GLD closing at 124.90. There are three trading days remaining until the next weekly expiration. Since the outlook is for GLD to stay around current levels for the next few days the middle strike options for this iron butterfly will be the GLD 125 call and GLD 125 put. To round out the iron butterfly a 123 put and 127 call could be purchased. This iron butterfly is comprised of these trades:

Buy 1 GLD 123 put at 0.40
Sell 1 GLD 125 put at 1.10
Sell 1 GLD 125 call at 1.00
Buy 1 GLD 127 call at 0.35

The net credit for this trade is 1.35 with a maximum potential loss of 0.65. Of course GLD needs to close exactly on the 125.00 price point at

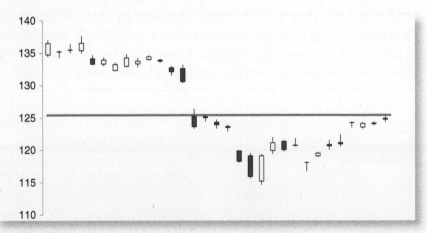

FIGURE 14.2 GLD Exchange-Traded Fund Meeting Resistance at 125.00

TABLE 14.3	Payoff at Expiration for a GLD 3-Day 123/125/127 Iron Butterfly					
GLD	123 Put	125 Put	125 Call	127 Call	Income	Profit/Loss
121.00	2.00	−4.00	0.00	0.00	1.35	−0.65
123.00	0.00	−2.00	0.00	0.00	1.35	−0.65
125.00	0.00	0.00	0.00	0.00	1.35	1.35
127.00	0.00	0.00	−2.00	0.00	1.35	−0.65
129.00	0.00	0.00	−4.00	2.00	1.35	−0.65

expiration for this trade to result in a profit of 1.35. The two inside strike options are the at-the-money contracts so as time passes the expectation is that they would lose value much quicker than the outside strike options.

The payout at expiration for this trade appears in Table 14.3. A perfect forecast with GLD at 125.00 on Friday of expiration results in all options expiring and a profit of 1.35. A more likely positive outcome would result in GLD very close to 125.00 near expiration. Again this maximum profit is realized at a precise price point. This can also be seen in the payoff diagram in Figure 14.3.

The price of GLD was 124.90 when this trade was initiated and it is highlighted on this payout diagram. If GLD does not move at all the profit would come in at 1.25, as the GLD 125 put would be 0.10 in-the-money. Usually the hope is for the stock or market to fall within the range between the downside and upside breakeven levels. On the downside the breakeven price is 123.65,

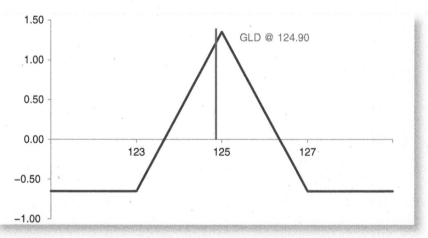

FIGURE 14.3 Payoff at Expiration for a GLD 3-Day 123/125/127 Iron Butterfly

which is determined by subtracting the premium received for the trade from the middle strike price. 123.65 is 1.35 lower than the middle strike price of 125.00. The upside breakeven is determined by adding 1.35 to the middle strike price, in this case it is 126.35. Therefore this trade is a profit as long as GLD falls between 123.65 and 126.35 at expiration. Of course a trader would like for GLD to close very near 125.00. The range between the breakeven levels also results in some sort of profit, not just the maximum profit.

Iron butterflies are very precise as far as the price target. Also, since they are often short at-the-money options the position will benefit from at-the-money time decay. Because of the precision needed to make close to the maximum profit iron butterflies are good candidates for very short-term trades—even for trades that last a single day. Figure 14.4 is again for the GLD exchange-traded fund, but the last price represented on this chart is a Thursday. GLD closed at 124.25 on this day so a trader that expects a flat day the next day and into weekly expiration might consider an iron butterfly with the middle strike being the 124 put and 125 call options.

The quotes in Table 14.4 shows markets for a variety of 1-day GLD put and call options. The expectation is for little change from GLD over the next day so the GLD 124 call and GLD 124 put options will be sold. The other lower strike put and higher strike call options will be considered to complete the iron butterfly.

The trading decision will be based on how much confidence there is that GLD is not going to move much on the following day. A 1-day 123/124/125 iron butterfly would be ideal if there was a strong feeling

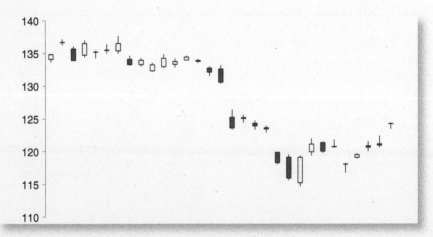

FIGURE 14.4   GLD Exchange-Traded Fund Daily Chart

TABLE 14.4	GLD 1-Day Option Prices	
Option	Bid	Ask
122 Put	0.08	0.10
123 Put	0.20	0.22
124 Put	0.49	0.51
124 Call	0.73	0.75
125 Call	0.30	0.32
126 Call	0.08	0.10

that GLD would close near 124.00 the following day. Another alternative could be a 1-day 122/124/126 iron butterfly. The GLD 122 put and GLD 126 calls are both offered at a dime each and at a lower premium than the 123 put and 125 call. Both alternatives will be investigated and then compared at the end of this section.

The first alternative would involve the following trades:

Buy 1 GLD 123 put at 0.22
Sell 1 GLD 124 put at 0.49
Sell 1 GLD 124 put at 0.73
Buy 1 GLD 125 call at 0.32

The net credit for this trade would be 0.68 as 1.22 in premium would be collected from selling the 124 put and 124 call while 0.54 would be paid out for the 123 put and 125 put.

The payoffs shown in Table 14.5 indicate that a very narrow range exists for this trade to result in a profit. The only price that shows a profit on this table is the middle strike price of 124.00. Adding and subtracting the premium from 124.00 results in breakeven prices of 123.32 and 124.68. It takes a price move of just 0.5 percent higher or lower than 124 to result in the trade turning into a loss instead of a gain.

TABLE 14.5	Payoff at Expiration for a GLD 1-Day 123/124/125 Iron Butterfly					
GLD	123 Put	124 Put	124 Call	125 Call	Income	Profit/Loss
122.00	1.00	−2.00	0.00	0.00	0.68	−0.32
123.00	0.00	−1.00	0.00	0.00	0.68	−0.32
124.00	0.00	0.00	0.00	0.00	0.68	0.68
125.00	0.00	0.00	−1.00	0.00	0.68	−0.32
126.00	0.00	0.00	−2.00	2.00	0.68	−0.32

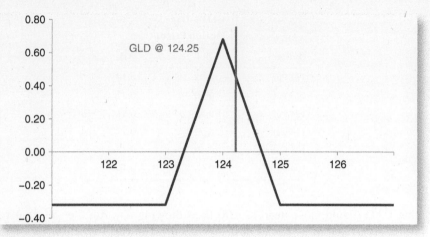

FIGURE 14.5 Payoff at Expiration for a GLD 1-Day 123/124/125 Iron Butterfly

Figure 14.5 is a good illustration of just how precise the 1-day price forecast needs to be for this iron butterfly to result in a profit. With 124.68 being the upside breakeven and GLD at 124.25, there is a pretty tight margin for error to the upside. GLD only needs to trade up 0.43 before reaching the upside breakeven on this trade. Of course, the ultimate goal of this trade would be for GLD to drop 0.25 and close at 124.00 even. On the downside there is a bit more margin for error; GLD would need to trade down by 0.93 in order for the breakeven level of 123.32 to be breached.

The second alternative to putting on a 1-day iron butterfly allows for a little more of a range before the trade goes from being a profitable trade to a losing one. The same middle strike options are sold, but a put and call with strike prices that are farther away from the current market are purchased. The second alternative would involve the following trades:

Buy 1 GLD 122 put at 0.10
Sell 1 GLD 124 put at 0.49
Sell 1 GLD 124 call at 0.73
Buy 1 GLD 126 call at 0.10

The net credit for this trade would be 1.02 as 1.22 in premium would be collected from selling the 124 put and 124 call while 0.20 would be paid out for the 122 put and 126 put. The result would be a trade that has a maximum pay out of 1.02 and a maximum potential loss of 0.98. Table 14.6 covers the profit and loss for this trade at a wide variety of settlement prices at expiration.

TABLE 14.6 **Payoff at Expiration for a GLD 1-Day 122/124/126 Iron Butterfly**

GLD	122 Put	124 Put	124 Call	126 Call	Income	Profit/Loss
121.00	1.00	−3.00	0.00	0.00	1.02	−0.98
122.00	0.00	−2.00	0.00	0.00	1.02	−0.98
123.00	0.00	−1.00	0.00	0.00	1.02	0.02
124.00	0.00	0.00	0.00	0.00	1.02	1.02
125.00	0.00	0.00	−1.00	0.00	1.02	0.02
126.00	0.00	0.00	−2.00	0.00	1.02	−0.98
127.00	0.00	0.00	−3.00	1.00	1.02	−0.98

A small profit, which would probably be offset by commissions, may be realized at 123.00 and 125.00. This wider profit potential comes at a cost of a maximum potential loss of 0.98 if GLD makes a big move higher or lower on the final trading day before expiration. In Figure 14.6 the wider payout for this iron butterfly versus the first example stands out tremendously. The margin for error as far as being wrong about the price of GLD not moving much the following day is wider in this case.

The choice between the two iron butterfly spreads may come down to the certainty that GLD is going to stay in a narrow range the following day and finish the trading day near 124.00. The dollar risk–reward favors the 123/124/125 spread where 0.68 may be made or 0.32 lost, while the 122/124/126 iron butterfly would payout 1.02 or lose 0.98 depending on

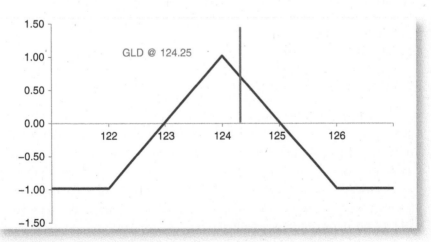

FIGURE 14.6 Payoff at Expiration for a GLD 1-Day 122/124/126 Iron Butterfly

the price change in GLD. The choice may also be based on historical price moves from GLD and the current implied volatility relative to expectations.

An iron butterfly put on the Thursday afternoon before expiration may often result in a small short-term profit. This is a very dynamic way to trade options on a short-term basis, take advantage of rapid time decay for at-the-money options, and have a defined risk and reward.

A great benefit behind trading iron butterflies relates to at-the-money time decay. Having a defined risk and reward in place combined with a trade that offers the benefit of rapid time decay results in an attractive short-term option spread.

■ Iron Condor

An iron condor is actually the more popular of the two option spreads discussed in this chapter. This spread is created in a very similar method to the iron butterfly, but the short call and put option do not share a strike price. Often the underlying market price is between the two short options that comprise an iron condor. Using options with two different strike prices often results in a wider range of potential profitability at expiration.

As with the iron butterfly, the iron condor is created by selling options that have higher premiums than the options that are purchased. The trade is done for a credit and the credit is the maximum profit if the options all expire out-of-the-money. With XYZ trading at 52.50, a basic example of a 30-day iron condor would be constructed in the following way:

Buy 1 XYZ 45 put at 0.10
Sell 1 XYZ 50 put at 0.80
Sell 1 XYZ 55 call at 0.85
Buy 1 XYZ 60 call at 0.10

Executing an iron condor at these prices would result in a credit of 1.45, as 1.65 would be taken in for selling the 50 put and 55 call while a total of 0.20 would be paid out purchasing the 45 put and 60 call for 0.10 each. Table 14.7 shows the profit and loss for this iron condor at expiration.

The payoff diagram in Figure 14.7 is a good visual of how the iron condor can have a wider range for a maximum payoff at expiration. Between 50.00 and 55.00 the maximum payoff for this spread, 1.45, would be realized. Like the iron butterfly there is a maximum loss for this spread in each direction, shown below 45.00 and over 60.00, in Figure 14.7.

TABLE 14.7 Payoff at Expiration for a 30-Day 45/50/55/60 Iron Condor

XYZ	45 Put	50 Put	55 Call	60 Call	Income	Profit/Loss
40.00	5.00	−10.00	0.00	0.00	1.45	−3.55
45.00	0.00	−5.00	0.00	0.00	1.45	−3.55
50.00	0.00	0.00	0.00	0.00	1.45	1.45
52.50	0.00	0.00	0.00	0.00	1.45	1.45
55.00	0.00	0.00	0.00	0.00	1.45	1.45
60.00	0.00	0.00	−5.00	0.00	1.45	−3.55
65.00	0.00	0.00	−10.00	5.00	1.45	−3.55

The iron condor does not necessarily have the same time decay benefit of an iron butterfly, but it does have a wider margin for error. A short-term trade is still an appropriate use of an iron condor as with an iron butterfly. However, the specific situations are slightly different when considering one versus the other.

■ Iron Condor Trading Examples

The first trading example of using a short-dated iron condor involves trading options on Google (GOOG). Figure 14.8 is a daily chart of GOOG showing there has been resistance at 900.00 and support around 860.00.

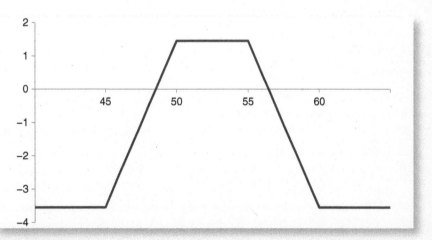

FIGURE 14.7 Payoff Diagram at Expiration for a 30-Day 45/50/55/60 Iron Condor

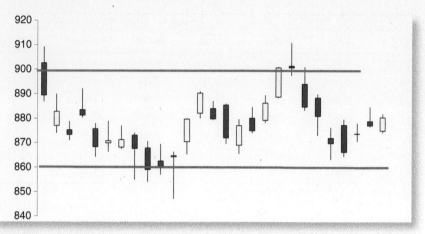

FIGURE 14.8 GOOG Daily Price Chart with Resistance and Support Highlighted

The last trading day on this chart has GOOG closing in the middle of this range at 880.40.

The closing price of 880.40 is on a Friday afternoon so a short-term iron condor would be constructed using options that expire the following Friday. If this support and resistance range is expected to stay in place over the next five trading days an iron condor that expires the following Friday would be worth exploring. Since the stock has support at 860.00 and resistance at 900.00 the following trades would be initiated to crease a five-day iron condor:

Buy 1 GOOG 850 put at 0.80
Sell 1 GOOG 860 put at 1.50
Sell 1 GOOG 900 call at 1.35
Buy 1 GOOG 910 call at 0.55

The net income from this trade would be 1.50. As long as GOOG closes between 860.00 and 900.00 the following Friday the result will be a profit equal to this credit. The worst case scenario is that GOOG drops to 850.00 or rallies up to 910.00 where the result would be a loss of 8.50. The various outcomes at expiration for this trade appear in Table 14.8.

Support for GOOG has been determined to be 860.00 and resistance is 900.00. On Figure 14.9 both these levels are where the spread starts to lose value with breakeven on the downside at 858.50 and breakeven on the upside at 901.50. The maximum loss of 8.50 on this diagram compared to the best-case scenario of a gain of 1.50 may appear to be a little intimidating.

GOOG	850 PUT	860 Put	900 Call	910 Call	Income	Profit/Loss
840.00	10.00	−20.00	0.00	0.00	1.50	−8.50
850.00	0.00	−10.00	0.00	0.00	1.50	−8.50
860.00	0.00	0.00	0.00	0.00	1.50	1.50
880.40	0.00	0.00	0.00	0.00	1.50	1.50
900.00	0.00	0.00	0.00	0.00	1.50	1.50
910.00	0.00	0.00	−5.00	0.00	1.50	−8.50
920.00	0.00	0.00	−10.00	5.00	1.50	−8.50

TABLE 14.8   Payoff at Expiration for a GOOG 5-Day 850/860/900/910 Iron Condor

Of course the stock has to move 30 points higher or lower to reach these points over a five-day period. This translates to a 3.4 percent move in five trading days. This 3.4 percent price change may be worth exploring further through historical weekly price changes for GOOG.

Since 860.00 and 900.00 are support and resistance levels they also may be utilized as stop-loss prices as well. This trade would result in a maximum loss if the stock had a breakout to the downside or a breakout to the upside. To manage this trade a stop loss could be implemented if GOOG breaches 860.00 on the downside or has a move higher that puts the stock over 900.00. Table 14.9 shows the profit or loss for this trade based on days left to expiration along with GOOG trading a point below or above the support and resistance levels.

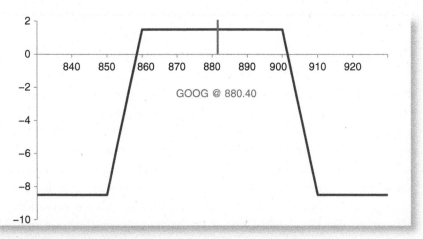

FIGURE 14.9   Payoff Diagram at Expiration for a GOOG 5-Day 850/860/900/910 Iron Condor

TABLE 14.9	Profit and Loss for GOOG 850/860/900/910 Iron Condor at 859.00 and 901.00 before Expiration	
Days	859.00	901.00
5	−1.95	−2.30
4	−1.95	−2.25
3	−1.90	−2.15
2	−1.80	−2.00
1	−1.60	−1.65
0	0.50	0.50

The losses appear to be a bit imbalanced when comparing a break on the downside to a break on the upside. For example, with four days remaining until expiration if GOOG is trading at 859.00 the estimated loss is 1.95 if the trade is exited. On the upside the estimated loss with GOOG at 901.00 would be 2.15. This is a function of the implied volatility at that time for the put options versus the calls used in this iron condor. The implied volatility is higher so the long GOOG 850 put component of the spread would have more value with GOOG at 859.00 than the comparable long GOOG 910 call would have if the stock trades up to 901.00.

What can be taken away from the table that shows the stop-loss levels if the spread is exited early is that the absolute risk versus reward for this 5-day iron condor is not risking 8.50 versus a gain of 1.50. If proper risk controls are in place, and the trade manages to avoid a gap move higher or lower, the losses incurred may be less than the maximum loss at expiration. Just because the maximum potential loss is 8.50 on the table, this does not mean the trade will result in this loss if the profit-risk controls are in place.

The next example of trading a short-term iron condor will be on the iShares Russell 2000 Index ETF (IWM) with the fund trading within a defined range. Figure 14.10 is a chart of the IWM with resistance at 99.00 and support at 96.00 both highlighted. As with GOOG there is a defined risk and reward range that would lend itself to being a good iron condor candidate. The final trading day on this chart is a Monday and IWM closed at 98.70.

The option quotes in Table 14.10 represent the contracts best suited to trade a short-term iron condor based on IWM support at 96.00 and resistance at 99.00. Note the lower premium for the 96 put related to the 99 call. At this time, with IWM at 98.70 there is very little income that would be realized by selling the IWM 4-day 96 put at 0.25 and buying the IWM 4-day 94 put for 0.10.

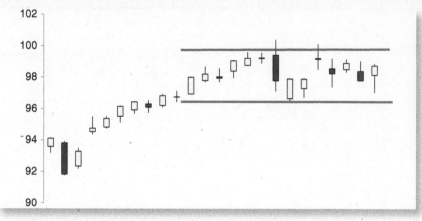

FIGURE 14.10 IWM Daily Price Chart with Resistance and Support Highlighted

When the underlying market appears to be range bound, but the market is closer to one side of the range or the other, it may actually make sense to leg into the iron condor. In this case only the call side of the iron condor would be entered with the anticipation of putting the other side on if there is any weakness in IWM over the next couple of days. The trades on the call side would entail the following two transactions:

Sell 1 IWM 99 call at 0.70
Buy 1 IWM 101 call at 0.10

Figure 14.11 shows the price action two days later for IWM with the same support and resistance levels highlighted as in the previous chart. The fund has traded lower the next couple of days after the first leg of the iron condor was traded. IWM is now resting on the support level of 96.00. At this point it is Wednesday, two days before option expiration, and the market is checked to see if it makes sense to leg into the put side of this trade.

TABLE 14.10	IWM 4-Day Option Prices	
Option	Bid	Ask
94 Put	0.08	0.10
96 Put	0.25	0.28
99 Call	0.70	0.73
101 Call	0.09	0.10

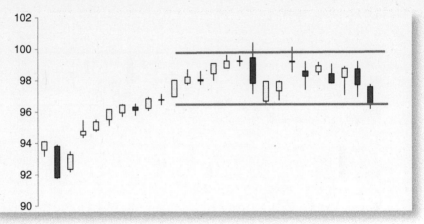

FIGURE 14.11 IWM Daily Price Chart with Resistance and Support Highlighted

The quotes in Table 14.11 are for the same options that were considered when IWM was trading close to the high end of the range. Also two days have passed along with the value of IWM moving lower. So these contracts are referred to as two-day options in the table.

There are a couple of things to note regarding the quotes for these options that now have two days remaining until expiration. The first has to do with legging into the other side of the iron condor. Now that IWM is trading at 96.40 the IWM 96 put may be sold for 0.60 and the IWM 94 put may be purchased for 0.10 and a net credit of 0.50. This is an improvement of 0.35 over the 0.15 credit that was available on Monday afternoon.

The other thing of note is that the two call options are practically worthless at this point. The IWM 99 call could be repurchased for 0.06 and the IWM 101 call could be sold for 0.01 and a net cost of 0.05. This is a trading decision that would involve some subjectivity as far as how certain a trader is that the two options will expire out-of-the-money versus spending 0.05 to

TABLE 14.11	IWM 2-Day Option Prices	
Option	Bid	Ask
94 Put	0.08	0.10
96 Put	0.60	0.63
99 Call	0.04	0.06
101 Call	0.01	0.02

TABLE 14.12 Payoff at Expiration for IWM 94/96/99/101 Iron Condor

IWM	94 PUT	96 Put	99 Call	101 Call	Income	Profit/ Loss
92.00	2.00	−4.00	0.00	0.00	1.30	−0.70
94.00	0.00	−2.00	0.00	0.00	1.30	−0.70
96.00	0.00	0.00	0.00	0.00	1.30	1.30
99.00	0.00	0.00	0.00	0.00	1.30	1.30
101.00	0.00	0.00	−2.00	0.00	1.30	−0.70
103.00	0.00	0.00	−4.00	2.00	1.30	−0.70

exit that side of the trade. Another thought that may come into play is possibly covering the short IWM 99 call at 0.06 and leaving the long position in the IWM 101 call open. If there is a tremendous run to the upside in IWM it may be possible that the 101 call could be sold for a little more premium. Gambling terms really have no place in the trading world, but think of the IWM 101 call as a lottery ticket.

If both sides have been legged into at this point the net credit received is 1.30. On Monday 0.70 was taken in for the call side of the iron condor, and on Wednesday 0.60 was taken in for the put side of the trade, to complete a IWM 94/96/99/101 iron condor that expires in two days. The iron condor payout in Table 14.12 assumes that all positions are held through expiration.

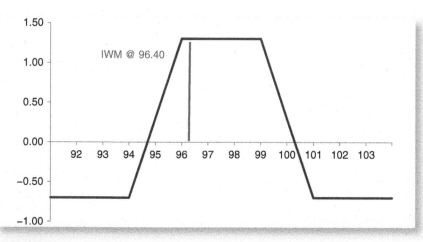

FIGURE 14.12 Payoff at Expiration for IWM 5-Day 94/96/99/101 Iron Condor

Successfully legging into this IWM 94/96/99/101 iron condor results in a very favorable risk–reward, with a maximum loss of 0.70 versus a gain of 1.30. In Figure 14.12 the price of IWM with two days remaining until expiration is highlighted. Note the closer risk is to the downside, but the chart analysis assumes the 96.00 level will hold. Also, on the other side 99.00 actually proved itself as a resistance level with IWM unable to trade over that price since the first leg of the trade was initiated on Monday.

Iron condors have some benefit from time decay, especially as expiration is approaching. They also offer a wider range of payout than a comparable iron butterfly. These popular spreads may be used to trade shorter-term outlooks where a forecast is for a stock to land between two strike prices just a few days in the future. They may also be used to replicate scalping a stock that moves up and down through legging into the call side of an iron condor when the stock is near a resistance level and working into the put side of an iron condor when a stock is near a support level.

CHAPTER 15

Split Strike Long Spreads

The value of an option contract is primarily based on the underlying market. A call and put option that share both expiration and a strike price are held together by what is commonly called *put–call parity*. Basically if the stock price, call price, or put price deviate too much from parity an arbitrage trade emerges. This arbitrage situation will arise, professional high-speed trading firms will take advantage of it, and the result will be that the stock, call, and put prices fall back in line with each other.

■ Synthetic Long and Short

A synthetic long or short stock position may be created by combining a put and call position that share the same strike price. In the case of a synthetic long, a call would be purchased and a put would be sold. As the stock price moves higher the long call would profit and if the stock price were to move down the short put would result in losses. Much like if a stock were purchased, there would be losses incurred through lower prices and gains would be earned if the stock moved higher.

To create a synthetic short position a call option would be sold and a put option would be purchased. A short stock position would lose value if a stock moves higher and a short call would also lose value as a stock moves up in price. Conversely if a stock moves down in price a short stock position benefits as does a long put position.

As a basic example consider the following prices:

XYZ stock at 45.00
XYZ 50 call at 1.50
XYZ 50 put at 1.50

To create a synthetic long position the XYZ 50 call would be purchased for 1.50 and the XYZ 50 put would be sold for 1.50. The net cost would be 0.00. This is an oversimplified example as normally there is a time value component related to the future value of XYZ stock based on the risk free rate. However, for the purposes of this chapter this should suffice.

Table 15.1 shows the payout at expiration for this synthetic long position. There was not a debit or credit incurred when selling the 50 put and purchasing the 50 call so the profit or loss is 100 percent based on the price action of the underlying stock. The stock is trading at 50.00 when this trade would have been initiated and Figure 15.1 shows the profit and loss for this synthetic long trade.

This payout diagram is pretty straightforward and mirrors a long position in XYZ from 50.00 a share. In addition, a long position with a net cost of 50.00 if this position is held through expiration. If the stock is below 50.00 at expiration the short put will be in-the-money. The short position in the XYZ 50 put carries the obligation to buy 100 shares at 50.00 if assigned. The result would be long 100 shares at 50.00. If the stock is above 50.00 at expiration the right to buy 100 shares at 50.00 would be exercised. Again, the result would be a long position in XYZ at 50.00.

There are positions that have a similar outcome to them, but do not mirror the underlying stock performance. The result can be some participation to the upside and potentially being assigned to buy a stock at a lower price. These types of spreads may also allow a trader to try to benefit from the time decay experienced from short-dated options.

TABLE 15.1	Split Strike Long Payoff at Expiration			
XYZ	Short 50 Put	Long 50 Call	Net Cost	P/L
40.00	−10.00	0.00	0.00	−10.00
45.00	−5.00	0.00	0.00	−5.00
50.00	0.00	0.00	0.00	0.00
55.00	0.00	5.00	0.00	5.00
60.00	0.00	10.00	0.00	10.00

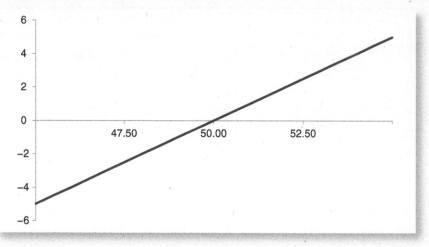

FIGURE 15.1 Synthetic Long Stock Payout

■ Split-Strike Positions

A version of the synthetic long or short position can also be created through using a call and a put with different strike prices. The basis behind doing something like this would be to purchase shares at a lower price or participate in a breakout to the upside. If the stock is between the strike prices at expiration the result is no position in the stock. The profit or loss is based on whether the trade was initiated with a credit or a debit. Typically, a goal should be to initiate one of these spreads at a credit so there may be a small profit if the stock price does not change too much over the life of the options.

As an academic example consider XYZ trading at 52.25. A trader thinks he may have an opportunity to buy XYZ below 50.00, but does not necessarily want to miss the stock if it takes off to the upside. The timing of this outlook is for the next 30 days. He decides to sell an XYZ 30-day 50 put taking in 0.90 in premium while buying a XYZ 30-day 55 call for 0.80. The net result is a credit of 0.10, which probably covers the commissions involved in the trade. Table 15.2 shows the potential profit or loss for this split-strike spread.

In addition to the traditional profit and loss information in this table, the resulting position in XYZ is shown in the final column. Between the strike prices of 50 and 55 the result would be no position in XYZ and a small profit based on the credit taken in when the trade was initiated. Below 50.00 and over 55.00 the result would be a long position in shares of XYZ.

TABLE 15.2	Split Strike Long Payoff at Expiration				
XYZ	Short 50 Put	Long 55 Call	Credit	P/L	Position
45.00	−5.00	0.00	0.10	−4.90	Long 100
50.00	0.00	0.00	0.10	0.10	None
52.25	0.00	0.00	0.10	0.10	None
55.00	0.00	0.00	0.10	0.10	None
60.00	0.00	5.00	0.10	5.10	Long 100

If the stock is below 50.00 at expiration 100 shares will be purchased at an effective price of 49.90. The trader is assigned an obligation to buy 100 shares at 50.00, but took in 0.10 from the split-strike spread when initiating the trade. If the stock is over 55.00 at expiration, the trader would exercise their right to buy 100 shares at 55.00. The effective cost in this situation would be 54.90 as 0.10 is subtracted from the 55.00 paid for shares when exercising the option.

Figure 15.2 shows the profit or loss for this XYZ 50 − 55 split-strike spread. Between 50.00 and 55.00 there is a small profit of 0.10. Below 50.00 and above 55.00 the profit and loss mirrors price changes in the underlying stock, plus the 0.10 credit received when the trade was initiated. A second line is included on this diagram showing the profit or loss if shares of XYZ are purchased as opposed to putting on the spread trade.

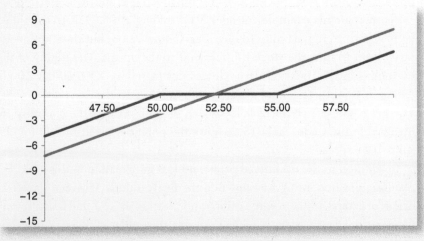

FIGURE 15.2 Split Strike Long versus Long Stock Position

■ Split-Strike Trading Example

A split strike synthetic long position makes sense if a trader would like to buy a stock at a lower price, but not miss the stock if it trades up to higher levels. The trading example of how to create a split strike long position uses shares and options on Facebook (FB). Figure 15.3 is a daily chart of FB price action along with what appears to be price support for FB around 23.00. This support is highlighted with a line below the price bars on the right side of the chart.

The final bar on this chart is a Friday and FB shares closed at 23.30. If a trader would be willing to try to buy shares on a dip below 23.00 they would consider selling a FB 23 put. If they are also concerned about FB shares trading up and missing the stock they might take the proceeds from selling the put option and apply it to purchasing a call. Looking to the options that expire the following Friday, a FB 5-day 23 put can be sold for 0.30 while the FB 5-day 25 call could be purchased for 0.10. The net result of these two trades is a credit of 0.20. The trade also results in the right to buy shares at 25.00 and the obligation to buy shares at 23.00 on the following Friday.

Table 15.3 covers the profit and loss along with positions that may result in FB, based on this five-day synthetic long split-strike trade. Below 23.00 the result is a long position with a net cost of 22.80 determined by subtracting the 0.20 credit from the put strike price of 23.00. If shares of FB take off to the upside and close above 25.00 the result would be a long position with a net effective cost of 24.80. This net effective cost of 24.80 is based on exercising the call option, paying 25.00 for shares and subtracting the credit of 0.20 from this cost.

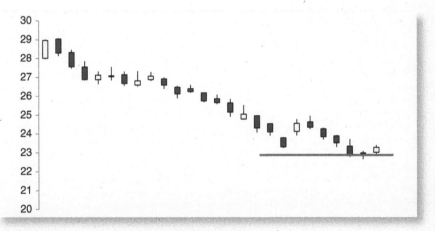

FIGURE 15.3 FB Daily Chart Support at 23.00

TABLE 15.3 **FB 23/25 Split Strike Long Payoff at Expiration**

FB	Short 23 Put	Long 25 Call	Credit	P/L	Position
22.00	−1.00	0.00	0.20	−1.20	Long 100 FB
23.00	0.00	0.00	0.20	0.20	None
24.00	0.00	0.00	0.20	0.20	None
25.00	0.00	0.00	0.20	0.20	None
26.00	0.00	1.00	0.20	1.20	Long 100 FB

If FB closes between 23.00 and 25.00, then both options would expire out-of-the-money. The net result in this case would be a small profit of 0.20, which was the credit received when the trade was initiated. Also, there would be no position in shares of FB.

Figure 15.4 shows the payout for this split-strike spread at expiration. FB is trading at a price where both options will expire with no value. The net result would be no stock position and a profit of 0.20 at that point. That 0.20 of profit that may be realized if FB is unchanged relates to time decay. Both the FB 23 put and FB 25 call were both out-of-the-money options when this trade was initiated. This means that 100 percent of the value of these two options is attributable to time value. Since there is 0.20 more of value for the put than the call the passage of time is a benefit to the position holder. Whenever a trader is considering a trade that gains in value based on time decay they should take a look at short-dated options. They also should consider trying to enhance the time-decay exposure if possible.

This next approach is going to be a multistep split strike synthetic long trade on FB. The situation is the same as the previous example. FB is trading

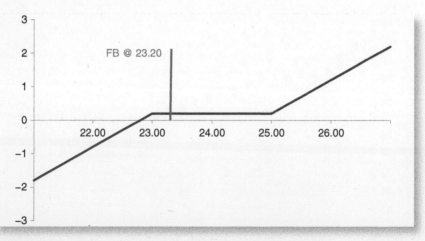

FIGURE 15.4 FB 23/25 Split Strike Long Payoff at Expiration

at 23.20 and an investor is considering putting on a spread that would result in a long position in FB below 23.00, but also benefits if FB stock begins to take off to the upside.

In this second case, the trader considers looking at different expiration dates for FB options. Since there are multiple consecutive weeks of options on FB there is a lot of flexibility around creating a split-strike spread using different expiration dates. There are 5-day and 15-day options available for trading. With the stock at 23.20, selling the FB 5-day 23 put for 0.30 again gains good time decay exposure. The 23 strike put options are the closest to being at-the-money. On the call side, the trader looks out a couple more weeks to call options that expire in 15 trading days. The reason behind exploring an option with more time to expiration is that through buying a longer dated out-of-the-money call there may be less short-term time decay from the long side of the trade. The decision is made to purchase a FB 15-day 25 call at 0.25. When combining this long call with the short FB 5-day 23 put, that was sold for 0.30, the result is a credit of 0.05.

The payout in Table 15.4 shows the profit and loss for the split trade synthetic long upon expiration of the 5-day option contract. At this point the FB 25 call still has 10 trading days remaining until expiration so there is some value remaining for this option at all prices on the table. Also, there is a substantial column that spells out the various positions that result at expiration. At any price above and including 23.00 the FB 10-day 25 call position is still open. Below 23.00, 100 shares of FB will be purchased and the 10-day 25 call position will still be open. In order to sell that option for anything more than 0.10 shares of FB needs to trade higher into expiration.

Figure 15.5 shows the payout based on this spread at expiration of the 5-day put. The shape has sort of a curved nature to it due to the time-value component of the long call that has 10 days remaining to expiration. It is worth noting the price of FB relative to the payout the following Friday. The

TABLE 15.4	FB 5-Day 23/15-Day 25 Split Strike Synthetic Long Payoff at 5-Day Expiration				
FB	Short 23 Put	Long 25 Call	Credit	P/L	Positions
22.00	−1.00	0.05	0.05	−0.90	Long 100 FB + Long 1 10-Day 25 Call
23.00	0.00	0.10	0.05	0.15	Long 1 10-Day 25 Call
24.00	0.00	0.30	0.05	0.35	Long 1 10-Day 25 Call
25.00	0.00	0.70	0.05	0.75	Long 1 10-Day 25 Call
26.00	0.00	1.30	0.05	1.35	Long 1 10-Day 25 Call

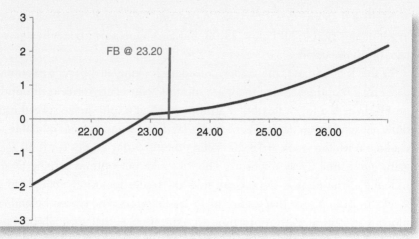

FIGURE 15.5 FB 5-Day 23/15 Day 25 Split Strike Long Payoff at 5-Day Expiration

trade would be a small winner and the spread also benefits from a price rise in FB, even if the stock has not topped the upper strike price of 25.00.

The 5-day put actually expired out-of-the-money as FB was trading at 23.65. Figure 15.6 shows daily chart of FB at this expiration date along with how the 23.00 price level has continued to hold as a support level.

With FB trading at 23.65 the long position in what is now the FB 10-day 25 call is worth 0.25. A trader would then check out the 5-day put options that expire the next Friday to see if there could be an opportunity to sell another put option. The FB 5-day 23 put can be sold for 0.25. The new split-strike position involves a short FB 5-day 23 put and long FB 10-day 25 call.

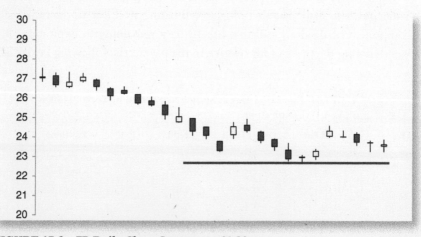

FIGURE 15.6 FB Daily Chart Support at 23.00

TABLE 15.5	FB 5-Day 23/10 Day 25 Split Strike Long Payoff at 5-Day Expiration				
FB	Short 23 Put	Long 25 Call	Credit	P/L	Positions
22.00	−1.00	0.00	0.30	−0.70	Long 100 FB + Long 1 5-Day 25 Call
23.00	0.00	0.05	0.30	0.35	Long 1 5-Day 25 Call
24.00	0.00	0.10	0.30	0.40	Long 1 5-Day 25 Call
25.00	0.00	0.50	0.30	0.80	Long 1 5-Day 25 Call
26.00	0.00	1.15	0.30	1.45	Long 1 5-Day 25 Call

Table 15.5 shows the payoff the following Friday along with what positions would be held based on a variety of closing stock prices for FB. Again, if FB is under 23.00 on this Friday then the short put will be assigned and 100 shares would be purchased. Now that a credit of 0.30 has been taken in the net effective cost of the shares could be considered 22.70. Also, if FB is under 23.00 on this expiration Friday the trader will still own 1 FB 25 call that expires in five days.

Selling another 5-day put option allows the trader a chance to take advantage of time decay while having the obligation to buy FB as a price where they would be a willing purchaser of the shares. Figure 15.7 shows the estimated profit and loss for this trade upon expiration of this second short-dated put option. Note FB shares at 23.65 are solidly at a price where the running profit of this trade is positive.

The breakeven price for this trade is about 22.70 at this point. The following Friday FB shares actually climbed to 24.50, which puts the net unrealized profit at around 0.65. This unrealized profit is based on the

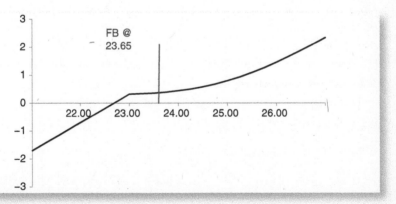

FIGURE 15.7 FB 5-Day 23/10-Day 25 Split Strike Long Payoff at 5-Day Expiration

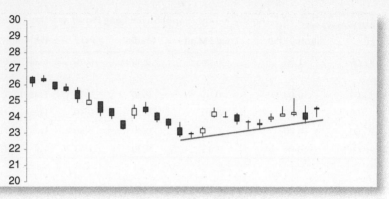

FIGURE 15.8 FB Daily Chart Beginning of Uptrend

income taken in of 0.30 through the two transactions combined with the estimated value of the open long position in the FB 25 call. This call option still has five trading days remaining until expiration and is trading at 0.35.

Figure 15.8 is a FB price chart for this following Friday with FB trading at 24.50. The stock appears to be starting an uptrend, which is indicated by the line on the chart beginning to slant higher as prices move to the right. The chart begins to confirm a bullish outlook for FB.

The stock is moving to the upside and support may be closer to 24.00 than 23.00. Taking this into consideration both the FB 5-day 23 put and FB 24 put prices are checked to determine if selling another put makes sense. Quotes for those two 5-day put options appear in Table 15.6.

Selling the FB 5-day 23 put would only bring in 0.09. In addition to not bringing in much premium, if FB were to trade down to 23.00 over the next few days that may be interpreted as a break of the developing uptrend. This new trend line that is sloping upward represents bullishness for FB, but also represents a support level. A violation of support may cause a trader to change from having a bullish outlook to having a more cautious outlook on FB. With a more cautious outlook they may be less inclined to take a long position in the underlying stock.

The bid price for the FB 5-day 24 put is 0.30. This price makes more sense from an income standpoint and a bullish outlook for FB. Trading close

TABLE 15.6	FB 5-Day Put Option Quotes	
Option	Bid	Ask
23 Put	0.09	0.11
24 Put	0.30	0.32

TABLE 15.7 FB 5-Day 24/5 Day 25 Split Strike Long Payoff at Expiration

FB	Short 24 Put	Long 25 Call	Net Credit	P/L	Position
22.00	−2.00	0.00	0.60	−0.65	Long 100 FB
23.00	−1.00	0.00	0.60	−0.40	Long 100 FB
24.00	0.00	0.00	0.60	0.60	None
25.00	0.00	0.00	0.60	0.60	None
26.00	0.00	1.00	0.60	1.60	Long 100 FB

to or just below 24.00 would not result in a break of the uptrend that is developing for FB shares. There are two factors to weigh regarding which option to sell. First, how much income may be brought in from selling the option? Second, at what price would the trader be obligated to purchase shares? Taking these two factors into account results in the trader selling the FB 5-day 24 put for 0.30.

Three put options have been sold and one purchased over the course of three weeks. (See Table 15.7.) The net credit over these three transactions is now 0.60 and the two open positions consist of being short 1 FB 5-day 24 put and long 1 FB 5-day 25 call. If FB is below 24.00 at expiration the obligation to buy shares will be assigned to the trader and the result will be a long position in FB with a net cost of 23.40. If the stock is over 25.00 upon expiration then the trader will exercise his right to buy shares and the net effective cost will be 24.40.

The payout diagram in Figure 15.9 shows the payout at expiration for both option positions. Note that the lines are not curves as in the previous two payoff diagrams. All options expire with no value so there is not a time

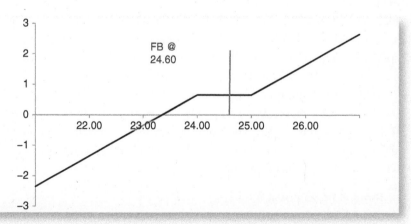

FIGURE 15.9 FB 5-Day 24/5-Day 25 Split Strike Long Payoff at Expiration

elements to the pricing in this diagram. Regardless of the price of FB on Friday the option contracts will both expire. The only possible position will be long 100 shares or no position at all. As there was a long-term bullish outlook for FB, at this point the profits from the option trades may be realized and, if a trader decides he still would like long exposure to FB, they will purchase the shares in the open market.

The split strike synthetic long is a great way for a trader to try to buy shares at a lower price, take in some income, and have some protection against missing a stock if it begins to trade higher. Combining a shorter-dated short position in a put and a longer-dated call option may result in benefitting from the time-decay difference between the short and long option contract. This is a perfect use of short-dated options by traders who have a longer-term focus for an underlying stock or market.

■ Bull-Put Spread Plus Long Call

Many investors and traders are not approved to initiate uncovered or naked short put positions. Also, some traders do not want to be exposed to the risk associated with a naked short option position. Different brokers have different rules in place regarding what types of trades they will allow clients to execute. These rules are based on trading experience and account capital. The riskier the option trade, the more trading experience and capital a broker desires from their client in order to allow that sort of trade to be executed. Unfortunately a naked short put position is one of those trades considered too risky for most traders. Because of this, many traders would not be able to initiate a split strike long trade as demonstrated in the previous section. However, there is a potential substitute that may be utilized by a wider number of traders. This substitute would involve combining a bull-put spread with a long call position. This alternative to a split strike synthetic long will be briefly demonstrated using an academic XYZ example. Then FB stock will be revisited using this unique spread.

With XYZ trading at 52.25 a trader has a 30-day outlook where they would buy XYZ on weakness to just below 50.00, but not want to miss out if the stock begins to rally. The trader is not approved to have an uncovered short put position. He decides to combine a bull-put spread with a long call. The trades to create this position are:

Buy 1 XYZ 45 put at 0.05
Sell 1 XYZ 50 put at 0.95
Buy 1 XYZ 55 call at 0.85

TABLE 15.8 Bull-Put Spread Plus Long Call Payoff at Expiration

XYZ	Long 45 Put	Short 50 Put	Long 55 Call	Credit	P/L	Position
40.00	5.00	−10.00	0.00	0.05	−4.95	None
45.00	0.00	−5.00	0.00	0.05	−4.95	Long 100
50.00	0.00	0.00	0.00	0.05	0.05	None
55.00	0.00	0.00	0.00	0.05	0.05	None
60.00	0.00	0.00	5.00	0.05	5.05	Long 100

The net result of these three trades is a small credit equal to 0.05. The trader also has two rights and a single obligation. He has the right to buy XYZ at 55.00 and the right to sell XYZ at 45.00. His obligation is to purchase XYZ at 50.00 which would be assigned to him if the price of XYZ is lower than 50.00 at expiration. The payout at expiration for this trade appears in Table 15.8.

The payoff table includes the value of these three options at expiration along with the credit of 0.05 received when this spread was initiated. Also, the final column indicates what the position in XYZ stock will be when the options expire. Note that on the top row, which shows the outcome if the stock is trading at 40.00, there is not a position in XYZ. The obligation to buy shares at 50.00 would be assigned, but the trader would also exercise their right to sell the shares at 45.00. The net result is a loss of 4.95 and also no position in XYZ. Between 45.00 and 50.00 the spread would result in a long position of 100 shares and if XYZ is above 55.00 at expiration the trade would result in a long position in XYZ.

Figure 15.10 is a payout diagram showing the result for this spread using three XYZ options at expiration. Note there is long exposure to XYZ

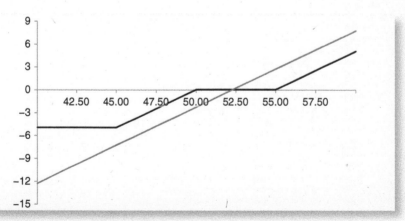

FIGURE 15.10 Bull-Put Spread Plus Long Call Payoff at Expiration

between 45.00 and 50.00 and then at any price over 55.00. Below 45.00 losses are capped at 4.95. Between 50.00 and 55.00 all options expire and the result is a profit equal to the small credit of 0.05 received when the spread was initiated. The goal of this trade is to try to buy on weakness, but not miss the stock to the upside. An additional benefit here is the potential loss is capped if XYZ trades below 45.00.

For a trading example using this hybrid form of a split strike long spread shares of Facebook will be used again. The exact same trading situation as in the previous section will be used as well. The only differences are either the trader wants to limit the potential downside or his broker does not allow him the ability to have uncovered short put option positions.

Figure 15.11 shows FB developing support at 23.00 a share. The trader decides to initiate a spread that will take in a credit, allow him to buy shares on weakness, but also allow him to participate to the upside if FB takes off to the upside.

The last trading day on this chart is a Friday and FB closed at 23.20. Based on their outlook the trader executes the following trades to have both a bull put spread and a long call:

Buy 1 5-day 22 put @ 0.10
Sell 1 5-day 23 put @ 0.30
Buy 1 5-day 25 call @ 0.10

The net result of these three trades is a credit of 0.10. Table 15.9 shows the profit and loss for this trade on the following Friday when all options expire. Below 23.00 the obligation to buy shares will be assigned, but below 22.00 the right to sell those shares would be exercised as well. The net result

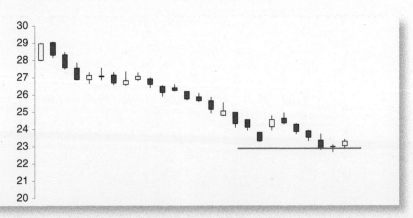

FIGURE 15.11 FB Daily Chart Support at 23.00

TABLE 15.9   FB 22/23 Bull Put + Long 25 Call Payoff at Expiration

FB	22 Put	23 Put	25 Call	Credit	P/L	Positions
21.00	1.00	−2.00	0.00	0.10	−0.90	None
22.00	0.00	−1.00	0.00	0.10	−0.90	Long 100 FB
23.00	0.00	0.00	0.00	0.10	0.10	None
24.00	0.00	0.00	0.00	0.10	0.10	None
25.00	0.00	0.00	0.00	0.10	0.10	None
26.00	0.00	0.00	1.00	0.10	1.10	Long 100 FB
27.00	0.00	0.00	2.00	0.10	2.10	Long 100 FB

with the stock below 22.00 would be a loss of 0.90, regardless of how much FB shares trade down in price.

Figure 15.12 shows the payoff structure of this spread upon expiration of all three options. Between 23.00 and 25.00 the small profit is equal to the credit of 0.10 that was taken in when this trade was initiated. Above 25.00 the profit rises in sync with FB stock moving higher. Finally, between 22.00 and 23.00 the trade loses value in line with FB moving lower with losses limited at 22.00 and lower.

This trade may also be executed in a way that time decay may work to the advantage of a trader. In the previous section a long call with slightly more time to expiration was combined with a shorter-dated short put. The result was more time decay benefit through multiple transactions being executed over a three-week period. This may also be accomplished by combining a short-dated bull-put spread with a long call that has more time to expiration.

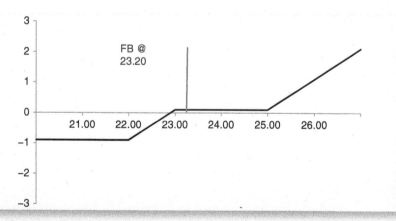

FIGURE 15.12   FB 22/23 Bull Put + Long 25 Call Payoff at Expiration

Using the same outlook for FB where a trader would like to buy on weakness, but not miss out on an upside move, a trader will initiate a five-day bull-put spread and buy a 15-day call option. The executed trades are:

Buy 1 FB 5-day 22 put at 0.10
Sell 1 FB 5-day 23 put at 0.30
Buy 1 FB 15-day 25 call at 0.25

One piece of the puzzle that may turn some traders off is that this trade is actually done for a small debit of 0.05. In the previous examples a credit was taken in when the trades were first initiated. In this case a debit is paid out, but after the first week the running cost of the trade will change over from being a debit to a credit.

Table 15.10 runs through the profit or loss of this spread trade at expiration of the five-day bull-put spread. The maximum loss of this trade is 1.05, which would occur if FB trades down to the low 20's. At this point the FB 25 call still has 10 trading days remaining until expiration, but the option is so far out-of-the-money it is doubtful there would be anything more than a penny or two bid for the contract. Trying to sell an option for 0.01 or 0.02 would not make much sense when commissions are figured into the net proceeds from the trade.

Also, do note that with the exception of between 22.00 and 23.00 there is not a stock position at any other price level on this table. The 25 call position is still open, so there is long exposure to FB regardless of the price of the stock at this time. However, this long exposure comes from the long call. In the window of prices between 22.00 and 23.00 the trader would also be long 100 shares in addition to having a position in the 25 call. A trading decision may need to be made regarding the long 25 call is the goal is to only be long 100 shares.

Figure 15.13 shows the payout for this trade at expiration of the bull-put spread. Note that despite the trade being initiated at a debit, if the stock

TABLE 15.10	FB 5-Day 22/23 Bull Call + FB 15-Day 25 Call Payoff at 5-Day Expiration					
FB	22 Put	23 Put	25 Call	Debit	P/L	Positions
21.00	1.00	−2.00	0.00	−0.05	−1.05	Long FB 25 Call
22.00	0.00	−1.00	0.05	−0.05	−1.00	Long 100 FB + Long FB 25 Call
23.00	0.00	0.00	0.10	−0.05	0.05	Long FB 25 Call
24.00	0.00	0.00	0.30	−0.05	0.25	Long FB 25 Call
25.00	0.00	0.00	0.70	−0.05	0.65	Long FB 25 Call
26.00	0.00	0.00	1.30	−0.05	1.25	Long FB 25 Call
27.00	0.00	0.00	2.15	−0.05	2.10	Long FB 25 Call

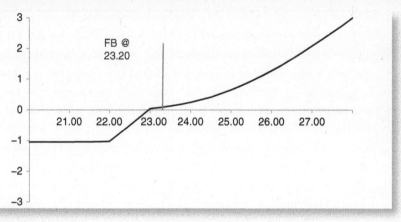

FIGURE 15.13 FB 5-Day 22/23 Bull Put + FB 15-Day 25 Call Payoff at 5-Day Expiration

price is unchanged at expiration of the put options the result is actually a small unrealized profit of 0.10. The long FB 25 call would be expected to be trading at around 0.15 at this time having lost some value due to time decay. Combined with the 0.05 debit incurred when the spread was initiated, this results in an unrealized profit of 0.10.

Also note that as the stock price rises the spread participates on the upside immediately. This participation is not necessarily one for one with the price of FB, but there is some appreciation in the value of the spread. This appreciation in the value of the spread increases the more the price of FB rises.

At expiration of the first bull-put spread FB closed at 23.65. Figure 15.14 shows the price action up to this Friday where the 23.00 level appears to

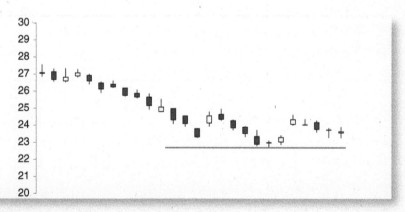

FIGURE 15.14 FB Daily Chart Support at 23.00

be holding as a support level. The opportunity to take in more premium through selling another FB 5-day 23 put for 0.25 and buy another FB 5-day 22 put for 0.10. The net credit for this bull-put spread would be 0.15

The open call position is priced at 0.25 and now has 10 days remaining until expiration. The net running cost of this trade has changed from being a debit to taking in a small credit of 0.10. At this point the maximum potential loss for this trade would be 0.90 instead of 1.05.

Table 15.11 shows the payout in five days when the second bull-put spread would expire. The debit of 0.05 has been replaced with a credit of 0.10. The position outcome is the same as it was in the previous example with a long position in FB being the outcome if the stock is between 22.00 and 23.00 at expiration. The long call option position would still be open as it still has five days remaining until expiration.

This trade will actually have an unrealized profit again if FB is unchanged over the next five days. The payoff diagram in Figure 15.15 shows FB trading at 23.65 when there are 10 days remaining for the long call option to expire and the second bull put spread is initiated. The profit of this spread moves up in line with an appreciation in FB shares, but is very linear if shares move lower. With FB below 23.00 there will probably be no value remaining in the long call with only five days remaining until expiration.

At the second expiration date, FB has traded up to 24.50 and it appears the stock is beginning to establish an uptrend. (See Figure 15.16.) The line on the chart defines this uptrend and if it is to hold it would result in the stock not necessarily trading down to the 23.00 level as in the previous two charts. A break of the trend would also result in a reevaluation of whether a trader would want to be long in the stock. Owning the lower strike put solves this issue.

TABLE 15.11	FB 5-Day 22/23 Bull Put + FB 10-Day 25 Call Payoff at 5-Day Expiration					
FB	22 Put	23 Put	25 Call	Net Credit	P/L	Positions
21.00	1.00	−2.00	0.00	0.10	−0.90	Long FB 25 Call
22.00	0.00	−1.00	0.00	0.10	−0.90	Long 100 FB + Long FB 25 Call
23.00	0.00	0.00	0.05	0.10	0.15	Long FB 25 Call
24.00	0.00	0.00	0.10	0.10	0.20	Long FB 25 Call
25.00	0.00	0.00	0.50	0.10	0.60	Long FB 25 Call
26.00	0.00	0.00	1.15	0.10	1.25	Long FB 25 Call
27.00	0.00	0.00	2.05	0.10	2.15	Long FB 25 Call

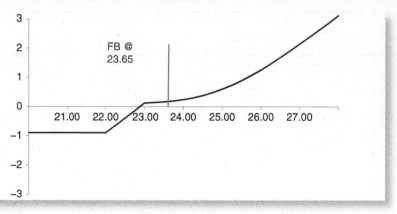

FIGURE 15.15 FB 5-Day 22/23 Bull Put + FB 10-Day 25 Call Payoff at 5-Day Expiration

With the stock now trading at 24.50, a bullish outlook may involve trying to buy the stock on a dip to 24.00 while still holding the long 25 strike call. The FB 5-day 24 put can be sold 0.30 while the FB 5-day 23 put would be purchased at 0.10. The net credit is 0.20 for this bull-put spread and now there is an obligation to purchase the stock at 24.00 with limited losses below 23.00 a share.

With the stock now trading at 24.50, a bullish outlook may involve trying to buy the stock on a dip to 24.00 while still holding the long 25 strike call. The FB 5-day 24 put can be sold 0.30 while the FB 5-day 23 put would be purchased at 0.10. The net credit is 0.20 for this bull-put spread and now there is an obligation to purchase the stock at 24.00 with limited losses below 23.00 a share. The payoff levels in Table 15.12 are based on all options

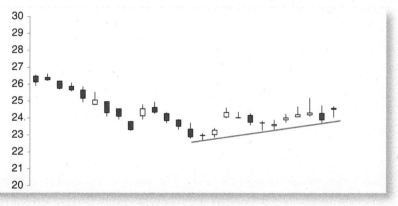

FIGURE 15.16 FB Daily Chart Beginning of Uptrend

TABLE 15.12	FB 5-Day 22/23 Bull Put + FB 5-Day 25 Call Payoff at Expiration						
FB	23 Put	24 Put	25 Call	Net Credit	P/L	Positions
21.00	2.00	−3.00	0.00	0.30	−0.70	None
22.00	1.00	−2.00	0.00	0.30	−0.70	None
23.00	0.00	−1.00	0.00	0.30	−0.70	Long 100 FB
24.00	0.00	0.00	0.00	0.30	0.30	None
25.00	0.00	0.00	0.00	0.30	0.30	None
26.00	0.00	0.00	1.00	0.30	1.30	Long 100 FB
27.00	0.00	0.00	2.00	0.30	2.30	Long 100 FB

expiring at the end of the following week. Between 22.00 and 23.00 the stock would be owned with a net cost of 22.70. If the stock rallies over 25.00 over the following week the FB 25 call would be exercised and, when including the 0.30 of premium taken in over this three-week period, the net cost would be 24.70.

The final payoff diagram for this trade (Figure 15.17) shows that FB is again trading at a level where the running net profit would result in positive outcome for this trade. The breakeven price for this trade is now 23.70 which is also the net price that would be paid for shares if it closes below 24.00 but above 23.00. Also, the profit begins to improve as the stock trades above 25.00. If the stock is over 25.00 at expiration the FB 25 call would be exercised. By exercising this option the paying 25.00 for 100 shares of stock. Including the 0.30 of income from the trading activity the net effective cost would be 24.70.

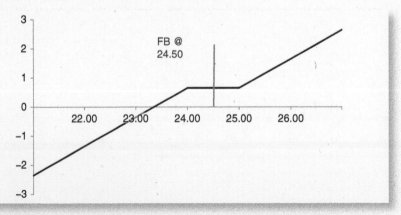

FIGURE 15.17 FB 5-Day 22/23 Bull Put + FB 5-Day 25 Call Payoff at Expiration

Selling a short-dated put option to enter a stock is an excellent use of the options market. A synthetic split-strike position can accomplish this and also allows a trader the ability to possibly take in credit. Also, if the stock moves up the long call part of the spread will allow the trader to benefit from this move. Finally, for traders who do not have the permission or risk tolerance for a naked short put position a bull-put spread combined with a higher strike long call is final way to get paid by the option market to take on the obligation to buy shares.

CHAPTER 16

Calendar Spreads

Taking advantage of time decay is a key component to option trading success. Calendar spreads are one of the best and most direct methods for taking advantage of time decay. Calendar spreads are price neutral by design, as they are most efficiently created using at-the-money option contracts. Before short-dated options were introduced, calendar spread opportunities did exist. Now, however, with an at-the-money option consistently expiring every week, the calendar spreading opportunities and the flexibility around trading these spreads has increased tremendously. In addition, now that there are short-dated options consistently available for trading it is possible to buy a long-dated option with the intent of selling more than one short-dated option over the life of the long-dated options. The goal behind this sort of trading is for the short options to expire slightly out-of-the-money and the long option to have enough value to be sold at a net profit.

■ Calendar Spread Overview

A calendar spread consists of a long and short option position. The strike price and type of option (call or put) is the same. The difference between the two contracts is the expiration date. Typically the short contract expires before the long-dated contract. First, consider the more common neutral example of a calendar spread. With XYZ trading at 35.00 a couple of examples are:

Short 1 XYZ Jan 35 call @ 0.50
Long 1 XYZ Mar 35 call @ 1.50
Short 1 XYZ Jan 35 put @ 0.45
Long 1 XYZ Mar 35 put @ 1.45

In these two examples, the January options have five days to expiration while the March contracts have 45 trading days to expiration. Also, all options are at-the-money contracts. With a neutral outlook for the underlying, a trader may consider selling the Jan 35 call and purchasing the Mar 35 call. This is due to the time decay difference for at-the-money option contracts, which varies dramatically for at-the-money put or call options that have different expiration dates. To illustrate this a little more, Figure 16.1 shows the time-decay difference between the XYZ Jan 35 call with five days to expiration and the Mar 35 call that has 45 days remaining until expiration.

This display of time decay assumes no change in the price of the underlying or change to any other option-pricing factor such as implied volatility. The chart isolates the passage of time and time decay. There are two five-day sections of this time-decay curve highlighted with squares. On the left side of the chart the expected time decay for the Mar 35 call is highlighted. Over that five-day period an at-the-money option contract would lose about 0.10 in value with the price changing from 1.50 to 1.40. On the right side of this time decay graph the last five days leading up to expiration are highlighted. In this case the option premium changes from 0.50 to 0.00 for a drop of 0.50.

Option contracts may expire several years into the future. These long-dated options are commonly referred to as LEAPS for Long-Term Equity Anticipation Securities. Any option that has more than nine months until expiration comes under the moniker LEAPS. Other than having more than nine months left until expiration, LEAPS contracts are just like traditional option contracts. Typically, LEAPS option contracts are issued during the third and fourth quarter over two years in the future. For instance, in September, October, and November of 2012 LEAPS expiring in January 2015 were

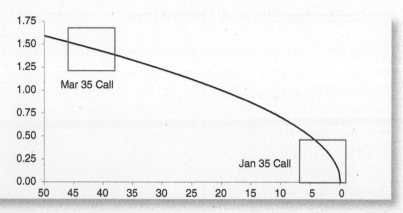

FIGURE 16.1 Time Decay Chart

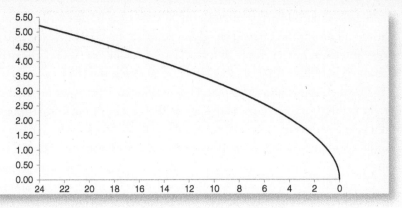

FIGURE 16.2 24-Month At-the-Money Time Decay Chart

listed. These LEAPS would expire anywhere from 25 to 27 months into the future on the third Friday in January 2015.

Figure 16.2 shows the time decay for at-the-money LEAPS going out for two years or 24 months. This chart was created using an option-pricing calculator, but the concept still holds up when considering the time decay of longer-dated option prices.

This time decay chart is based on a stock trading at 35.00 with 25 percent implied volatility and 24 months until expiration results in a premium of about 5.20. All 5.20 of premium are time value since this is an at-the-money option. The number of months until expiration appears at the bottom of the chart. At first sight, the shape of this curve is very similar to the shape of the curve over 50 days in Figure 16.1. However, the rate of time decay occurring with more time to expiration is much slower with much more time to expiration. For instance this theoretical 24-month option loses about 0.02 of value over the first five days shown on the chart. An option with the same pricing factors lost 0.10 of value between 45 and 50 days to expiration, and lost 0.50 over the last five days leading up to expiration. Calendar spreads are typically traded with two near-dated options; however, it is always possible to buy a LEAPS call or put and sell near-term options against the much longer-dated LEAPS.

■ Time Value and Implied Volatility

Since the nature of time decay and implied volatility are important relative to calendar spreads, a quick review of both concepts is a worthwhile exercise. The value of an option contract can be divided into two components, intrinsic value and time value. The intrinsic value is the amount an option contract is in-the-money or the value of an option contract if it could be exercised at that very moment. For example, if a stock were trading at 40.00 a 35 strike call option would have 5.00 of intrinsic value based on the right to buy a stock at 35.00 when it is trading at 40.00. That option has 5.00 of value based on that right to buy. Option contracts that are at-the-money or out-of-the-money will not have any intrinsic value. For example, with the stock trading at 40.00 a call option with a strike price of 40 would be the at-the-money call and have no intrinsic value. There is no economic value in exercising the right to purchase a stock at 40.00 when it may be purchased at 40.00 in the open market. As an example an out-of-the-money call option may have a strike price of 45 and like the at-the-money contract would have no intrinsic value either. As with the 40 call, the 45 call would have no economic value, as exercising the right to buy a stock at 45.00 when it is trading at 40.00 makes no sense at all.

The other pricing component that contributes to the value of an option contract is time value. Time value is the market price of an option that is in excess of the intrinsic value of an option contract. For instance if the 35 strike call is trading at 5.50 when the stock is at 40.00 there is 5.00 of intrinsic value and 0.50 of time value in that option contract. For the 40 and 45 strike call options any quoted value would be 100 percent time value. An example of this appears in Table 16.1, where the 40 strike call is trading at 2.45 and the 50 strike call is at 0.75.

Calendar spreads are all about benefitting from time decay differences and time decay for at-the-money option contracts is the best method to take advantage of time decay differences. At-the-money contracts have the most time value and, as expiration approaches, the decay of this time value accelerates. Since time decay accelerates when expiration approaches for at-the-money options these are the contracts most commonly used for a calendar spread. At-the-money options have the greatest amount of time value relative to in-the-money and out-of-the-money options, but also experience the nonlinear time decay that is the key motivation for entering into a calendar spread.

TABLE 16.1 At Intrinsic Value and Time Value

	Premium	Intrinsic Value	Time Value
35 Call	5.50	5.00	0.50
40 Call	2.45	0.00	2.45
45 Call	0.75	0.00	0.75

Another pricing factor that can come into play with respect to calendar spreads is a change in implied volatility. A change in implied volatility only will impact the time-value component of an option contract. Implied volatility may also vary from expiration to expiration. Options that expire on different dates will often have different levels of implied volatility. This may be based on market forces or due to the timing of some sort of company event such as an earnings release. Whatever the reason, these differences will contribute to the potential profitability of a calendar spread.

■ Option Skew

Before jumping into some actual calendar-spread examples we will have a quick review on the impact of different implied volatility levels across different expiration dates. This is commonly known as *horizontal skew* and may have a great influence on calendar-spread pricing. Consider Facebook (FB) shares trading at 27.32 on a Thursday afternoon. If you have a slightly bullish outlook on FB but expect the stock to stay below 28.00 over the near term, you may consider a calendar spread using 28 strike call options. Table 16.2 shows the market prices for FB 28 calls along with the respective implied volatility levels.

These are the final quotes for the next few FB option expiration dates. The number of trading days is substituted for the expiration months to give a proper perspective on the different time values relative to time to expiration. The FB one-day option that expires the next day is omitted. This means the nearest expiration is the following Friday or in six trading days. Beyond that there are standard FB options expiring in 16, 33, 73, and 141 trading days currently available. Note the implied volatility for these FB 28 calls trends up and then off a little for the June contracts. A typical calendar spread involves selling a near-dated contract versus buying a long-dated contract. In terms of implied volatilities this would mean selling a contract with slightly lower implied volatility and buying an option with higher implied volatility.

TABLE 16.2   **FB 28 Call Quotes with Implied Volatilities**

Time to Expiration	Bid	Ask	Implied Volatility
6 Days	0.40	0.45	43.69%
16 Days	0.90	0.95	44.57%
33 Days	1.55	1.60	45.92%
73 Days	2.65	2.70	50.64%
141 Days	3.60	3.80	48.56%

The one outlier on this table is the 73-day call option with an implied volatility that is elevated a little compared to the other options. This slightly higher implied volatility relates to the timing of expiration for those options. The 73-day call expires after the expectation of shares coming off lockup and possibly being sold into the open market. The market being aware that a future company-specific event may impact the price of FB stock is reflected by the higher implied volatility of the 73-day call option.

■ Trading Example

The first trading example for a calendar spread will stick with the options trading on Facebook. Figure 16.3 is a daily price chart that shows FB shares had quite a run and closed under 28.00 at 27.32.

If a trader felt the stock was going to stall out at 28.00 for a while they may consider a calendar spread. The calendar spread would involve selling the six-day call and buying a farther dated at-the-money option contract. For a short-term trade the two choices may be buying the FB 16-day call for 0.95 or the FB 33-day call for 1.60. Both choices are going to be analyzed and then compared at the end of this section. The first alternative would involve the following transactions:

Sell 1 FB 6-day 28 call at 0.40
Buy 1 FB 16-day 28 call at 0.95

This trade would cost a net of 0.55 from taking in premium from selling the short-dated call for 0.40 and paying out 0.95 for the long-dated call option. Table 16.3 illustrates the estimated payout at expiration of the

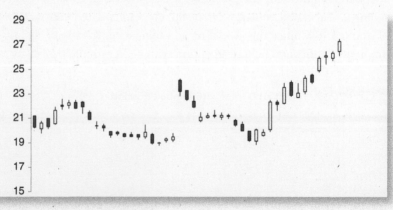

FIGURE 16.3 FB Daily Price Chart

TABLE 16.3   FB 6-Day/16-Day 28 Call Calendar Spread Payoff

FB	6-Day 28 Call	16-Day 28 Call	Cost	P/L
25.00	0.00	0.10	−0.55	−0.45
26.00	0.00	0.25	−0.55	−0.30
27.00	0.00	0.55	−0.55	0.00
28.00	0.00	1.00	−0.55	0.45
29.00	−1.00	1.60	−0.55	0.05
30.00	−2.00	2.35	−0.55	−0.20
31.00	−3.00	3.15	−0.55	−0.40

short-dated option. An assumption that the implied volatility does not change for the 16-day call is used to determine the value of that contract. Upon expiration of the 6-day call, the 16-day call will still have 10 trading days remaining until expiration, so the value of that option is a best guess depending on market factors such as implied volatility.

The prices for the six-day options are based on holding the option to expiration. This means there would time value remaining in the short option. The 16-day calls will have 10 trading days remaining until expiration. The breakeven level for this trade on the downside is 27.00 and breakeven on the upside is very close to 29.00. If FB lands between these two prices the trade would be expected to be some sort of profit at expiration of the near-dated option.

Figure 16.4 is a payoff diagram from this trade at expiration of the six-day call. Note that FB is trading a little lower than the maximum profit level of

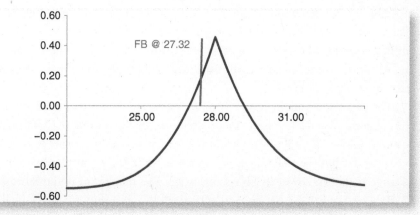

FIGURE 16.4   FB 6-Day/16-Day 28 Call Calendar Spread Payoff

TABLE 16.4	FB 6-Day/33-Day 28 Call Calendar Spread Payoff			
FB	6-Day 28 Call	33-Day 28 Call	Cost	P/L
25.00	0.00	0.50	−1.20	−0.70
26.00	0.00	0.80	−1.20	−0.40
27.00	0.00	1.20	−1.20	0.00
28.00	0.00	1.70	−1.20	0.50
29.00	−1.00	2.25	−1.20	0.05
30.00	−2.00	2.95	−1.20	−0.25
31.00	−3.00	3.60	−1.20	−0.60

28.00 and there is more room to the upside than the downside before this trade turns into a loss. Also notice that it is not the normal linear shape that depicts a payoff at expiration. Also note as FB moves farther away from the strike price of 28.00 the losses begin to level off. The loss on this trade is limited to the premium paid when the trade was initiated. The maximum loss for this FB 6-day/16-day 28 call calendar spread is 0.55.

This trade might also be created by selling short the six-day call and buying a farther-dated call option. The next expiration date for FB options is 33 days in the future so the second alternative would involve the following transactions:

Sell 1 FB 6-day 28 call at 0.40
Buy 1 FB 33-day 28 call at 1.60

This trade would be a little more costly than the calendar spread combining the six- and 16-day options. This trade takes in 0.40 and pays out 1.60 for a net cost of 1.20. This also means that the maximum potential loss is greater than the

Table 16.4 shows the payout for this spread at expiration of the near-dated option. At that time the long call option would have 28 days remaining until expiration. The first thing to note on this table is that the breakeven levels for this trade are practically the same as with the spread that combined the short-dated options.

The payoff diagram in Figure 16.5 does a good job of showing what is different about this trade. There is a greater potential loss using the long-dated call option as the long position in this calendar spread. The gain at 28.00 is very similar but the risk of loss is much greater in the event of a large price change higher or lower in FB's share price. The maximum potential loss is 1.20 versus only 0.55 for the first spread trade and it shows up very well in this payoff diagram.

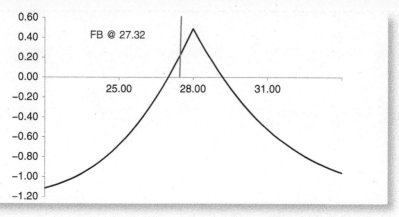

FIGURE 16.5 FB 6-Day/33-Day 28 Call Calendar Spread Payoff

To get a better direct comparison of the two spread trades Table 16.5 is a side-by-side comparison. The most startling difference is the maximum potential loss of the spread using a 33-day call option compared to the spread using a 16-day call option as the long component of the calendar spread.

It appears from this table that the better of the two trades would involve selling the FB 6-day 28 call at 0.40 and buying the FB 16-day 28 call for 0.95 and a net cost of 0.55. The maximum potential gain favors purchasing the 33-day call option, but only by 0.05, which may not justify the maximum potential risk. However, there may be a reason a trader would prefer to buy the FB 33-day 28 call instead of the 16-day 28 call.

With weekly options available there is always a near-dated expiration series being rolled out and available to trade. In this case, if the outlook is for FB to trade around the 28.00 level for several weeks, a trader may consider buying the FB 33-day call.

Figure 16.6 shows FB trading up to expiration of the six-day option contract. FB closed at 27.50 on this Friday so the FB 6-day 28 call expired out-of-the-money. Both the long option alternatives were out-of-the-money as well, but they did have some time value remaining. If a trader chooses to close out the trade the profit net profit would be 0.30 for the spread created with the 6- and 16-day options. The open long position could be sold for

TABLE 16.5 FB 6-Day/33-Day 28 Call Calendar Spread Payoff

Spread	Lower Breakeven	Higher Breakeven	Maximum Gain*	Maximum Loss
6/16 Day	27.00	29.05	0.45	−0.55
6/33 Day	27.00	29.05	0.50	−1.20

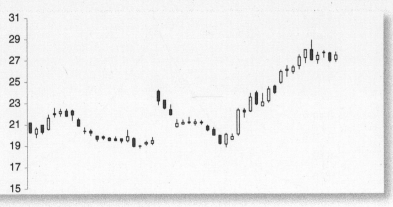

FIGURE 16.6 FB Daily Price Chart

0.85 and after subtracting the 0.55 cost of the spread the net result is 0.30. The spread created with the 6- and 33-day options would result in a profit of 0.40. This profit is determined by selling the long-dated call for 1.60 and subtracting the spread cost of 1.20.

In addition to closing out the trade there is another choice that a trader may make at this time. The FB 16-day 28 call now has 10 days and the FB 33-day 28 call now has 28 days remaining until expiration. Also, there is now a short-dated FB option with five days remaining until expiration. The markets for each of these three options appear in Table 16.6.

If a trader was going to consider potentially selling multiple call options against a long call position they would be more inclined to consider originally purchasing a longer-dated alternative. However, in the case of a very short time frame, the long position in the 16-day call would have been the preferable choice, even if they were only going to sell short-dated options twice.

With FB trading at 27.50 the next expiration FB 5-day 28 call could be sold for 0.45. Taking this 0.45 of income and adding it to the original debit of 0.55 results in net running cost of 0.10. Table 16.7 shows the estimated running potential payout for the two short options and one long option trade.

TABLE 16.6	FB 28 Call Quotes	
Time to Expiration	Bid	Ask
5 Days	0.45	0.50
10 Days	0.85	0.90
28 Days	1.60	1.65

TABLE 16.7	FB Short 5-Day/Short 6-Day/Long 16-Day 28 Call Payout			
FB	**5-Day 28 Call**	**16-Day 28 Call**	**Cost**	**P/L**
25.00	0.00	0.00	−0.10	−0.10
26.00	0.00	0.10	−0.10	0.00
27.00	0.00	0.30	−0.10	0.20
28.00	0.00	0.70	−0.10	0.60
29.00	−1.00	1.35	−0.10	0.25
30.00	−2.00	2.10	−0.10	0.00
31.00	−3.00	3.05	−0.10	−0.05

If FB moves dramatically higher or lower the worst outcome is a loss of 0.10. If FB closes at 28.00 the net result is a profit of 0.60 based on the 10-day call having five trading days remaining to expiration. The long FB call in this case is starting to experience faster time decay than the long-dated option. The payout diagram in Figure 16.7 highlights this low risk versus return further.

This payout diagram depicts a potential profit and loss for a pretty attractive trade. Do remember that many factors need to fall into place for the trade to result in a maximum profit. Also, the opportunity to sell a near-dated 28 strike call may not always come up two weeks in a row.

The other alternative to the FB calendar spread involved buying a long-dated call option. The upfront cost was higher and led to a greater risk relative to the potential outcome of the trade. If that choice was made and a trader felt FB was going to continue to trade around 28.00, the FB 5-day call could be sold for a credit of 0.45. The net running cost in this case would

CALENDAR SPREADS

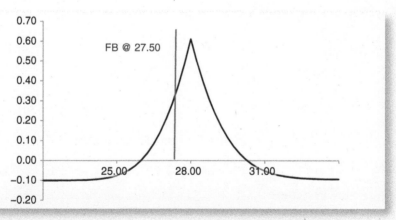

FIGURE 16.7 FB Short 5-Day/Short 6-Day/Long 16-Day 28 Call Payout

TABLE 16.8   FB Short 5-Day/Short 6-Day/Long 33-Day 28 Call Payout

FB	5-Day 28 Call	33-Day 28 Call	Cost	P/L
25.00	0.00	0.40	−0.75	−0.35
26.00	0.00	0.70	−0.75	−0.05
27.00	0.00	1.05	−0.75	0.40
28.00	0.00	1.55	−0.75	0.80
29.00	−1.00	2.15	−0.75	0.40
30.00	−2.00	2.75	−0.75	0.00
31.00	−3.00	3.55	−0.75	−0.20

now be 0.75, as the original cost was 1.20, and through taking in 0.45 of credit this cost has now been reduced to 0.75.

Table 16.8 shows the payout at expiration for the five-day call. The potential reward is 0.80 and potential loss is 0.75 with a large outlier move in FB. It would actually take a pretty large price change in FB shares for the result to be a loss of 0.75 at five-day expiration. Figure 16.8 shows the estimated payoff at expiration of the second short option contract.

Note FB shares were priced to give a little more cushion to the upside than downside on this payout diagram. Also note the very wide range of profitability for this trade. FB shares closing between 26.00 and 30.00 at expiration would be estimated to result in some sort of profit for the trade.

Table 16.9 is a comparison of the two sets of trades. The maximum loss of 0.10 versus the gain of 0.60 for the spread that originally purchased a 16-day call is more attractive than the other spread that has a risk of 0.75 for a potential reward of 0.80. However, at this time, the potential benefit of having gone with the long-dated call will be demonstrated.

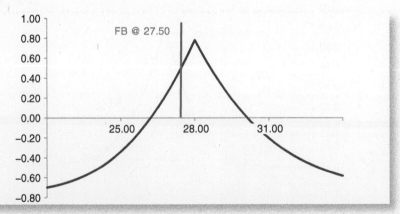

FIGURE 16.8   FB Short 5-Day/Short 6-Day/Long 33-Day 28 Call Payout

TABLE 16.9

Spread	Lower Breakeven	Higher Breakeven	Maximum Gain*	Maximum Loss
5/6/16 Day	26.00	30.00	0.60	−0.10
5/6/33 Day	26.00	30.00	0.80	−0.75

TABLE 16.9 FB 6-Day/33-Day 28 Call Calendar Spread Payoff

AU : Provide some note for this asterisk

FB shares closed at 26.80 upon expiration of the second short-call option. Figure 16.9 shows the daily price changes up to the expiration date. Everything looked to be in good shape for a FB close near 28.00 until the last day before expiration.

This price action is less than ideal for either of these running calendar spreads. The two long option choices now have either five trading days or 23 trading days remaining to expiration. The markets for the two potential long option choices appear in Table 16.10.

This price action is less than ideal for either of these running calendar spreads. The two long option choices now have either five trading days or 23 trading days remaining to expiration. The markets for the two long option choices appear in Table 16.10.

If the short-dated option was chosen for the long component of this running trade it could be sold for 0.30 and a net profit of 0.20. The long-dated call could be sold for 1.25 and would result in a net profit of 0.45. A couple of other choices remain as well. If there is a feeling that FB shares may rebound in the next few days the long option may be held with the intent of selling the option for a higher premium. Over the following week this opportunity actually comes up. Table 16.11 is a summary of FB prices over

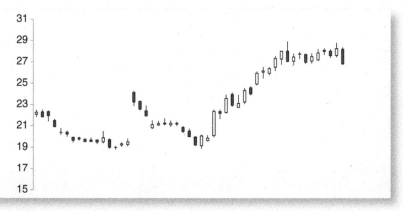

FIGURE 16.9 FB Daily Price Chart

TABLE 16.10	FB 28 Call Quotes	
Time to Expiration	Bid	Ask
5 Days	0.30	0.35
23 Days	1.25	1.30

the next five trading days along with the bid price for what would be the FB 5-day call and the FB 23-day call at this time.

If the long-dated option had been the original choice there would have been a bit more flexibility around this trade. The dip in FB stock into the second expiration date impacted both the near-dated and long-dated long call positions. Even though FB stock rallied up to 27.70 the Tuesday after expiration the short-dated call option did not improve at all. Time decay is quickly taking premium out of this option that has just a few days left to expiration.

Calendar spreads are one of the most direct methods that an option trader may utilize to take advantage of time decay. The different impact that the passage of time has upon two options that share a strike price, but have different expiration dates, makes a calendar spread an ideal trade when there is a neutral outlook for the underlying market or stock.

The decision of which expiration dates to choose should be primarily based on the price and timing outlook for the underlying market. However, the time decay impact on the long contract that will occur after the short option has expired should be taken into consideration as well.

Finally, with short-dated options, buying a long-dated option can result in multiple opportunities to sell short-dated option contracts with the result being a very favorable risk-to-reward scenario.

TABLE 16.11	FB Stock FB 28 Call Quotes and Potential Profit/Loss				
Day	FB Close	5-Day 28 Call	5-Day 28 Call P/L*	23-Day 28 Call	23-Day 28 Call P/L*
Friday	26.80	0.30	0.20	1.25	0.45
Monday	26.75	0.20	0.10	1.10	0.35
Tuesday	27.70	0.30	0.20	1.45	0.70
Wednesday	27.40	0.15	0.05	1.30	0.55
Thursday	27.35	0.10	0.00	1.20	0.45
Friday	26.25	0.00	−0.10	0.75	0.00

CHAPTER 17

Diagonal Spreads

D iagonal spreads are similar to calendar spreads as a diagonal spread consists of a long and short position in option contracts sharing the same underlying. A calendar spread consists of two options that are the same type (put or call) and have the same strike price, but have different expirations. Diagonal spreads expand on this with the spread consisting of options that have different strike prices as well as different expiration dates.

A diagonal spread builds on the concept in the previous chapter where a trader benefits from time decay. Diagonal spreads will often have a directional bias to them. This means that in addition to a profit from a neutral outlook, there may be a profit from a bullish or bearish move out of the underlying market. When the correct strike prices are chosen, options with more time to expiration can experience less time decay than comparable options with less time to expiration. Also, when different strike prices are thrown into the mix, the difference in time decay can be even more dramatic.

■ Diagonal Spread Overview

The two examples below are typical diagonal spread positions. The underlying XYZ is trading at 35.00 a share. January expiration is in five trading days and March expiration is in 45 trading days.

Short 1 XYZ Jan 35 call @ 0.50
Long 1 XYZ Mar 33 call @ 2.70
Short 1 XYZ Jan 35 put @ 0.45
Long 1 XYZ Mar 37 put @ 2.65

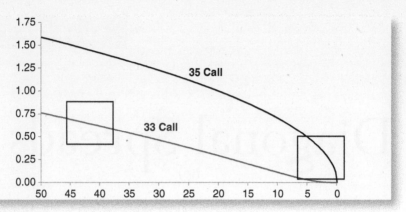

FIGURE 17.1 Time Decay Chart

Focusing first on the diagonal spread using call options the short-dated option is an at-the-money 35 strike call with only five days remaining to expiration. Since this is an at-the-money option 100 percent of the premium may be attributed to time value. The long 33 strike call is in-the-money by 2.00 so only 0.70 of this option's premium may be attributed to time value. Even though there are 40 more days to expiration, the 33 strike call has only 0.20 more time value than the 35 strike call. Figure 17.1 is a chart of the time decay of both call options.

This figure compares the time decay of the at-the-money call with five days remaining until expiration and the in-the-money call that has 45 days remaining until expiration. The higher (dark gray) line on the chart represents time decay for the 35 call, which is the at-the-money contract. The lower (light gray) line shows time value decaying for the in-the-money 33 strike call option. Note that the long-dated in-the-money option has 2.00 of intrinsic value, so the chart only shows the time value of this option and subtracts out the intrinsic value. Over this five-day period the long-dated in-the-money call would experience about 0.10 of time decay while the five-day at-the-money option would lose 0.50 attributed to time decay.

▪ Short-Term Diagonal Spreads

Diagonal spreads can be the combination of two options that have just a week or two separating the expiration dates or even years. Since the motivation behind a trade combining options that both expire within the next few weeks would be different than the motivation behind combining a long position in an option that expires several months or even years in the future these two types of trades will be addressed separately.

Often a short-term diagonal spread is going to benefit more from time decay than a price move in the underlying market. The forecast may be slightly bullish or slightly bearish, but in many cases a dramatic price move would result in lower profits or even a loss if a stock trades dramatically past the forecasted price.

■ Short-Term Bullish Diagonal Spread

Pricing on Nike (NKE) is used to demonstrate a diagonal spread using call options. Figure 17.2 is a daily price chart of trading action in NKE through a Friday afternoon. On this particular Friday shares of NKE closed at 64.75.

Shares of NKE have made a run up to 65.00 and appear to be hitting some resistance. This resistance level of 65.00 is highlighted with the horizontal line on the upper right hand side of the chart. A trader may approach NKE believing that this 65.00 level will hold, but that the trend is still favoring an upside move. If the risk of a big price move is to the upside, a trader might explore putting on a short-term bullish diagonal spread. The specific trade should be profitable if the stock trades close to 65.00 or breaks through this resistance level and trades to the upside. Based on this outlook the trader executes the following trades:

Short 1 NKE 5-day 65 call at 0.60
Buy 1 NKE 29-day 60 call at 5.20

The net cost of this trade is 4.60 when the credit of 0.60 is summed with the 5.20 cost of the long-dated call. Something worth noting is the time value of each option contract. The NKE 5-day 65 call has 0.60 worth of time

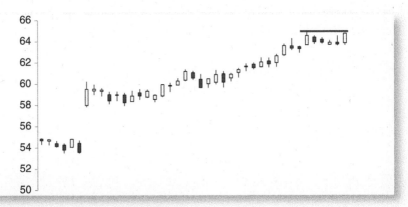

FIGURE 17.2   NKE Daily Price Chart

value while the NKE 29-day 60 call has 0.55 of time value. If at all possible, when creating a diagonal spread using relatively short-dated options, buying an option with less time value than the option that is sold is preferable. Through selling more time value than the amount purchased, a price move in one direction will hurt profitability, but not result in a trade turning into a loss. Both the payout table and diagram will highlight this point. Table 17.1 shows the payout at expiration of the five-day call for this diagonal spread.

The net cost of this trade is 4.60 which is the maximum potential loss for this trade. However, the worst outcome on this table shows a loss of 3.90 if NKE is trading down at 57.50 at expiration of the near near-dated short call. The prices for the longer-dated call option have some time value remaining in addition to intrinsic value if NKE shares move higher. The deeper an option is in-the-money, the lower the time value of that contract. At the high end of the price table, 72.50, there is 0.05 of time value for the 60 call despite there being 24 trading days until expiration.

The payout diagram in Figure 17.3 shows the estimated profit or loss at expiration. The curved nature of this diagram relates to the time-value component of the open long call position at expiration of the near-dated option contract.

This spread trade works out best if NKE trades 0.25 higher and closes at 65.00 on the following Friday. However, the trade can be considered neutral to bullish since a move higher for shares of NKE would still result in a profit. The profit does tail off a bit as the price of NKE goes higher.

This version of a diagonal spread that has a neutral-to-bullish focus is one method to benefit from time decay when there is an expectation that a stock price is going to settle around a certain price on an expiration date. This method allows a trader to be wrong about this outlook, but still profit if the stock rallies despite a neutral stock forecast. A diagonal spread may also be created with a bias to the downside.

TABLE 17.1	NKE 60/65 Diagonal Call Spread Payoff			
NKE	5-Day 65 Call	29-Day 60 Call	Cost	P/L
57.50	0.00	0.70	−4.60	−3.90
60.00	0.00	1.70	−4.60	−2.90
62.50	0.00	3.30	−4.60	−1.30
65.00	0.00	5.30	−4.60	0.70
67.50	−2.50	7.65	−4.60	0.55
70.00	−5.00	10.10	−4.60	0.50
72.50	−7.50	12.55	−4.60	0.45

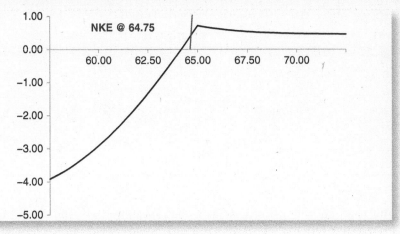

FIGURE 17.3 NKE 60/65 Diagonal Call Spread Payoff

■ Short-Term Bearish Diagonal Spread

When a trader has an outlook that is neutral to bearish a diagonal spread may be created that will offer profits for both outcomes. This sort of diagonal spread would be created with put options. A put with a higher strike price and more time to expiration is purchased. Simultaneously a near-dated put option with a lower strike price is sold. Typically this short option will have a strike price that is closer to the underlying market price.

A short-term diagonal trade created from put options is demonstrated based on price action in the Potash Corp (POT) stock. The chart in Figure 17.4 shows that shares of POT will make a new high and then retrace a little periodically. This sort of price activity shows up a couple of times on

FIGURE 17.4 POT Daily Price Chart

TABLE 17.2   POT 43/45 Diagonal Put Spread Payoff

POT	4-Day 43 Put	19-Day 45 Put	Cost	P/L
40.00	−3.00	5.00	−1.60	0.40
41.00	−2.00	4.00	−1.60	0.40
42.00	−1.00	3.00	−1.60	0.40
43.00	0.00	2.05	−1.60	0.45
44.00	0.00	1.25	−1.60	−0.35
45.00	0.00	0.65	−1.60	−0.95
46.00	0.00	0.25	−1.60	−1.35

this chart and the pattern seems to be repeating itself. The second-to-last day on this chart is a Friday where shares made a new high of 43.67. The following trading day was a Monday when shares backed off a little down to 43.11. Based on an outlook that is neutral to slightly bearish a diagonal spread using near-dated put options is considered.

The next short-dated expiration is just four trading days off, but with POT closing at 43.11 a POT 4-day 43 put may be sold for 0.40. The next standard option expiration date is 19 trading days off and an in-the-money POT 19-day 45 put would cost 2.00. The net debit or cost of this trade comes to 1.60. This 1.60 is the maximum potential loss for this trade; however, this much of a loss does not show up on the profit-and-loss payout shown in Table 17.2.

There is not much margin for error for this trade on the upside. The breakeven level for this trade is about 43.50 at expiration. The payoff diagram in Figure 17.5 highlights this, as the closing price for POT on the day

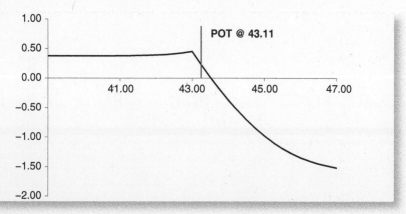

FIGURE 17.5   POT 43/45 Diagonal Put Spread Payoff

TABLE 17.3 **POT 43/45 Diagonal Put Spread Stop Loss Summary**

Days to Expiration	43 Put	45 Put	P/L
3 Days	0.03	1.28	−0.35
2 Days	0.01	1.26	−0.35
1 Day	0.00	1.25	−0.35
Expiration	0.00	1.25	−0.35

the trade would be initiated is just 0.39 lower than the point where this trade goes from being a profit to a loss at expiration.

All trades should be entered into with a combination of alternatives for exiting the trade. Even if the intent is to hold a winning or losing trade until expiration that decision should be made when entering the trade. With such a narrow margin for error with this POT 43/45 diagonal put spread a stop loss may be worth exploring.

The day before this trade was initiated POT made a new high, closing at 43.67. A close above this level might be the beginning of another move up in the price of POT stock. To give a little wiggle room for normal market activity, 44.00 would be a good stock price to use as a stop loss price for this trade. Table 17.3 shows the estimated price for two options in this diagonal spread, based on POT closing at 44.00 each day, up to and including expiration.

This outcome is fairly interesting as the estimated loss for this spread would be 0.35 at any time leading up to expiration based on POT trading at 44.00. Of course, there is no assurance that the stock may not gap higher, resulting in a larger loss than 0.35. However, sticking with an exit plan based on the price of POT making a new high would be a good risk-management decision.

■ Long-Term Diagonal Spreads

Traders and investors often associate option trading with short-term trading. A good portion of this book is based on short-term trading. However, there are options—specifically, Long-Term Equity Anticipation Securities (LEAPS)—that will expire over nine months and up to almost three years into the future. Positions in these long-dated versions of option contracts may be held for several months and even a couple of years, which in this day and age is thought of as a long-term holding. As with short-dated option contracts there is a time-value component to the price of a LEAPS contract. A method of reducing the cost associated with the time value of these long-dated options is to opportunistically sell short-dated at-the-money options. These short positions will have time decay that benefits the seller and offsets the time-value cost of the long-dated option.

A long-term trade that incorporates a diagonal spread has more of a directional bias than diagonal spreads put on for a short-term trade. The short-term trades were benefitting from time decay differences and a neutral price outlook. The bullish or bearish bias was more about if the trade does not work as planned as opposed to the optimal price projection. A long-term trading strategy would involve expecting a stock to move higher or lower over a period of months. At times the price move may get ahead of itself. Stated another way, if a stock is moving in a steady trend higher or lower the price may accelerate ahead of this trend and may be expected to backtrack to the trend line. Also, a bullish trend may hit a short-term resistance level and, at that time, a short-dated at-the-money call may be sold. In the case of a stock that is in a downtrend, the stock may find a support level and a short-term at-the-money put could be sold. In both instances the goal would be to sell an option that will expire with no value.

■ Long-Term Bullish Diagonal Spread Trade

The trading example of combining a LEAPS call with opportunistically selling short-dated call options against the position will use Apple (AAPL) price history. The first chart (see Figure 17.6) shows AAPL stock coming under pressure after several months of a downtrend. AAPL shares closed at 390.50 and a trader considers taking a long position over the next few months. Possibly based on a combination of fundamental analysis and technical

FIGURE 17.6   AAPL Daily Price Chart

FIGURE 17.7 AAPL Daily Price Chart—Stock Hitting Short-Term Resistance

analysis, a trader manages to make an excellent trade and purchases an AAPL 190-day 300 call at 100.00. At this time the AAPL call has 190 trading days until expiration. Also note the time value of this contract. Despite this option having several months remaining until expiration there is only 9.50 of time value in this AAPL call.

Figure 17.7 is a second AAPL chart that shows the AAPL 300 call purchase has been a good one. The stock has rebounded to 453.00 over the course of just 15 trading days. The long-dated call option now has 175 days remaining until expiration and it is trading at 160.00. It appears after this pretty impressive run to the upside that AAPL shares may be ready for a retracement. In fact, a minor downtrend line demonstrates this outlook on the chart.

The trader believes in the long-term prospects for the stock, but wants to take advantage of this short-term pause in the uptrend. Being a Friday, the trader looks at the five-day call options on AAPL that expire the following week. An AAPL 5-day 450 call can be sold at 7.50. This call does have 3.00 of intrinsic value and 4.00 of time value, based on the appearance of topping in shares of AAPL, so the feeling is the stock will be under 450.00 when this short-call option expires on the following Friday. This short AAPL 450 call trade worked well and a profit of 7.00 was realized as AAPL closed the following week below 450.00.

Over time, shares of AAPL do retrace some and then head back higher. The 450 resistance level where the stock stalled out before is tested again. Figure 17.8 shows where AAPL is trading now along with a resistance level based on the last move to the upside. Fourteen trading days have passed and now the long-term 300 call has 160 days remaining until expiration and is trading at 156.00 based on AAPL trading at 449.75.

FIGURE 17.8 AAPL Daily Price Chart—Stock Hitting Short-Term Resistance

Believing that 450.00 is going to hold as a resistance level, and the next short-term option expiration being in five days, an AAPL 5-day 450 call is sold for 4.75. A little less premium is taken with this trade relative to the first instance of selling a 450 call since there is 3.00 of intrinsic value. With AAPL trading at 449.75 the premium is all time value. The 450 level is a formidable one and AAPL backs off in price again resulting in a profit of 4.75 from this short-dated option sale.

When the long-dated AAPL 300 call was purchased, a trader paid 100.00 for the option that had several months remaining until expiration. Based on AAPL trading at 390.50 at the time there was 9.50 of time value. On two occurrences AAPL stock reached a resistance point where the opportunity arose to sell a short-dated call option and take in premium. Table 17.4 is a summary of the three AAPL option trades.

The AAPL short-call trades resulted in profits of 7.50 and 4.75 for a realized profit of 12.25. With just two well-timed trades the time value of the original call purchase has been eliminated. Also, upon expiration of the second short call position, there is still 155 days remaining until expiration of the long call. With this much time remaining until expiration of the long

TABLE 17.4	AAPL Short Term Option Sale Summary	
Days to Option Expiration	**Action**	**Result**
190	Buy 1 AAPL 190-Day 300 Call at 100.00	Open Position
175	Sell 1 AAPL 5-Day 450 Call at 7.50	7.50 Profit
160	Sell 1 AAPL 5-Day 450 Call at 4.75	4.75 Profit

option position there is a good chance of more option selling opportunities before the long-call expires.

■ Bearish Diagonal Spread Trade

When a trader has a long-term short bias regarding a stock one way to trade this outlook is through purchasing a long-dated put option. The amount of time value for this long-term option depends on the amount of time remaining until expiration, the strike price of the option relative to the underlying market, and the implied volatility of the put. In order for the trade to be successful the stock will often need to move down in price to overcome this time value. Selling short-dated put options to take advantage of time value decaying rapidly is a way to offset time value.

Price action in the SPDR Gold ETF (GLD) will be used to demonstrate how short-dated puts may be sold against a long position in a put option that has a much longer time period remaining to expiration. Figure 17.9 is a daily price chart for GLD with this fund closing at 155.35. Through a combination of fundamental and technical reasons a trader believes the price of gold is in for a downturn. With this outlook a GLD 195-day 160 put may be purchased for 11.00. This put option has 5.35 of intrinsic value and 5.65 of time value.

This put purchase turns out to be a very good trade as a few days later the GLD fund comes under pressure. Figure 17.10 is a chart that shows this price action. After the drop to about 130.00 GLD starts to develop some support. This support is indicated by the trend line on the left side of the chart. This trend line shows how after the fall in price each day the price action for GLD shows how the fund is putting in higher daily low prices.

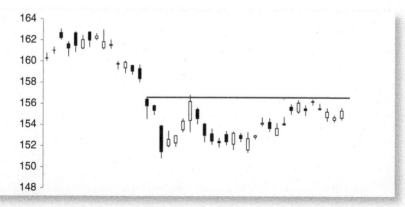

FIGURE 17.9   GLD Daily Price Chart

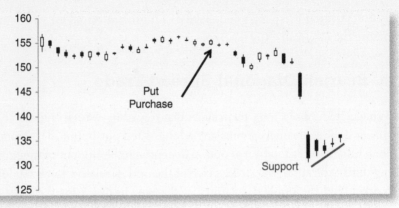

FIGURE 17.10   GLD Daily Price Chart

With support developing there appears to be an opportunity to sell a short-dated put option and take in some income to offset the original cost of time value when the long-dated put was purchased. The final price bar on this chart is a Friday and GLD is trading at 135.45. Based on the support level that appears to be developing on the chart a trader could sell a GLD 5-day 135 put for 2.25. The long position in the GLD 160 put is still open and has 179 trading days until expiration. With GLD trading at 135.45 the long-dated 160 put is trading at 26.50 or 15.50 higher than the original purchase price.

Over the next few weeks GLD continues to trend higher then roll over returning to the low 130s. This price area is a significant support level for GLD as it held after the previous dramatic drop in price. Figure 17.11 shows the price action in GLD leading up to the next put option sale. The last closing price on this chart is 131.05 and this occurs on a Friday.

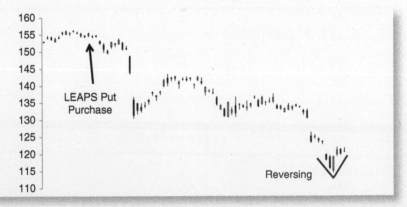

FIGURE 17.11   GLD Daily Price Chart

With the belief that GLD will not break support a GLD 5-day 131 put is sold for 2.00. This would be a pretty aggressive trade as the near-term trend is definitely favoring a bearish one. It would be prudent to keep a close eye on the support level and if the market were to breach this support be prepared to buy back the short put position. Also, at this point on the chart, the long-dated put position has 159 trading days remaining until expiration.

This support level holds, at least for the short term and then is broken with a pair of gaps to the downside in GLD. The price behavior toward the end of this chart shows a dramatic one-day push to the downside followed by a rebound that is just as dramatic. Figure 17.11 shows this price action that appears to indicate a reversal of the downtrend developing.

The last day on this price chart is actually a Thursday, so options with six days remaining until expiration are considered to generate income through a short-term trade. The closing price on this Thursday was 120.75 so the GLD 6-day 120 put is sold for 1.70. The long 160 put is still an open position and now has 127 days remaining until it expires. This GLD 6-day 120 put expires out-of-the-money as GLD closed at 124.13 the following Friday.

At this point there have been three option sales for a total of 5.95, and the long put option still has 121 days remaining until expiration. Through opportunistically selling short-dated near at-the-money put options, enough premium has been brought in to offset the time value of the long-dated put option that was originally purchased with 195 trading days until expiration. Table 17.5 is a summary of the four trades.

Periodically creating a diagonal spread from a long option position is a good method of lowering the cost of a long option position and take in premium. When a long-term opinion regarding a stock or market is in place in the form of a long-dated put or call option this method of trading works very well. Any time a market appears to have hit a point where the trend may pause or have a short-term reversal selling a short-dated option could be a profitable short-term trade.

TABLE 17.5   **GLD Short-Term Option Sale Summary**

Days to Option Expiration	Action	Result
195	Buy 1 GLD 195-Day 160 Put at 11.00	Open Position
179	Sell 1 GLD 5-Day 135 Put at 2.25	2.25 Profit
159	Sell 1 GLD 5-Day 131 Put at 2.00	2.00 Profit
127	Sell 1 GLD 6-Day 120 Put at 1.70	1.70 Profit

CHAPTER 18

Trading Earnings Releases with Short-Dated Options

A major reason for the success of short-dated option contracts is the ability to trade options that have very little time left to expiration around a pending event. Probably the best example of an event would be quarterly earnings releases. Other examples include a new product announcement or regulatory ruling, such as a court case or product approval. Of the different events that will result in a large stock price move, earnings are the easiest events for individual traders to consider trading. Earnings dates are widely known and a historical perspective on how a stock has reacted in the past to earnings releases may be used as a guide for a trade.

■ Stock Prices and Earnings

The reason traders care so much about earnings has to do with the price changes experienced by stocks during the trading session that comes just after an earnings announcement. Table 18.1 is a summary of price reactions for 10 of higher-priced stocks that have weekly options available for trading.

	AAPL	AMZN	CF	CMG	FDX
	AAPL	**AMZN**	**CF**	**CMG**	**FDX**
Average Earnings % Change	3.97%	7.11%	3.70%	8.37%	3.81%
Average Daily % Change	1.30%	1.53%	1.89%	1.52%	1.27%
Maximum Earnings % Change	12.35%	15.75%	6.87%	21.51%	8.17%
Maximum Daily % Change	12.35%	15.75%	12.45%	21.51%	8.17%
Minimum Earnings % Change	0.16%	1.00%	0.41%	1.11%	0.91%
	GOOG	**ISRG**	**MA**	**NFLX**	**PCLN**
Average Earnings % Change	6.75%	5.71%	3.63%	19.17%	3.97%
Average Daily % Change	1.11%	1.44%	1.33%	2.64%	1.30%
Maximum Earnings % Change	12.98%	12.68%	13.39%	42.22%	12.35%
Maximum Daily % Change	12.98%	12.68%	13.39%	42.22%	12.35%
Minimum Earnings % Change	2.38%	0.14%	0.47%	5.19%	0.16%

TABLE 18.1 Average Earnings Report Reactions

The data in Table 18.1 represent the 12 quarters of earnings results for each stock from the middle of 2010 through the middle of 2013. The percent changes all represent absolute values as the focus is on the magnitude of price moves. The first row for each stock represents the average of the absolute value of the percent move for the first full trading session after a company reports their earnings results. The next row is the average of the absolute value of percent price changes for each stock over this three-year period. For example, AAPL shares have an average daily price change of 1.3 percent. The average price change for the session after earnings is 3.97 percent or just over three times the average daily price move. Note that the average price move for each stock is at least two times the average daily price change for the stock on any random trading day. It is this magnitude of one-day price changes that makes trading earnings so tempting.

The third row shows the maximum one-day price change for each stock based on a reaction to earnings. Remember these are absolute values; for example, 12.35 percent for AAPL was actually a day that AAPL shares lost 12.35 percent in a single trading session. Also, 12.35 percent was the largest price change for AAPL over this three-year period as indicated by the next row. Every stock, with one exception, experienced the largest one-day change in reaction to earnings. CF Industries Holdings (CF) was the lone stock that had a larger price change on a trading day that was not in reaction to an earnings announcement. CF is a fertilizer producer and the big price not attributed to earnings was due to a scheduled government corn-crop report. The outcome of this crop report was as significant for future profitability at CF as any earnings report.

The final row on this table shows the minimum one-day price change based on an earnings release. It is interesting to note that there are several instances where a stock was practically unchanged the day after earnings, but there are also several instances where the smallest price change for a stock after earnings is larger than an average trading day price change.

These large one-day price changes can be rewarding but, as with any big potential reward, there are large risks as well. Despite the large stock price change, the timing of the announcement is anything but a surprise to the market. Traders know that stocks like AAPL or GOOG are going to report earnings and are going to be in the news for a day. They are just unsure of the direction or magnitude of the price change.

■ Option Prices and Earnings

Option traders are well aware of pending earnings announcement dates. These dates are usually set months in advance. Option market makers and other professional traders will adjust option premiums in anticipation of the larger-than-average stock price change that will accompany an earnings announcement. As the pending news announcement date approaches option premiums will adjust on a daily basis. This adjustment balances time until the announcement with the expected accentuated price movement from the underlying stock. The option-premium adjustment will be attributed to a rise in implied volatility. Figure 18.1 is an example of how implied volatility increased as an earnings release date approaches and then drops after the earnings announcement has passed.

CBOE publishes implied volatility indexes on a handful of individual stocks. The same method that is used to determine the widely followed CBOE Volatility Index (VIX) is applied to option pricing on individual stocks. This method results in a measure of anticipated 30-day volatility for the underlying instrument. The chart of CBOE Equity VIX on Google (VXGOG) shows the daily close for a couple of weeks leading up to an earnings release and a couple of weeks following that earnings announcement.

The peak of this chart is in the middle and coincides with GOOG making their earnings announcement regarding results for the previous quarter. At this time, GOOG reports their earnings after the market closes and the stock and option price reactions occur the following trading day. Note as the

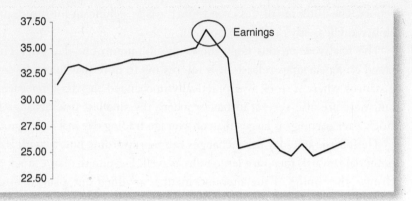

FIGURE 18.1 CBOE Equity VIX on Google before and after an Earnings Announcement

earnings date approaches the implied volatility, as indicated by option pricing on GOOG stock, continues to move up. Then, as the event happens—in this case, the earnings announcement—the implied volatility quickly drops. This is typical of many stock option series leading up to and following an earnings announcement. The risk of a quick short-term price move is now out of the market, at least until the next earnings announcement, and the result is lower option premiums and lower implied volatility.

A phrase that is often associated with a company-related event, such as earnings, that will move a stock price is the *known unknown*. That is, the market is aware an event is coming up and the unknown is what sort of price reaction will occur in the stock price as a result of this event. Sometimes the reaction that a stock has relative to an earnings announcement is a head scratcher for many individual and professional traders.

■ The Earnings Announcement

Every company has their own process for issuing their earnings results each quarter. The vast majority of companies report earnings outside of regular trading hours. They will also hold a conference call that is open to the public to discuss their earnings results and field questions from analysts and investors.

Despite the stock and option markets not being open when earnings announcements are made, there is stock trading going on in what is often referred to as *extended hours trading*. Currently, with the exception of some exchange-traded funds, option trading is only available from 9:30 to 4:00 Eastern Standard Time each day. After an earnings report, option traders will wait until the market opens to exit positions or see what the updated profit or loss is for a position. Also, during extended hours trading, there is a little less liquidity for stock trading so the price moves may be a bit accentuated.

Most companies will release earnings results along with other important financial information in the form of an extensive press release. The financial news organizations will take that information and condense it down into a handful of headlines that will come across the various quote systems that traders use to follow the markets. The stock will quickly react in after-hours trading to these headlines.

After the press release there will be a conference call hosted by the company. The call traditionally will begin with comments from the CEO that reflects language that is already in the press release. There also may be some forward-looking statements that are to be used as guidance for analysts in projecting earnings results in the future. After statements the call will be opened up for questions. Depending on the results, the tone of the questions may be anywhere from complimentary to argumentative. Responses to questions may also result in the stock price moving around in after-hours trading.

At this point the company is done making their results known to the public and fielding any resulting questions. The financial press and Wall Street analysts will follow up on the results with commentary of their own. This may include analysts changing their recommendations or discussion of the repercussions of these results for suppliers and competitors.

Finally, the stock and option markets will open and the full impact of this new news will be reflected in trading. The direction of the stock price reaction will be in question leading up to the earnings report, but a quick drop in implied volatility of near-dated options is a certainty.

■ Earnings Trades

Something that is continually emphasized in this book is that any trade begins with an outlook for the underlying stock or market. This holds true for a short-term trade based on earnings. An earnings report occurs outside of market hours. Therefore, option traders will have to wait until the option market opens to exit any trades or see what their profit or loss is for a position. Despite being the third factor mentioned, a change in implied volatility cannot be underemphasized with respect to an earnings release.

In the case of trading an earnings reaction the price forecast may have a unique twist to it. The forecast may be a normal bullish or bearish outlook based on a fundamental opinion on the company. Also, if a stock has a track record of moving higher or lower based on earnings this may come into play for the price forecast. Finally, the magnitude of the price forecast can be based on historical price changes based on an earnings announcement.

The timing of the trade directly relates to the earnings announcement. A trade based on earnings would most likely be exited after the announcement, but also may be in place to hold through expiration. A trade that is based on options expiring with no value will be held to expiration. Typically, a trade that is net long options should be exited after the stock price reaction or a target is reached to avoid time decay or implied volatility continuing to move down as the news is digested by the market. Finally, when short-dated options are being used to trade earnings, assuming no time-value component for an option after earnings is a method that results in a small bonus if there is any time value remaining when the option is exited post-earnings.

Finally, projecting an expected change in implied volatility is as much an art as it is a science. History may be a good guide as the pattern of changes in volatility may repeat. Another method of estimating a change in implied volatility is to look at the implied volatility of similar options that expire a month or two after the earnings release. These options are not the contracts that are being bought or sold to take a position on an earnings release so they may offer a clue as to where implied volatility may be after earnings.

■ Earnings Trading Strategies

Earnings announcement dates are known well in advance. For instance Google is known to consistently release their earnings every three months on the third Thursday of each month. A visit to any of the free earnings calendars available on the Internet will yield dates that are quarters—if not years—into the future.

Three different general earnings trading strategies will be discussed in this section. The first will cover having a directional outlook for a stock that is to report earnings and initiating a trade that will benefit from the expected price change either higher or lower. The other two strategies will be based on the magnitude of a price move out of the underlying market. For earnings, a popular strategy is often an option spread that will benefit from the magnitude of a price change that occurs in the underlying market based on earnings. This trade may benefit if the move is less than a certain amount or if it is greater than a certain amount.

Lowering the Cost of a Directional Outlook

The first trade is based on shares of Nike (NKE). Fifteen days before NKE is to report earnings the stock is looking strong, but meeting resistance. Figure 18.2 is a price chart with NKE closing at 98.97.

The stock failed to break through the 100.00 level and is testing this resistance price three weeks before earnings. The thought is NKE is fundamentally sound and the added boost of a positive earnings report means the stock could break through the 100.00 barrier. The day after NKE reports earnings is the third Friday of the month, or standard option expiration. These options have 16 trading days remaining until expiration. Based on the timing of the news and a price outlook that puts NKE over 100.00, a trader decides to buy a NKE 16-day 100 call for 1.85.

NKE also has weekly options that expire in six days available for trading. There is a strong feeling that NKE will not break through 100.00 until the earnings announcement. Based on NKE shares staying under 100.00 over the next couple of weeks the trader also decides to sell a NKE 6-day 100 call for 0.45. The net NKE option position is:

Long 1 NKE 16-day 100 call at 1.85
Short 1 NKE 6-day 100 call at 0.45

FIGURE 18.2   NKE Daily Price Chart 15 Days before Earnings

FIGURE 18.3 NKE Daily Price Chart Nine Days before Earnings

The net cost of this position is 1.45 which is the net potential loss of this trade if shares move to the downside. The goal for this trade is that NKE shares languish around current levels and then rally on the earnings report in three weeks. The NKE price chart in Figure 18.3 shows the stock six days after the initial trade with NKE closing at 98.60.

At this point the earnings announcement is in nine trading days and the long call has 10 days remaining. There is also a short-dated option series that expires in five trading days. Checking quotes, the NKE 5-day 100 call may be sold for 0.35 to further offset the cost of the long option contract. The long option is now trading at 1.60 so the net current position is:

Long 1 NKE 10-day 100 call at 1.60
Short 1 NKE 5-day 100 call at 0.35

The net running cost of this position is now 1.05 based on the initial long option cost of 1.85 and a net credit of 0.80 taken in from the two option sales. Figure 18.4 shows the price action has been fairly range bound for NKE and the result is the second short option expiring out-of-the-money. NKE is actually at the low end of a range and the long call is trading at 1.05.

At this point in time there are only four trading days until NKE reports earnings. After the earnings report there is only one trading day remaining until expiration. The long NKE call is now a five-day option that expires the day after earnings are released. There is a final alternative to reduce the cost of the NKE call option. This alternative is to sell a higher strike five-day NKE call option.

Two factors would come into play when deciding whether to sell a call option that shares expiration with the long option. First would be the price

FIGURE 18.4 NKE Daily Price Chart Four Days before Earnings

forecast for the underlying stock. A check of NKE's earnings history over the past 12 quarters leading up to this release results in the figures in Table 18.2.

These results are shown in reverse order so the move down by 1.14 percent was the most recent quarter followed by the one-day loss of −9.40 percent. The one-day gain of 5.33 percent was the price change for NKE 12 quarters ago. The average price change comes to 5.30 percent, with the maximum day just over 10 percent. A 10 percent move from current prices would place NKE shares around 106.60, while an average price move would place the stock around 102.05. The willingness to sell an out-of-the-money call and create a bull call spread would be dependent on what price forecast a trader is using. The historical price changes based on earnings are often a good guide to create a forecast for trading.

The other factor that comes into play is the amount of income that would be taken in when selling a higher strike option. The next strike higher is the NKE 5-day 105 call that can be sold for 0.20. This option would expire

TABLE 18.2	Last 12 NKE Earnings Report Reactions
One-Day %	One-Day %
−1.14	4.81
−9.40	−9.16
−3.22	−5.80
2.91	2.45
5.30	−3.99
10.14	5.33

FIGURE 18.5 NKE Daily Price Chart One Day after Earnings

out-of-the-money if an average move to the upside occurs. If it is a larger price move, similar to the 9 to 10 percent price changes that accompanied earnings results in the past, then the NKE 5-day 105 call may be in-the-money and some profits would be left on the table. The logical move in this case would to be forgo selling the NKE 105 call that would only bring in 0.20.

Figure 18.5 is a final chart showing price action in NKE. This shows the forecast was correct that NKE would have a positive reaction to the earnings announcement. The closing price for NKE was 99.00 the day before earnings were announced. The following day the stock opens at 102.50 and closed at 105.10 on the day for a gain of just over 6 percent. The NKE 100 call was worth 5.10 on the close or about 2.60 on the open, with the outcome for the trade dependent on when the option would have been sold.

A forecast can be traded in this manner when a long-dated option is going to be purchased based on a bullish or bearish outlook for a stock around earnings. An option will start to experience rising volatility two to three weeks in advance. Trying to take a long position ever a few weeks in advance will subject a trader to time decay. Buying early and selling short-dated options is a good method to take an inexpensive option position in front of earnings.

Expecting High Volatility

A common reaction when a trader sees a big stock move on earnings is they wish they had purchased a call or put. Of course this depends on the direction that the stock has moved. A secondary thought is often to the effect of knowing that since earnings were coming out maybe the trader should have

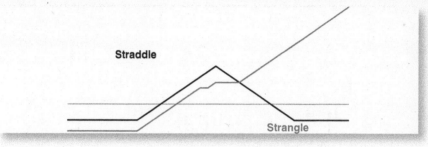

Straddle

Strangle

FIGURE 18.6   Generic Straddle and Strangle Payoff Diagram

bought both a put and call. The common strategies that buy a call and put that share an expiration are called the *straddle* and *strangle*. Upon first glance these strategies look very attractive. Figure 18.6 is a generic payoff diagram showing a straddle or strangle at expiration.

The payout that looks like the letter V is the straddle while the payoff diagram that has a flat area in the middle represents a strangle payoff at expiration. These two payoff diagrams look deceptively easy. Stock prices are always changing so buying a straddle or strangle is a relatively easy method of profiting from stock price movement, right? This statement could not be further from the truth.

These two spreads are comprised of two long option positions. This means two options experiencing time decay. Also, two long option positions result in exposure to a drop in implied volatility. If a trader is considering a straddle or strangle just before an earnings announcement they are probably buying options when implied volatility has reached a peak or when implied volatility is most expensive.

The key to trading a straddle or strangle in front of earnings is having an opinion that is different than what the market is pricing in. This statement can be made about most any trading situation, but in the case of a straddle or strangle buying (or selling) one is taking a stand that is different than the market consensus. With respect to earnings these spreads are a prediction of what sort of price move is expected out of the underlying security based on the impact of an earnings announcement. What is interesting is at times the most recent earnings announcement seems to have more weight than the average earnings announcement.

Facebook (FB) will be used as an example of buying a straddle into an earnings announcement. Figure 18.7 shows FB daily trading activity leading up to an earnings report.

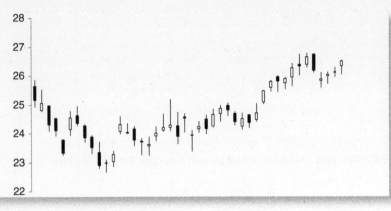

FIGURE 18.7 FB Daily Price Chart Day before Earnings

After a slight drop the stock works its way higher each day into the earnings release. This trade is more concerned with the magnitude of a price movement than the direction of the move. In order to determine what is priced in by the market, the at-the-money straddle will be priced for four days leading up to earnings. The first line shows the at-the-money straddle four days before the earnings report. The percent move to breakeven is an average of the move higher and move lower to break even since they are slightly different price moves.

Table 18.3 shows the closing prices for FB stock and the at-the-money call and put options that expire two days after the earnings report date. The stock is closer to 26.00 than 26.50 for the first three days on the table. Then the stock closes at 26.51 which results in the best at-the-money straddle being the 26.50 call and 26.50 put. The interesting aspect of this table is that the cost of the straddle is relatively consistent when measured relative to the price change to breakeven on the straddle. The percent move is in the 7 to 8 percent range and actually least expensive on the closing prices just before the report.

TABLE 18.3 FB Straddle Pricing Leading Up to Earnings

	FB Stock	ATM Strike	Call Premium	Put Premium	Straddle Cost	% Move to Break Even
Friday—4 Days	25.88	26.00	1.00	1.10	2.10	8.11
Money—3 Days	26.05	26.00	1.05	1.00	2.05	7.87
Tuesday—2 Days	26.13	26.00	1.10	1.00	2.10	8.04
Wednesday—1 Day	26.51	26.50	0.95	0.95	1.90	7.17

Just before the market closed the at-the-money straddle is pricing in a 7.17 percent move in Facebook in order to breakeven. The options will have two days remaining until expiration, and if the stock moves over 7 percent in one direction or another it is a safe assumption that there will be no time value remaining and one of the options will be 100 percent intrinsic value. Before considering a straddle this move should be compared to the historical average move.

At this time, Facebook had reported earnings only four times as a public company. There was limited price history to work with, but it is fairly interesting price history. The previous four quarter FB price reactions appear in Table 18.4.

The first top two one-day price changes are the more recent FB earnings result reactions. The last earnings release resulted in a move of 5.61 percent higher and the move before that was basically FB shares hardly moving on the day. Before that there were some interesting results, with a jump of 19 percent and a drop of 11.7 percent. The average price move for FB's limited history is 9.30 percent. This would result in FB trading up to 29.98 or down to 24.04 after the earnings report. The cost of the straddle is 1.90 just before earnings. A 9.30 percent move in FB would result in the FB put at 2.46 or the FB call at 2.48. This is the risk to reward that may be weighed when considering this spread. The risk is the cost of 1.90 and an average return of 2.47. The payout diagram in Figure 18.8 shows this payout with the assumption that FB moves higher or lower based on this average highlighted.

Although the maximum potential loss for this spread is 1.90, this is highly unlikely since this would result from FB closing at 26.50 or 0.01 lower than where the stock was trading before earnings. Even the small drop of 0.83 percent that occurred a couple of earnings releases in the past would place the stock at 26.28 and this would mean without any time

TABLE 18.4	Last Four FB Earnings Report Reactions
One-Day %	
5.61	
−0.83	
19.13	
−11.70	

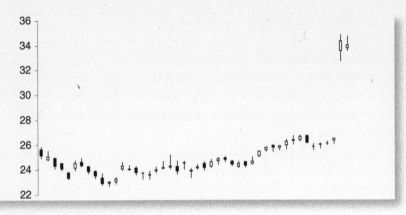

FIGURE 18.8 FB 26.50 Straddle Payout at Expiration

value associated with the FB 26.50 put that it could be sold for 0.22 and a net loss of 1.68.

The outcome for this trade was better than all expectations as FB rallied tremendously after earnings; Figure 18.9 is a price chart showing the gap in FB trading that occurred post-earnings. This should not be taken as an example of what typically happens around earnings, but every earnings season there seems to be a few stocks that gap higher or gap lower and get the attention of traders. This sort of price action is what makes trading earnings so tempting.

Initiating a straddle or strangle is an easy trade conceptually, but more difficult to profit from on a consistent basis. This is especially true with respect to

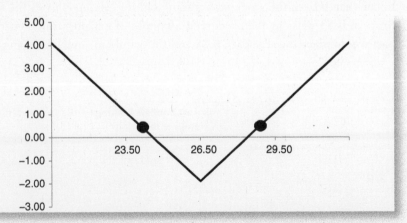

FIGURE 18.9 FB Daily Price Chart after Earnings into Option Expiration

trades around events such as earnings. When an earnings event is being antici-pated by the option market implied volatility rises and options become more expensive. Since a straddle or strangle will consist of two long option posi-tions, often a trader is taking on an expensive position. When trading around earnings or any other event, the outlook for the underlying market or stock should be dramatically different than what is being priced in by the market.

Expecting Low Volatility

An earnings trade that is based on a low-volatility outlook would be a strat-egy that pays off if a stock does not move as much as the market is an-ticipating. Again, the market anticipation is being priced in by the option premiums of at-the-money options that expire shortly after the earnings announcement. Normally the option series that is the first to expire after an earnings announcement are the options that are pricing in the expected change from the underlying stock. This is a direct result of those options being the contracts most likely to be traded based on an earnings outlook.

Buying a straddle or strangle is the most logical method of trying to ben-efit from a large move out of the underlying stock. The most logical trade would be selling a straddle or strangle based on an earnings outlook. How-ever, this may not be the best trade for a couple of reasons. The first reason has to do with your broker and the second reason that a trader would con-sider avoiding selling a straddle or strangle has to do with risk.

First, many brokers shy away from allowing individual traders initiate un-covered short call or put positions. This is not to say that they never allow it, they just only tend to allow this sort of trade for very experienced traders or traders who have a substantial amount of capital in their account. In either case, the average option trader is often not permitted to have uncovered short option positions in their account.

The other reason has to do with risk control. The theoretical risk of a short-option position is unlimited in the case of a short call and substantial in the case of a short put. A short put is a little less risky because a stock may not trade under 0.00. Note the average price moves based on earnings releases that appeared back in Table 18.1. Being on the wrong side of one of those moves with unlimited or substantial risk could be a pretty painful experience. For this reason alone, if a trader is considering shorting volatility in front of an earnings announcement, an iron butterfly or iron condor are the two best strategies to consider with the iron condor being the best. Figure 18.10 is a generic payout diagram showing an iron butterfly and iron condor.

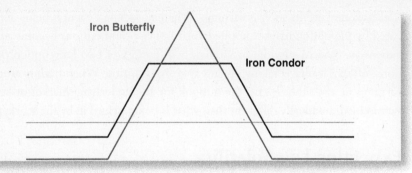

FIGURE 18.10 Iron Butterfly and Iron Condor Payoff Diagram

The downside risk for both of these spreads is limited to the outside strike prices. At these levels this is where the short-option positions are covered by a long put to the downside or a long call to the upside. This sort of risk management is highly recommended when trading an earnings report. Stock price reactions to earnings reports may be very dramatic, so a trader should consider spread trades that have a defined maximum loss when approaching an earnings related trade.

As a low volatility example, an earnings release out of IBM will be used. The price chart for IBM leading up to the close before earnings were released appears in Figure 18.11.

IBM has traded lower and seems to have found some support around 190. The 200 level was a good support area that gave way a few weeks before earnings. A rule of thumb regarding support is that it becomes resistance when a stock breaks below it. So, going into earnings, the 190 level is a

FIGURE 18.11   IBM Daily Price Chart

TABLE 18.5	IBM Earnings Price Reactions
One-Day %	One-Day %
−8.28	−4.12
4.41	5.67
−4.91	3.44
3.77	−0.39
−3.53	3.35
4.43	−3.36

support level and 200 is a resistance level. This, along with some earnings history, will play into the trade.

The price reaction for IBM post-earnings over the past 12 quarters appears in Table 18.5. The first price change, a loss of 8.28 percent, is actually the largest price change over the past three years. What is often interesting about the option market is how shortsighted it is relative to history. The average move for IBM over these three years is just over 4 percent. However, based on this recent move of 8 percent, the market is actually anticipating another big move in IBM postearnings.

IBM closed at 194.55 before the company was set to release earnings. An iron condor can be created using options that expire just two trading days after the earnings report. The iron condor in this case will sell an IBM 2-day 190 put and sell a IBM 2-day 200 call. The next strike lower is 185 and the next strike higher is 205 so the 185 put and 205 call will be purchased. The actual trades to create this short term iron condor are:

Buy 1 IBM 2-day 185 put at 1.05
Sell 1 IBM 2-day 190 put at 2.25
Sell 1 IBM 2-day 200 call at 1.75
Buy 1 IBM 2-day 205 call at 0.65

The net credit for this trade comes to 2.30. The payoff diagram, if this iron condor is held through expiration, appears in Figure 18.12. The maximum payout occurs if IBM lands between the strike prices of 190.00 and 200.00 at expiration. In addition to establishing these price levels as support and resistance there is another factor that contributes to using the specific options chosen to create this iron condor.

The downside breakeven level for this trade is 187.70 and the upside breakeven is 203.30. On a percentage basis this means the stock needs

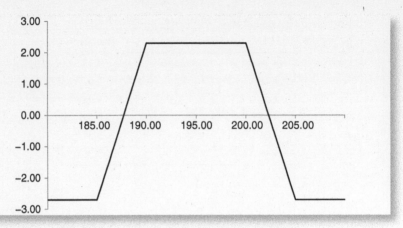

FIGURE 18.12   IBM 185/190/200/205 Iron Condor Payoff

to drop 3.5 percent or rally 4.5 percent postearnings for the result to be outside of breakeven. An average move on earnings is about 4 percent, so breakeven with the limited loss is in line with an average move. The trader's expectation is for a move out of IBM that is below average or less than 4 percent. The outcome for this trade if held to expiration can be illustrated by the IBM price chart in Figure 18.13.

Over the two days following earnings and leading up to option expiration IBM stays between 190.00 and 200.00, managing to close at 193.54 with all options expiring with no value. The initial one-day price change based on the earnings release was a 2.3 percent rise to 197.99 that was safely between the two short option strike prices.

FIGURE 18.13   IBM Daily Price Chart after Earnings

Trading earnings is a tempting method of using options. When considering an earnings trade focus on the historical gains and losses that have occurred over recent earnings releases and develop a forecast for the earnings release. Finally, consider what the option market is pricing in, and if your forecast varies from what the market is expecting, consider an option trade—but consider an option trade that has some defined risk to it. Every earnings season a handful of stocks post a surprise that will result in a large move higher or lower. Defined risk is key to limiting the damage if a trader is on the wrong side of such a move.

CHAPTER 19

Leveraged Exchange-Traded Products

The SPDR S&P 500 (SPY) exchange-traded fund (ETF) was introduced in 1993 to much fanfare and some doubt. The question of who was going to invest or trade using the SPY ETF created many doubters. Well, the answer was a lot of people. As of June 2013 the average daily volume for SPY was over 140 million shares and the assets under management for SPY was $130 billion.

Many investment banks witnessed the growth and acceptance of SPY and sought to create funds that would replicate this success. Now there are exchange-traded funds and exchange-traded notes that allow all levels of traders and investors the ability to gain niche market exposure. In 2006 the first exchange-traded funds that sought to leverage performance of a certain market sector or strategy became available to the overall market. Many of these unique exchange-traded products (ETPs) have not gained market acceptance due to complexity or overlapping strategies with existent ETPs. However, there are a handful that are actively traded enough to warrant having short-dated option series available for trading.

■ Leveraged Long

There are three exchange-traded funds that offer leveraged long exposure to the equity market which have consistently been among the instruments with short-dated option trading available. They are the ProShares Ultra S&P

500 ETF (SSO), Direxion Daily Small Cap Bull 3× Shares ETF (TNA), and Direxion Daily Financial Bull 3× Shares ETF (FAS). Also, the ProShares Ultra Silver ETF (AGQ) was created to offer two times the daily return for the price of silver on a daily basis.

The ProShares Ultra S&P 500 ETF was designed to offer double the return of the S&P 500 on a daily basis. Figure 19.1 is a 12-month, one-day line chart for the S&P 500 and SSO from July 2, 2012, through June 28, 2013. Both the ETF and S&P 500 are indexed to 100 in order to display a direct comparison.

For the 12 months shown on this chart, $100 invested would have grown to about $140 while $100 in the S&P 500 would have grown to about $117. Due to compounding, SSO has actually outperformed the S&P 500 by more than two times the index.

Implied volatility on SSO options usually ranges from the up to 20 percent to a low 30 percent range, which leads to what appear to be expensive option contracts. However, when a trader has a bullish or bearish outlook for the equity market the result can be taking in more premium than if a comparable trade were done with SPY or SPX option contracts.

For example, on a Friday afternoon a five-day at-the-money call on SPY was pricing in implied volatility of 12.8 percent, while the at-the-money SSO call was pricing in implied volatility of 26.1 percent. If a trader is considering a market-related vertical spread or iron condor, SSO options may be a good alternative to SPY options based on the higher at-the-money volatility.

The Direxion Daily Small Cap Bull 3× Shares ETF offers an investor three times the daily performance of the Russell 2000 Index. A one-year chart of the performance of the Russell 2000 versus TNA appears in Figure 19.2.

FIGURE 19.1 S&P 500 versus SSO Daily Price Performance

FIGURE 19.2 Russell 2000 versus TNA Daily Price Performance

The Russell 2000 and TNA ETF have both been indexed to 100 at the beginning of this chart to allow for a direct performance comparison between the two.

If SSO was not enough as far as leverage for the equity market goes, TNA options maybe another alternative. There is dramatic underperformance and outperformance of the Russell 2000 index depending on the trend of the market. For the 12 months on the chart, $100 in TNA would result in a return of almost 70 percent and $170. $100 in the Russell 2000 index would have returned 20 percent and taken $100 and turned it into $120.

The best fund for gaining unleveraged exposure to the Russell 2000 is the iShares Russell 2000 Index (IWM). The implied volatility of IWM options is often at a premium relative to SPY options. Taking it a step further, IWM options' implied volatility is usually right around one-third of the implied volatility of TNA options.

What is interesting is that even though TNA options consistently have three times the implied volatility priced in as IWM, the average weekly price change since inception in 2008 is 8.1 percent while the average change for IWM is 2.7 percent. The implied volatility of TNA reflects the assumption that TNA is going to move three times as much as IWM.

Ever since the market implosion of 2008 the financial sector has taken on price behavior that is expected more for technology or biotech companies. The Direxion Daily Financial Bull 3X Shares ETF is constructed to offer three times the performance of the Russell 1000 Financial Services Index on a daily basis. This is three times the performance of a sector that has been prominent in the news for some time.

Figure 19.3 shows that $100 in FAS over a 12-month period turns into almost $210. The underlying index returns come to $128. There is not a

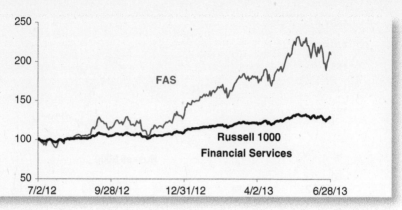

FIGURE 19.3 Russell 1000 Financial Services Index versus FAS Daily Price Performance

comparable unleveraged ETF that offers exposure to the Russell 1000 Financial Services Index. However, on an absolute basis the average daily price change for FAS is over 4 percent and average weekly change is 9 percent. Third-day implied volatility oscillates between 40 and 55 percent, but also does something that is interesting relative to most ETF's. There appears some seasonality to the implied volatility of FAS around earnings periods.

The final leveraged long exchange-traded fund is based on the price of silver. The ProShares Ultra Silver (AGQ) exchange-traded fund offers a return that is two times the daily price change for silver. A comparable unleveraged ETF is the iShares Silver Trust (SLV). A comparison of these two ETFs indexed to 100 appears in Figure 19.4.

As a leveraged version of SLV, $100 in the AGQ fund would be worth $44 while $100 in SLV would have dropped to $71. This is a 56 percent drop in

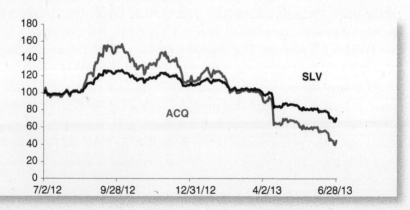

FIGURE 19.4 Proshares Ultra Silver versus iShares Silver Trust

AGQ and a 29 percent drop in SLV. The leveraged AGQ fund does an excellent job matching SLV on a daily 2-to-1 basis as far as performance goes. The average daily move for ACQ since inception in 2008 is 3.2 percent while it is 1.6 percent for the price of silver. ACQ implied volatility is about two times that of SLV, having a range between 40 percent and 100 percent over this time period.

■ Leveraged Short

There are three exchange-traded funds with short-dated options that offer leveraged short exposure to the equity market. The ProShares UltraShort S&P 500 ETF (SDS), Direxion Daily Small Cap Bear 3× Shares ETF (TZA), and Direxion Daily Small Cap Bear 3× Shares (FAZ) all offer leveraged short exposure to the equity market, with FAZ focusing on the Russell 2000. Also, the ProShares UltraShort 20+ Year Treasury ETF (TBT) is based on two times the daily inverse return of the Barclays U.S. 20+ Year Treasury Bond Index.

The ProShares UltraShort S&P 500 ETF offers daily investment returns that correspond to two times the inverse of the daily performance of the S&P 500. Figure 19.5 shows how being short the S&P 500 would compare to having a position in SDS. SDS is 35 percent, while being short the S&P 500 over this period would be down 16 percent. There is a little extra underperformance in SDS in this bullish market phase. This is something that is worth keeping in mind if considering an option position based on a market opinion. A short-term bearish forecast for the S&P 500 may be benefit a little more from a position in SDS.

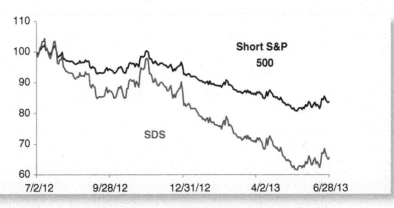

FIGURE 19.5 **Short S&P 500 versus SDS Daily Price Performance**

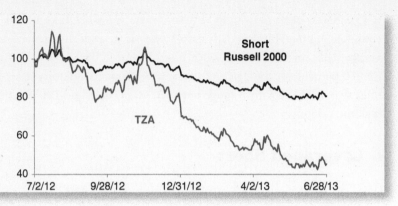

FIGURE 19.6 Short Russell 2000 versus TZA Daily Price Performance

Despite underperforming in a bull market, SDS implied volatility is consistently about two times SPX implied volatility. This may result in a slightly less expensive long option when compared to SPY or SPX index options.

The Russell 2000 is more volatile than the S&P 500 on a consistent basis. The Direxion Daily Small Cap Bear 3× Shares ETF (TZA) offers the holder three times the daily short performance of the Russell 2000 and prices in more than three times the implied volatility of IWM options (Figure 19.6).

On a daily basis, TZA moves 3.8 percent and the average week sees a price change of 7.9 percent. This is interesting as it is not the same as the leveraged long version of this fund. The result is some unusual spread-trading opportunities that come up from time to time between TNA and TZA or even IWM and TZA.

The Direxion Daily Financial Bear 3× Shares (FAZ) ETF is the inverse of the bullish version in the section above. Again, there is not a comparable ETF so the comparison is with the underlying index. FAZ is down 62 percent on the chart in Figure 19.7, which reflects the expected performance of a leveraged short fund in a bullish market.

FAZ has an average daily price change of 4.2 percent and an average weekly price change of 8.8 percent which differs slightly from the daily and weekly changes for FAS.

Finally, a very popular inversed leveraged ETF is the ProShares Ultra-Short 20+ Year Treasury ETF (TBT). There is a comparable unleveraged long ETF that is based on the same index. The iShares Barclays 20+ Year Treasury Bond ETF (TLT) is designed to match the same index. Figure 19.8 shows a side-by-side price comparison of these two ETFs.

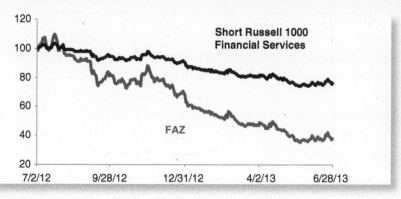

FIGURE 19.7 Short Russell 1000 Financial Services Index versus FAZ Daily Price Performance

The equity market has been very trendy over the year leading up to the charts in this section. The treasury market had not been trending and the result is a good example of how well the leveraged ETFs can do when a trader has a neutral outlook. TLT looks basically like a moving average of TBT. A short position in TLT would be up 12 percent, while owning TBT would result in a 16 percent return. The TBT return is not exactly two times being short this market.

Despite being a leveraged product, the implied volatility of TBT options only ranges between 20 and 30 percent. TLT, as expected, fluctuates between 10 and 15 percent. The performance comparison between the two reflects this as well, as TLT performance is very close to half of TBT performance over these shorter time periods.

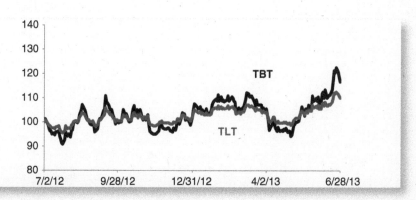

FIGURE 19.8 TBT versus Short TLT Daily Price Performance

This chapter is an overview of leveraged exchange-traded funds that have short-dated options available for trading. These markets are not for the faint of heart or anyone who is not experienced in dealing with high volatility. In addition to considering directional plays with the individual markets, there are many unusual spread opportunities that arise between ETFs based on a similar index. The website that accompanies this book dives much deeper into these sorts of trades, along with providing descriptions of more leveraged products that have short-dated options available for trading

CHAPTER 20

VIX-Related Exchange-Traded Products

The growth of VIX futures and options trading has been tremendous over the past few years. Following on this success, exchange-traded products have been introduced that follow a volatility related strategy. There are only a handful of volatility-related exchange-traded products. Despite only a relative small number of them being available, they have become very popular with short-term traders. The iPath S&P 500 VIX Short Term Futures ETN (VXX) and ProShares Ultra VIX Short-Term Futures ETF (UVXY) consistently have short-dated options available for trading.

■ iPath S&P 500 VIX Short Term Futures ETN (VXX)

VXX was the first exchange-traded product to be listed based on a volatility-related strategy. It was issued in 2009 when VIX was near 50. Since 2011 VIX has been in a more subdued mood, averaging around 20. This lack of implied volatility in the overall equity market has resulted in VXX continuously grinding lower. Figure 20.1 is a chart of VXX since inception through June of 2013.

The chart shows that, on a split-adjusted basis, VXX has traded down from 1900 to around 20. This is a function of the index that VXX was created

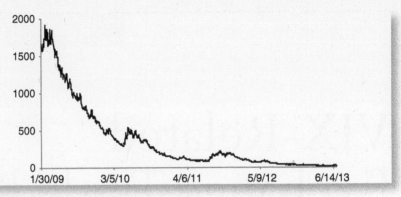

FIGURE 20.1 VXX Daily Price Chart, January 2009 through June 2013

to follow. The performance of VXX is based on a portfolio that holds the front two-month VIX futures contracts. In a low-volatility environment VIX futures prices are higher the longer there is until expiration. VXX focuses on a weighting between the front two months; on a daily basis the portfolio sells the first month and buys second-month futures. Because of this there is a consistent drag on VXX regardless of what is going on in the spot VIX index. Estimates have been made that VXX will lose 4 percent on average if VIX is flat for a month. That 4 percent figure can vary based on other market factors. The important point is VXX is constantly fighting a headwind to move higher. During the 230 weeks VXX has been listed, over 62 percent of the time VXX has closed down for the week.

One other aspect to keep in mind about VXX is that when VIX spikes, VXX does as well. Table 20.1 shows the 10 biggest percent moves higher for VXX since inception.

So despite the headwind when the S&P 500 comes under pressure and VIX moves up, so does VXX. VXX was issued in 2009; however, the index that it is based on has data going back to 2007. In 2008, if VXX were

TABLE 20.1	VXX 10 Largest Percent Moves Higher		
Date	% Move	Date	% Move
8/18/2011	20.70	5/20/2010	14.14
8/4/2011	19.98	2/25/2013	13.70
11/9/2011	18.86	8/10/2011	12.51
8/8/2011	14.75	2/22/2011	12.13
11/1/2011	14.49	5/7/2010	11.98

available, it would have been up over 100 percent. The point is that despite the constant grind lower in VXX for over four years, VXX will move up if volatility increases in the markets.

The 30-day implied volatility of VXX options ranges from 50 to 80 percent, which is justified based on the potential one-day moves as demonstrated in the previous table. VXX options may be traded with an outlook for volatility, but also may be traded based on an equity market outlook. VIX and the S&P 500 have an inverse correlation over time. The correlation between the daily change for VIX and the S&P 500 is –0.75. The relationship between VXX and the S&P 500 is a bit more negative at –0.80. So the opportunity to trade SPY options in conjunction with VXX options exists as well.

■ ProShares Ultra VIX Short-Term Futures ETF (UVXY)

UVXY is a leveraged version of VXX. The result is similar long-term performance, but worse. However, like VXX, UVXY is a good vehicle to be long volatility for a short period of time. Figure 20.2 is a split-adjusted price chart of UVXY since inception in October 2011.

This is not the chart of an exchange-traded product that any individual or institution would consider for a buy-and-hold strategy. Weekly performance for UVXY has been negative 70 percent for weeks since inception. In fact, as a buy-and-hold instrument for the long term, the same comments may

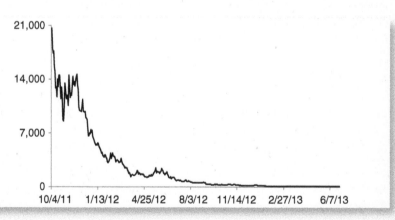

FIGURE 20.2 A Split-Adjusted Price Chart of UVXY since Inception in October 2011

ABOUT THE AUTHOR

Russell Rhoads, CFA, is an instructor with the Options Institute at the Chicago Board Options Exchange. He joined the Institute in 2008 after a career as an investment analyst and trader with a variety of firms including Highland Capital Management in Memphis, Tennessee, Caldwell & Orkin Investment Counsel in Atlanta, Georgia, and Balyasny Asset Management in Chicago, Illinois. He is a financial author and editor who has contributed to technical analysis of Stocks and Commodities and Active Trader magazines and has edited several books for John Wiley & Sons. In addition, he wrote Candlestick Charting For Dummies in 2008 and he is the author of Option Spread Trading: A Comprehensive Guide to Strategies and Tactics, released in early 2011. Before 2011 he also published Trading VIX Derivatives: Trading and Hedging Strategies Using VIX Futures, Options, and Exchange-traded Notes.

He is a double graduate of the University of Memphis with a BBA (1990) and an MS (1994) in Finance and also received a Master's Certificate in Financial Engineering from the Illinois Institute of Technology in 2003. In addition to his position with CBOE, Mr. Rhoads serves as an instructor for The Options Industry Council and is an Adjunct Instructor at Loyola University in Chicago, Illinois.